ETHICS

and

ON THE IMPROVEMENT
OF THE UNDERSTANDING

The Hafner Library of Classics

Ethics

Preceded by

On the Improvement of the Understanding

by **BENEDICT DE SPINOZA**

Edited with an Introduction by

JAMES GUTMANN

HAFNER PRESS
A Division of Macmillan Publishing Co., Inc.
New York
Collier-Macmillan Publishers
London

HAFNER PRESS
A Division of Macmillan Publishing Co., Inc.
866 Third Avenue, New York, N.Y. 10022

Collier Macmillan Canada, Ltd.

Printed in the United States of America

printing number
8   9   10

CONTENTS

NOTE ON THE EDITION

This edition of Spinoza's works has been prepared on the basis of many years' experience reading the texts not only with classes in ethics but also with beginning students in philosophy including students in the general Humanities course in Columbia College during the last decade. That Spinoza can be read by beginners in philosophy and that, despite technical difficulties, he can be approached directly in the context of the humanistic tradition of Western literature may seem surprising to those who have not made the attempt,

There are, of course, difficulties. But we can without triviality paraphrase the conclusion of the "Ethics": If the way seem difficult it can nevertheless be found. . . . But all excellent things are as difficult as they are rare.

"Of Spinoza it is probably more true than of any other philosopher that his thought cannot be divorced from his life and character without grave risks of total misapprehension." So wrote Professor A. Wolf in his edition of "The Oldest Biography of Spinoza," and the Introduction to this volume was written with this conviction in mind. One of the satisfactions of planning this volume was provided by the opportunity to include in it Woodbridge's brief essay on Spinoza. Originally delivered as an address at Columbia University for the Spinoza tercentenary in 1932 it was subsequently published in the *Columbia University Quarterly* and reprinted in a pamphlet. But it has long since been out of print and to make it available is a service to the memory of two philosophers as well as to students who find it here.

The text of the "Ethics" in this volume is based on the translation by William Hale White (1883) as revised by Amelia Hutchinson Stirling (1894, 1899) and the text of the "Improvement of the Understanding" is the translation by R. H. M. Elwes (1884). Anyone who has himself performed the task of translation must hesitate before tampering with the work of another translator when scholarship and literary art have been combined as in the case of both these texts. To amend them is almost like changing an original. Almost but not quite, for in this case the original is available as a check. Wherever changes have been made in the basic versions this check has been used and counterchecked by reference to other translations. The chief changes follow the suggestion of Dr. Joseph Ratner, in his "Selections from the Philosophy of Spinoza" in the Modern Library (1926), that White's translation is clarified by substituting the word "emotion" for "affect" in rendering the original *affectus*, and "modifications" or "modes" for Spinoza's *affectiones*, where White uses "affections." No matter how much of a Latinist a reader may be nor how often he be reminded that "affects" are emotions and that "affections" have nothing in common with what the word currently means to everyone, constant confusion results from continuing to use the White-Sterling text unamended in this regard. Virtually all other changes in the text of the "Ethics" incorporate some felicitous phrases of Elwes' in the White-Sterling version.

In both texts I have capitalized the term "Nature," especially when Spinoza's *Deus sive Natura* makes the English "God or nature" an evident distortion of his meaning.

J. G.

INTRODUCTION

"To UNDERSTAND any prophet thoroughly," wrote Matthew Arnold in his essay on *Spinoza and the Bible,* "we ought to know the life, character, and pursuits of that prophet, under what circumstances his book was composed, and in what state and through what hands it has come down to us." Arnold was, of course, referring to the prophets of the Bible but his statement applies to other authors as well. It certainly applies to Spinoza.

The history of Spinoza's name tells much about the man. When Benedict Spinoza was born in Amsterdam, in 1632, he was called Baruch de Spinosa or Baruch Espinosa. His family had come as refugees from the Inquisition and had found a home in the Netherlands, whose people had themselves but recently gained political independence from Spain. This national freedom as well as the economic prosperity which accompanied it the Dutch were willing to share with newcomers from the south of Europe.

The change of the form and spelling of the family name suggests Spinoza's assimilation to the culture of his native land. Something of what its freedom meant to him is made explicit in his "Theologico-Political Treatise":

> Now, seeing that we have the rare happiness of living in a republic, where everyone's judgment is free and unshackled, where each may worship God as his conscience dictates, and where freedom is esteemed before all things dear and precious, I have believed that I should be undertaking no ungrateful or unprofitable task, in demonstrating that not only can such freedom be granted without prejudice to the public peace, but also, that without such freedom, piety cannot flourish nor the public peace be secure.

The alteration of Spinoza's first name involved a decision concerning which we know the bare facts but which had profound and, indeed, dramatic implications. Whatever the details of Spinoza's separation from Judaism and the Jewish community, the record of which will be outlined presently, he himself marked it by dropping his Hebrew name, Baruch, and taking the Latin equivalent Benedictus. The name means Blessed, and it will be important to note wherein Spinoza came to consider himself to be blessed.

If we turn from Spinoza's name to his occupation, the simple facts again illustrate the significance of his life and character for an understanding of his philosophy. History lists Spinoza among the greatest of philosophers, but had his neighbors in the cities and towns of Holland where he made his home been asked his occupation, they would have answered that he was a grinder of optical lenses. This calling by which he supported himself points — like his name — in two directions. The traditions of the Jewish education in which he was reared required that he be trained in a manual skill along with his scholarly instruction. The choice of the work of an optician not only gives evidence of special dexterities and aptitudes but reflects the scientific civilization so important in seventeenth century Europe, to which Dutch scientists were making notable contributions.

It is, then, in the double aspect of the barest and simplest facts of Spinoza's life and also in terms of the setting of his life in the culture — social, religious, scientific — of seventeenth century European civilization that the relationship of Spinoza's biography to his thought can be most fruitfully considered.

The world in which Spinoza was born had characteristics which we of the mid-twentieth century may recognize as all too familiar. In 1632, Northern Europe was in the midst of a Thirty Years War which in sheer destructiveness and in violence of ideological fanaticism remained unequalled until our own era. The Netherlands had freed themselves from Spain in the previous century, making good their declaration of independence of 1581 by a twelve year truce in 1609, at the same time that they surmounted the religious dissension between their own Calvinists and the followers of Arminius by establishing a principle of freedom of conscience which enabled them to remain aloof from the struggles of the Thirty Years War. Yet the proximity of the war not only provided a chief concern for the statesmen of the newly established nation whose independence was unsuccessfully contested by Spain in the peace settlement of 1648, but preoccupied the political thought of the day. This is notably illustrated on the work on "The Laws of War and Peace" of Hugo Grotius [Huigh de Groot — (1583–1645)].

Despite rebellions and wars, the progress of science and the increase of economic wealth were, perhaps, nowhere more readily visible in the middle of the seventeenth century than in the Netherlands. To what extent these were interrelated need not concern us here; the facts themselves may, however, impress a student of Spinoza's biography. The canvasses of Franz Hals (1580–1666) and of Rembrandt (1606–1669) give vivid examples of scenes not at all remote from his life. Their opulence and variety suggest, at very least, goods and values from which Spinoza deliberately turned away.

More positively, it was toward the new sciences that Spinoza turned, sciences in which contemporary Europe was achieving unexampled heights. The "Dialogues" of Galileo (1564–1642) were published in the year of Spinoza's birth. Johannes Kepler had died only two years before. Though the invention of the telescope is usually credited to Galileo in 1609, in the Netherlands the claim was made that Jan Lipperhey had designed such an instrument even earlier. There, too, Christian Huygens perfected his large telescope with which, in 1656, he observed the ring of Saturn and its fourth moon. While Spinoza, the lens grinder, made his telescopic and microscopic glasses, his mind saw Nature in terms of what these lenses were revealing to astronomers and physicists.

When one turns from the background of Spinoza's life to biographical details there appear to be a number of problematic and even paradoxical considerations. What had long been considered to be the earliest and most authoritative "Life of Spinoza" was the work of a German Lutheran minister, Johann Köhler, latinized as Colerus. He came to Holland in 1679, two years after Spinoza's death, and later occupied rooms in which the philosopher had lived for a brief time. Colerus became interested in Spinoza's career and devoted himself to gathering facts about him though he had little interest in his thought and less than little evident sympathy with it. The biographical data are, moreover, confused to some degree by the circumstance that several elements of uncertainty continue to attach to the earliest records. Both the authorship and the date of the "Earliest Biography" present problems. Up to comparatively recently it had been thought that it had been written later than the longer work by Colerus. Even though some uncertainties remain, it seems to be established as more than twenty-five years older than Colerus' *Life* and as the work of one who actually knew Spinoza, whether it be Saint-Glain or Jean Maximilian

Lucas to whom it has generally been ascribed. In addition to these two documents, the primary record of Spinoza's life includes voluminous correspondence, more than eighty letters written by or to Spinoza in the years between 1661 and 1676. Some of these letters were included in the "Posthumous Works," published in the year of Spinoza's death; others were found, as were three lost works by Spinoza, during the latter half of the nineteenth century. "The Correspondence of Spinoza" was translated into English and edited by Professor Abraham Wolf, the outstanding Spinoza scholar, in 1928. Professor Wolf also edited, in 1927, "The Oldest Biography of Spinoza," the work referred to above. Beside these primary accounts there are brief records by friends and acquaintances of Spinoza or by contemporaries who received reports from such sources. These may be found in Carl Gebhardt's "Spinoza: Lebensbeschreibungen und Gespräche" (Leipzig, 1914), and most of them are translated in Professor Wolf's edition of the "Oldest Biography."

It is from these records that all later biographies of Spinoza are drawn. Their facts, their omissions, and even their conjectures have constituted the basis of subsequent accounts. In considering the relationship of Spinoza's life to his philosophy, we may happily seek to eliminate the elements of surmise though they are the more obviously dramatic, and even melodramatic items in some of the stories. Whether there was a single romance in Spinoza's life — an attachment to the daughter of his Latin teacher — is unimportant in regard to his clear statements concerning sexual passion and the relationship between the sexes. Whether or not a Jewish zealot made an attempt on Spinoza's life, the putative dagger left as little mark on Spinoza's thought as it was said to have made on his flesh.

But this does not imply that the authentic facts of Spinoza's life lack dramatic interest or that they lack relevance to his thought. On the contrary, as Professor Wolf observed in his introduction to the "Oldest Biography" (p. 36): "Of Spinoza it is probably more true than of any other philosopher that his thought cannot be divorced from his life and character without grave risks of total misapprehension."

Spinoza was born on November 24, 1632, in Amsterdam, where, as has been noted, his family had settled as refugees from the Inquisition in Spain and Portugal. His grandfather, Abraham, came to Holland with a group of Jews who had fled from southern Portugal and, after remaining for a time in France, reached the Netherlands early in the last decade of the sixteenth century.

By the time of Spinoza's birth this group of Jews were fairly well established in Amsterdam. They had secured permission to build a synagogue for their community of which Abraham Spinoza seems to have been the acknowledged leader. The family had prospered as merchants, and Abraham's son, Michael, had married another refugee, a Portugese Jewess who had come to Holland from Lisbon. Michael had three children — two daughters, Rebecca and Miriam, and his son, Baruch. The daughters may have been stepsisters; in any case little is known of the family and of Spinoza's relations with its members. His mother died in 1638 when Spinoza was six years old, and only one of his sisters seems to have survived the father, who died in 1654.

In or about 1638, the year of the mother's death, a Jewish school was established in Amsterdam and Michael Spinoza became an official of this institution as well as being an officer of the synagogue and president of a philanthropic organization. Biblical and Talmudic studies formed the core of education in the Hebrew school where Baruch received his first schooling. His further instruction included the study of the works of mediaeval Jewish philosophers, such as Abraham Ibn Ezra (1092–1167), Moses Maimonides (1135–1204), and Chasdai Crescas (c.1340–c.1410).

Of Spinoza's other studies little is known. It was in these years that he learned to make lenses and to use many languages. All studies in the school were Hebrew, but Spanish was spoken there as it was in Spinoza's home. Dutch he learned as a member of the community and later used it as well as Latin in his philosophical writing, though, it is said, never with ease. His earliest instruction in Latin he received from a German scholar from whom he may also have learned some German. His further classical studies he owed to Francis van den Ende, an ex-Jesuit physician who opened a private school in Amsterdam in 1652. Spinoza not only continued his own studies in this school but was an assistant teacher there between 1656 and 1660.

These were critical years in Spinoza's life. According to Colerus it was in the latter year that Spinoza was cast off from the synagogue, but later evidence shows that this happened in 1656, two years after Michael Spinoza's death and four years after the founding of van den Ende's school. The sequence of these events may well be significant though their effect on Spinoza's development is uncertain. Moreover the change in Spinoza's life and thought appears to have been gradual and not to be understood as a simple conflict between strict orthodoxy and violent negation. For one thing his earlier teachers had by no means represented a narrow doctrinalism, and this statement applies both to his actual instructors and the teachers whose writings he studied with them. Rabbi Saul Levi Morteira, the most influential of the teachers in the Amsterdam school, was an Italian by birth, a physician and, after 1638, the chief Rabbi of Amsterdam. Manasseh Ben Israel was a native of Portugal. He was brought to Amsterdam in early childhood and became a Rabbi there in 1622 and later a leader in the Hebrew school.

There are numerous, more or less assured accounts concerning Spinoza's relation to his teachers and their congregation. It is not surprising to hear of him as an outstanding scholar for whom the greatest expectations were entertained. There are reports of the efforts of jealous fellow-students to lead him to express heterodox opinions and then to betray him to the authorities. There are accounts of efforts to bribe or cajole him into silence or conformity. The details even as to the nature of his heresy are uncertain. That they involved the accusation of atheism has been a tradition, but even if this is assumed it must be remembered that atheism has time and again been the charge against an accused because he professed to conceive divinity in ways unfamiliar or unacceptable to his accusers. The spirit of Inquisition seems indeed to have infected those who but a short time before had been its victims or had fled from its terrors. That they were now only precariously established in a new home may help to explain, if not to excuse, their own excesses. Spinoza was only one of several who in Amsterdam incurred the displeasure of the synagogue. He is said to have witnessed the tragedy of Uriel da Costa who, after excommunication, reacceptance and a second excommunication, committed suicide in 1640. If so it does not seem to have made him cautious but it may have added to his own toleration of those with whom he himself came to differ.

Despite the harsh language of the edict which expelled Spinoza from the Jewish community there is no evidence of resentment on his part toward the people of whom he ceased being one. Indeed the antecedents of Spinoza's convictions have been traced to writings which he studied in the Hebrew school. Though he was no longer counted a Jew, by himself or others, he never spurned his heritage. Though excommunicated he did not share the intolerance or the timidity of those who banished him. But he now called himself Benedict, Blessed.

According to Colerus, when Spinoza was expelled from the synagogue and became a teacher in van den Ende's school, he abandoned the study of theology and devoted himself entirely to physics. Even the suddenness of this shift must be doubted. Mathematical and scientific studies were not foreign to rabbinical traditions and interest in physics was widespread. Moreover, van den Ende, despite his medical studies, seems to have been more of a humanist than a follower of the new science. His influence on Spinoza has been thought more decisive with regard to social and political ideas perhaps because he himself is known to have put these ideas into action and to have suffered execution for political conspiracy in France. It has been suggested that Spinoza's interest in the writings of Machiavelli may have derived from van den Ende. Indeed, in his "Political Treatise" Spinoza wrote of Machiavelli as a "most ingenious" and farsighted man, but it is well to note the grounds for his statement (chapter V, sec. 7):

> He perhaps wished to show how cautious a free multitude should be of entrusting its welfare absolutely to one man, who, unless in his vanity he thinks he can please everybody, must be in daily fear of plots, and so is forced to look chiefly after his own interest, and, as for the multitude, rather to plot against it than consult its good. And I am the more led to this opinion concerning that most farseeing man, because it is known that he was favourable to liberty, for the maintenance of which he has besides given the most wholesome advice.

But the nature of van der Ende's influence on Spinoza is conjectural and hardly more credible than the romance with the schoolmaster's daughter, Clara Maria, reported by Colerus. He remarks that Clara was singularly ill-favored physically, though of superior mentality, but he fails to mention that she was only twelve years old at the time of Spinoza's supposed infatuation. What has the earmarks of a bit of a jest was given currency by Colerus and repeated, indeed with sombre, moral implications, by later biographers.

That despite Colerus' assertions concerning Spinoza's shift of

intellectual interest at this time one should be cautious in accepting
such a view is fairly clear. His religious and even theological interests
certainly did not come to an end with his excommunication from the
synagogue, as is evident from his writings. Moreover mathematical
studies and interest in the physical sciences which are supposed to
have replaced the intellectual preoccupations of his youth were by no
means foreign to the rabbinical traditions in which he had been reared.
Those who have been concerned to emphasize the suddenness of the
transition have assumed that Spinoza himself set religious faith as
such against the teachings of science, an assumption by no means
warranted.

It might better be said that both Spinoza's religious and his scientific
interests underwent a striking development at this time. Together
with a group of friends, religious dissenters who called themselves
"Collegiants" and who sought to practice simple forms of worship
without clergy or ritual, he undertook the study of the new science
embodied in the work of René Descartes (1596–1650). Though
Spinoza never joined the Collegiants, he lived among them and guided
their Cartesian studies in group discussion and later by correspondence.
It was, indeed, from this activity that his first published work derived,
the only work published during his lifetime that bore his name, his
"Principles of Cartesianism Geometrically Demonstrated." That
Spinoza was no disciple of Descartes even at this time is evident in
the critical attitude which characterizes this work. It may be noted
here that he subsequently endured an opposition from Cartesians
hardly less hostile than the enmity of zealots of synagogue and
churches.

The men who formed or were connected with the Amsterdam group
of Collegiants were the most loyal friends and supporters of Spinoza
not only in the years immediately following his excommunication but
largely to the end of his life. Jan Rieuwertsz, for example, was not
only the publisher of Spinoza's first book in 1663, but also published
his "Posthumous Works" in 1677, which required no little loyalty
and, perhaps, courage. Lodewijk Meyer wrote the preface to the
aforementioned first book, was one of the editors of the "Posthumous
Works," and may have been the physician-friend present at Spinoza's
death. (Colerus identifies the friend who was alone with Spinoza
when he died as "Dr. L. M.," but Professor Wolf has disputed this

identification with evidence that seems rather less cogent than his other findings.) Jarig Jelles payed for the publication of the work on Descartes and wrote the preface for the "Posthumous Works" of which he was also an editor. Simon de Vries was an Amsterdam merchant as was Jelles. In a letter to Spinoza written in 1663 (Letter VIII, Wolf ed. p. 102) he gave an account of how the study group in Amsterdam was conducted after Spinoza had left the vicinity and while he continued to write for them:

> As to the society, this is how it is conducted; one member (but each takes his turn) reads through, explains according to his conception, and, moreover, proves everything, following the sequence and order of your propositions; then, if it happens that we cannot satisfy one another, we think it worth while to make a note of it, and to write to you, so that, if possible, the matter may be made clearer to us, and that under your leadership we may be able to defend the truth against those who are superstitiously religious or even Christian, and to stand firm against the onslaught of the whole world.

De Vries showed his devotion to Spinoza by offers of financial assistance and later by wishing to make him his sole heir. Spinoza declined both offers urging the claims of De Vries' brother to his estate. When Simon De Vries died, in 1667, Spinoza once again declined the annuity of five hundred florins bequeathed to him but accepted a stipend of three hundred florins, and this annuity he received regularly.

Spinoza lived among the Collegiants, first, between 1656 and 1660, in the house of one of the members of the group on the road to the town of Ouwerkerk, near Amsterdam, and later at the Collegiant headquarters at Rhynsburg, near Leyden. Here he stayed from 1660 to 1663, and during this time wrote not only his study of Descartes but also his "Short Treatise on God, Man and his Well-being" (part of which was also written for the Collegiant study group), the first book of the "Ethics" and the unfinished work "On the Improvement of the Understanding." The opening passages of the last mentioned work are autobiographical in a way not unlike the beginning of Descartes' "Discourse on Method." But whereas in Descartes' work the search for a new method is presented as the outcome of purely intellectual difficulties, Spinoza emphasizes the ethical conflicts from which he and other men suffer and seek release.

The "Principles of Cartesianism" were apparently dictated to a young student, perhaps Albert Burgh whom Spinoza taught during the time he lived at Rhynsburg. In 1675, this Burgh, newly converted to Roman Catholicism, wrote to Spinoza (Letter LXVII, Wolf ed. p. 311), whose "penetration and acuteness of mind" he had "formerly admired." Granting that Spinoza was "a lover of truth, indeed eager for it," he went on to ask him: "How do you know that your Philosophy is the best among all those which have ever been taught in the world, or are actually taught now, or ever will be taught in the future?" · Another acquaintance of the Rhynsburg period was the Danish geologist Niels Steensen (Nicholas Steno). He also became a Roman Catholic and "persuaded that the memory of an old companionship still preserves a mutual love" (Letter LXVIIA, Wolf ed. p. 325) tried to influence Spinoza in the same direction. It is possible that Steensen never despatched this letter and, in any case, there is no evidence that Spinoza ever received it. He did, however, reply to Albert Burgh (Letter LXXVI, Wolf ed. p. 350 f.). He reminded his correspondent "that in every Church there are many honest men who worship God with justice and charity" — hardly the words of an enemy of all religion! And after replying to Burgh's question that "I do not presume that I have found the best Philosophy, but I do know that I think the true one," he turned Burgh's words on his own claim to have found the best religion.

Of all the acquaintances of this period the most important in some ways was Henry Oldenburg. A German by birth, Oldenburg spent much of his life in England, partly as diplomatic representative of his native city of Bremen and partly as a teacher and advocate of the new sciences. In the latter role he became the Royal Society's first secretary or co-secretary with Dr. J. Wilkins. Oldenburg visited Spinoza at Rhynsburg in 1661 and professed an immediate admiration for him. He encouraged Spinoza in his work and brought him in contact with the researches of other men of science. Their exchange of letters constitutes more than a third of Spinoza's extant correspondence.

In 1663, Spinoza left the Collegiants in Rhynsburg and moved to Voorburg, a suburb of the Hague. Here he turned to the completion of the book known to us as the "Ethics" but which he had planned as a work to be called "On God, the Rational Soul and the Highest Happiness of Man." Projected as a work in three parts it had evidently been conceived in terms similar to the "Short Treatise." In his method of presentation Spinoza reverted to the geometrical procedure which he had found useful in expounding Descartes' Principles and abandoned the form of dialogue which — possibly in imitation of Giordano Bruno — he had considered and of which a brief specimen remains embodied in the "Short Treatise."

By the publication of his work on Descartes' "Principles" at this time Spinoza evidently hoped to prepare the way for the "Ethics." As has already been mentioned, Jarig Jelles defrayed the cost of publishing the "Principles" and another friend, Lodewijk Meyer, wrote the preface. In introducing the work, Meyer assured Cartesian readers that Spinoza was not so presumptuous as to seek "to correct that most distinguished man," Descartes, while also asserting that he did not share the opinions he was expounding. If it was hoped that all this would gain a welcome for the publication of the "Ethics," the plan miscarried. But the publication of the "Principles" brought Spinoza some friendly and possibly influential acquaintances: Willem van Blyenbergh, a grain broker of Dordrecht; Hugo Boxel, Secretary and later Pensionary of the town of Gorkum, whose belief in ghosts elicited a notable letter from Spinoza; Johan Hudde, Sheriff and later Mayor of Amsterdam; and, above all, Jan de Witt, Grand Pensionary of Holland.

The failure of the "Principles" to clear the way for the "Ethics" may account for the fact that Spinoza turned from the almost completed work to write his "Theological-Political Treatise." Under the circumstances the passage quoted early in the Introduction from Spinoza's preface to the Treatise is doubly interesting. It seems likely that his praise of republican freedom was hortatory rather than strictly descriptive, written with the double hope of preparing a better attitude for his own work as well as strengthening the Republic under de Witt. The Treatise was published anonymously and secretly at Hamburg early in 1670, and in the spring of that year Spinoza moved from Voorburg to the Hague. He was known by many persons to be the author of the "Treatise." Though it roused widespread hostility he never denied his responsibility for it but he prevented its publication in Dutch so as to avoid stirring up useless contention. It was repeatedly republished in Latin and provoked the fanatical opposition of Calvinists, who disputed Spinoza's view of the Bible. The writing of the Treatise had taken him back to his early scriptural studies and led him to begin the composition of a Hebrew Grammar. This was destined to remain unfinished and, in the midst of polemical attacks, Spinoza turned again to his "Ethics."

He worked on this between 1670 and 1675, but his life, though he sought quiet, touched the world of political affairs at several points during these years. In 1672, the French armies invaded Holland. Lack of military preparation to resist the invasion was blamed on the Republican leadership by the Monarchists, and a mob seized the Grand Pensioner Jan de Witt and his brother, Cornelius, and murdered them. Whether or not Spinoza had personal relationship to the de Witts, as the early records indicate, he and his friends felt the murder of the brothers as a shocking and terrible blow. This, at very least, is the essence of Colerus' account of Spinoza's effort to confront the mob and to proclaim his abhorrence of their crime. It was during the same period of French invasion that Spinoza was, in turn, confronted by a hostile crowd and threatened with the fate of the de Witts. The headquarters of the French army were at Utrecht and the Prince de Conde sent for Spinoza through a Colonel Stoupe, one of his subordinates. The motives for this unusual invitation are obscure and have been attributed to Conde's intellectual interests, Spinoza's courteous sense of special obligation to one of lofty station, and Stoupe's concern to mend his own damaged reputation as a renegade Calvinist. It seems also that the French gave hints of a pension from Louis XIV in return for the dedication of a book by Spinoza — a story strange alike because of the reputation of Spinoza's work and his lack of interest in pensions from any source. There was, however, also the suggestion that Spinoza hoped that he might help to secure peace between France and Holland. These hopes came to nothing and the episode almost resulted in tragic consequences when people of the Hague, hearing that Spinoza had been at the French headquarters, suspected him of disloyalty.

In the same year, 1763, Spinoza received an invitation from Prince Karl Ludwig, Elector Palatine, to accept a professorial appointment at the University of Heidelberg. The letter of invitation has been preserved and so has Spinoza's reply in which he declined the position: "For, first, I think that if I want to find time for instructing youth, then I must desist from developing my philosophy. Secondly, I think that I do not know within what limits that freedom of philosophizing ought to be confined in order to avoid the appearance of wishing to disturb the publicly established Religion" (Letter XLVIII, Wolf ed. p. 267).

So he kept himself free to complete his "Ethics," which was at last finished in 1675 and circulated among his friends. The publication of the work was, however, postponed to the evident relief of timorous correspondents. And Spinoza undertook what was destined to be his last work, the "Political Treatise," which, like the "Improvement of the Understanding" and the Hebrew Grammar, remained uncompleted at the time of his death. Considering the recent course of events in Holland and his own involvement in them, Spinoza once again showed his courage and integrity in expressing support for democratic institutions. Hobbes' influence on Spinoza's political theory is often emphasized, but he himself remarks in a letter to Jarig Jelles: "With regard to Politics, the difference between Hobbes and me, about which you inquire, consists in this that I preserve the natural right intact so that the Supreme Power in a State has no more right over a subject than is proportionate to the power by which it is superior to the subject" (Letter L, Wolf ed. p. 269).

The last two years of Spinoza's life continued the activities and preoccupations for which he had expressed preference when he refused to become a professor at Heidelberg. His simple way of life was aided by a pension from de Witt which supplemented the earnings of his lens polishing and de Vries' annuity. The heirs of de Witt disputed his right to the pension but, when Spinoza declined to contest their action, they relented and he received this assistance for the brief balance of his life.

During these last years his fame — for good or ill — had spread and visitors and correspondents sought him out. To some extent his interest in optics rather than his major philosophic concerns may have accounted for this. As has been noted, optics was a focus of much contemporary scientific work. Gottfried Wilhelm Leibniz wrote to him first, in 1671, because he had heard of Spinoza's "great skill in optics." In 1676, Leibniz visited him at the Hague as had another German scientist, Ehrenfried Walther von Tschirnhaus a year previously. It was Tschirnhaus who, on a visit to London at that time, met Henry Oldenburg and his great friend Robert Boyle, the physicist.

Tschirnhaus brought about the resumption of the correspondence between Oldenburg and Spinoza, and the latter's indirect contact with Boyle, which had been interrupted during the war between England and Holland.

The years of Spinoza's life were drawing to an end. Whether or not an inherited predisposition to consumption existed, which accounted for the failure of his never robust health, it may well be that glass dust, incident to polishing lenses, had its part in weakening him. In mid-February, 1677, he sent to Amsterdam for his physician whom Colerus — and later biographers — identified as his old friend Dr. Lodewijk Meyer, though Professor Wolf believes it to have been a younger friend, Dr. Georg Hermann Schuler. In any case it was in the presence only of a physician-friend that Spinoza died, quietly as he had sought to live, on Sunday afternoon, February 20, 1677.

His landlord and landlady, the Hendrik van der Spycks, were at church at the time of Spinoza's death. He had made his home with them for the last six years of his life in what is now the Domus Spinozana. From their recollections of the philosopher virtually all detailed impressions of his intimate personality and habits of life are derived. Colerus, who sought them out and knew them well, recorded their memories in great detail. These first-hand impressions convey an authority far more convincing than accounts which he gives at second-hand or even less direct evidence, and they are confirmed by the less ample and circumstantial descriptions contained in the "Oldest Biography" and by others who knew Spinoza or knew acquaintances of his. Some of the latter were persons far from friendly to Spinoza, and when they report well of him add their astonishment that a man whose views they deplore should have lived so excellent and, indeed, moral a life.

JAMES GUTMANN

SPINOZA[1]

By Frederick J. E. Woodbridge

On 27 July, 1656, the Jews of Amsterdam expelled Spinoza from the Congregation of Israel. It is reported of them that they passed judgment upon him in words like these:

> The heads of the Ecclesiastical Council hereby make known that already well assured of the evil opinions and doings of Baruch de Espinoza, they have endeavored in sundry ways and by various promises to turn him from his evil courses. But as they have been unable to bring him to any better way of thinking; on the contrary, as they are every day better certified of the horrible heresies entertained and avowed by him, and of the insolence with which these heresies are promulgated and spread abroad, and many persons worthy of credit having borne witness to these in the presence of the said Espinoza, he has been held fully convicted of the same. Review having therefore been made of the whole matter before the Chiefs of the Ecclesiastical Council, it has been resolved, the Councillors assenting thereto, to anathematize the said Espinoza and to cut him off from the people of Israel, and from the present hour to place him in Anathema with the following malediction . . . .
>
> Let him be cursed by the mouths of the Seven Angels who preside over the seven days of the week, and by the mouths of the angels who follow them and fight under their banners. Let him be cursed by the Four Angels who preside over the four seasons of the year, and by the mouths of all the angels who follow them and fight under their banners. Let him be cursed by the mouths of the seven principalities. Let him be cursed by the mouth of the prince of the Law, whose name is Crown and Seal. In a word, let him be cursed by the mouth of the strong, powerful, and dreadful God.
>
> Let God never forgive him his sins. Let the wrath and indignation of the Lord surround him and smoke forever on his head. Let all the curses contained in the book of the Law fall upon him. Let God blot him out of his book. Let God separate him to his own destruction from all the tribes of Israel, and give him for his lot all the curses contained in the Book of the Law . . . .
>
> And we warn you, that none may speak with him by word of

[1] A lecture delivered in Havemeyer Hall, Columbia University, 26 January, 1933.

mouth nor by writing, nor show any favor to him, nor be under one roof with him, nor come within four cubits of him, nor read any paper composed by him.[2]

The man thus driven out from the fellowship of his own people found no welcome from Christian congregations. They feared his influence and called him atheist. Yet this atheist would have the first commandment this: "Thou shalt love the Lord thy God with all thy *mind*." He would have it this for the unusual reason that he was convinced that God loves all his creatures equally and so has a preferential love for none. God's care is for the whole of what he has created, not for a part of it preferred to some other part. He has no chosen people. He loves man no more and no less than he loves the sands of the desert. The "atheist" wrote a book to show how this is so. He gave it the odd title *Ethica in ordine geometrico demonstrata*, or *Ethics Geometrically Demonstrated*. It has given him a place among the great philosophers, and current interest in its philosophy has led to the commemoration of Spinoza in many parts of the world during the three-hundredth anniversary of the year of his birth, 1632.

Condemned by Christian and Jew alike, with few friends, with little recognition in his own day and for years after, living so largely a life of isolation, persecution, and poverty, Spinoza presents personally a tragic figure. It is natural to picture him among humanity's saints and martyrs. I shall not, however, try to estimate how far his life reflected the philosophy which he expounded. Just now, my interest, and I would have it yours, is in his convictions and his book. It is not his only book, but it is the one by which he is remembered and which has made his others precious and revealed them as indications of those convictions to which he tried to give final and persuasive expression in the greatest of all his books. Nor shall I attempt to place his book in its historical setting, to deal with it in relation to the preceding currents of philosophical thought which flowed together in the making of it. These are matters for the historian and ought not to be omitted from a course in the history of philosophy. But today is exceptional. We want to remember a great book and what it says to those who are interested in the love of wisdom as that love discloses itself through the years in the words of those who have encouraged it.

[2] Abraham Wolfson, *Spinoza. A Life of Reason* (New York, 1932), 74 ff.

Historically considered, Spinoza confronted the philosophical attitude which had found an energizing spokesman in Descartes, with a distillation of scholastic theory, transformed into a theory of nature. With him, to consider God was to consider Nature and to consider Nature was to consider God. He would transform the formula, *Deus et natura* into *Deus sive natura*. He confronted modern philosophy, at the start, with the union of that which it deliberately separated — not "God *and* nature," but "God *or* Nature." The names were irrelevant, that which was named was essential. Spinoza chose the name "God" and made "Nature" its equivalent, because he found in nature not only something to explore, but also something to admire and worship. The order of nature is not fully disposed of in associations for the advancement of science: a man must dispose of it in his living, for it is a disposition in his mind which controls his affections. Something like this may be said in sum about Spinoza's historical position. I turn to his book.

Its subject is Ethics. If we want to know what ethics is in general, we may go to the dictionary for a definition. We shall find there a variety of definitions conformable to the usage of writers. If we want to know what ethics is for Spinoza, we should go to his book and examine it. It has five parts: the first about God; the second about the origin and nature of the mind; the third about the nature and origin of the affections; the fourth about human slavery or the forces of the affections; the fifth about the power of the intellect or human freedom. On the face of it, the book would carry the reader from a consideration of God to the discovery of human freedom, by leading him to a knowledge of what his mind is, what his affections are and how they enslave him to them, and what the power is which can free him from that slavery. Ethics is thus for Spinoza the study of the life of freedom — the exposition of a way of thinking and the recommendation of a way of living, which, together, will free us from our unruly wills and affections which are the causes of our misery. We would be delivered from them. To get deliverance from them we should begin, not with them, but with God.

In the study of philosophers, I have found it good to try to discover their convictions first and their methods of expounding them second. The attempt to convince another is often unconvincing. It involves an argument, and the following of an argument is something quite different from entertaining a conviction. I am convinced that you are men and women, here in this room on 26 January, 1933. I doubt if you or I doubt this at all. But if I should try to convince you of our mutual convictions, I am sure that you would be more interested in my argument than in being what you are. We should soon be on debatable ground and possibly quarrelling about the soundness of the argument. The convictions of philosophers are often more interesting and frequently better than the arguments they use in supporting them. Consideration of the argument is largely a consideration of logical consistency and thorough consistency is difficult to attain. Consideration of convictions leads one to reflect on their character and their power, on what they do or may do to us. Sometimes, when the argument fails to support them, they do not lose their power. It is well, therefore, to find out what a philosopher's convictions are before worrying much about his argument in support of them.

This is important in the case of Spinoza. His argument is developed in a form unusual and involves words, the sound of which is impressive and the sense obscure. Often, simply by repeating the words, "intellectual intuition," "infinite substance," "infinite attributes," "eternity," "essence," "existence finite and infinite," "the intellectual love of the mind for God is part of the infinite love with which God loves himself" — often simply by repeating such words, one experiences an elevation and mistakes the elevation for clear thinking. It is difficult to express the convictions of Spinoza without using some of these words, but using them is an exhibition of their power even when their sense escapes us. "Slavery" and "freedom" are less troublesome words. We usually know what we mean when we use them. We know what we mean when we say that a man is the slave of habit or convention instead of the master of them. There is slavery to ambition, to prejudice, to riches, to pleasure, to circumstances. There is slavery to the affections, to what we love and hate, to what we hope for and fear; slavery to society, to the state, to the church; to family, to husband, wife, and children. From all such slavery we think it would be good to be free. We have to pay in some way or other for all that we possess and enjoy, to find ourselves more or less slaves to the price. Spinoza saw mankind as thus enslaved — creatures in bondage to their affections, to what they love and want, yet wanting what they love in freedom from the bondage which it brings. Above all Spinoza sees us enslaved by what he calls *Perturbationes mentis* or mental anxiety. We must care for what we love and want and that care is anxious care. We may lose, are daily in danger of losing, all that on which our affections are set. Those things which we call the goods of life, health, wealth, esteem, pleasure, friends, all that we hold dear — all these are precarious. They are held at an anxious risk which impels us to fortify ourselves against it by trying to get security, by concessions to others, by propitiations of others, of the fates, of God, by sacrifices of all sorts. In trying to get security, we must secure ourselves against others. There arise, consequently, hatreds and jealousies and enmities. We may shut and lock ourselves in, but anxiety sits outside on the step, waiting for us to come out. A mind without anxiety, undisturbed and at peace, would be free.

By what methods do people usually try to relieve the great burden of human anxiety? Some by indulgence in pleasure. Spinoza sees in this nothing but folly. It leads to satiety, disgust, disease and final wretchedness. Others try stoical indifference. There is the appearance of nobility in this, and there is certainly courage and fortitude. But it is courage and fortitude, and not freedom from anxiety. It commands the troubled waters of the mind to be still, but does not still them. Stoicism and asceticism of all sorts are really bewilderment in despair, marked by fortitude. Some there are who try to relieve anxiety by cultivating a belief in a god who will be well disposed towards man, if he is properly worshipped and propitiated. This is superstition which leads to religious bigotry and persecution. It is even worse, for it makes of God a whimsical person moved by human likes and dislikes, a jealous god who takes revenge, a judicial god who punishes and rewards, a changeable god who is flattered by attention. More thoughtful people try philanthropy. They encourage the instrumentalities and institutions which work for the lessening of human misery and distress. But philanthropy is medicine, not emancipation. It defines the human problem instead of solving it. It is intensified anxiety. It is, dispassionately considered, only organized slavery to the affections. As Spinoza saw indulgence, stoicism, the belief in providence and philanthropy, he saw human slavery only magnified. He did not see freedom or anything like it. The closer he examined them the clearer he saw in them exaggerated examples of human bondage, examples of anxious care, of being put to trouble with the consciousness of being put to trouble, and with being put to trouble for one's reward. This is not freedom. This is not happiness. It is slavery. Philanthropy is good. Thoughtful men will promote it to the best of their ability. They will, however, recognize it as bondage to the affections.

The essential character of this bondage, however, suggests the possibility of escape from it. Here I paraphrase the opening sentence of Spinoza's unfinished tract on the *Improvement of the Understanding*. "After experience had taught me how futile life usually is, when I became convinced that things are good and evil, not in themselves, but only as our affections are aroused by them, I finally decided to ask whether there is a true good, one that gives its goodness of itself and by which alone our affections might be aroused; nay, rather, whether there were something which when found and possessed, could be kept forever with perfect and unbroken joy." This sentence converts the slavery into the possibility of emancipation. Perhaps it would be better to say that slavery is here revealed as a possibility of transforming itself by its own method. We can not, Spinoza is convinced, escape the dominion of our affections. We are slaves of the love of something. The character and scope of our slavery depend on the character and scope of what we love. Is there then something, and can this something be found, which has the power to evoke a love which no other love can hinder or impair? Such a love would be slavery, but it would be so different from all other kinds that it would claim the name of freedom. It would invoke no denial of man's affectionate nature. It would involve the supreme exercise of that nature freed from envy, hatred, malice and jealousy, freed from the aching anxiety of the mind. The loves that enslave can be overcome only if there is and can be found an object which inspires a love that frees.

Can such an object be found? Spinoza thinks that we ought rather to ask, What is the way to find it? What does trying to find it involve? His answer is: "It involves the discovery of the union of the mind with the whole of Nature." This is to involve a good deal. Before being staggered by the immensity of it, and exclaiming that a discovery so vast is beyond ordinary human power, one may pause to reflect whether the object could be found without that discovery. Change it to *our* union with the whole of nature or to our place in the scheme of things, and then it looks inevitable that, could we discover that union or find that place, we should know whether that object can be found. This is what Spinoza means. It reveals two of his deep-seated convictions. One is that we are what we are because of our place in nature and for no other reason, and the other is that we are bound to be miserable and unhappy so long as we are ignorant of what that place is. This second conviction throws a new light on our bondage and our anxiety of mind, and also on the possibility of escape from them. We are dissatisfied with the place we imagine ourselves to occupy. We find in it a competition of loves and not one sustaining love. We are haunted by the suspicion that it is not our proper place, that it is not where we really belong. All this, thinks Spinoza, is clear proof that we are ignorant of what our place is. For if we were not, how could we have all these doubts and perplexities about it? We have the sense of belonging to something and we want to belong to something which will fill us with an overmastering love, but we are ignorant of what that something is. If we knew what it is, Spinoza is convinced that our whole mental attitude would be changed. We should then see life in a different perspective from that of from day to day. He tells us our place is in nature and to nature we belong. And that, he thinks, ought to make us happy and free. It sounds easy. Spinoza tells us it is difficult and rare.

Having a place in nature and belonging to nature is not having a place in New York and belonging to New York. It might be a helpful exercise in understanding Spinoza, to put the two places side by side and observe their contrasted effects upon our attitude of mind. Which is the larger place; which the securer? In which are we the more cabined and confined? In which is the imagination the ampler and the more expansive? In which are we the more lifted out of ourselves to the contemplation of imperishable things? In which do we feel the more intimately the pressure of something "deeply interfused whose dwelling is the light of setting suns, and the round ocean and the blue air and in the mind of man?" Placed over against nature, in contrast and in opposition to it, we may shrink to well-nigh nothing. Placed in nature, as completely belonging to it — is there then shrinkage or something else? Being in and belonging to New York, Chicago, London, Paris, Berlin, Moscow, Amsterdam, and being in and belonging to nature — Spinoza would have us reflect on the difference and discover what difference it makes, what difference in our attitude of mind and in the affections that arise within us.

He would have us carry the contrast into particulars. How do hunger, thirst and nakedness, poverty and riches, love and jealousy, friendship and enmity, health and disease, happiness and misery, life and death — how do they all look when we put ourselves in New York and belong to New York and when we put ourselves in nature and belong to nature? We may try the experiment at our leisure. Spinoza is convinced that if we try it thoroughly, our minds will find something different from that aching anxiety which destroys their peace.

But what is our place in nature? The question is now no longer one of geography. It is not a matter of latitude and longitude. It is not even a matter of length of days or of personal biographies. It is not ascertained by chart and compass or by reference to the calendar. It is discovered by the mind. It is the same place as that of the sands of the desert, or of the stars, if you will. It is a necessary place, a place, that is, which nature does not and can not get on without and without which neither we nor the sands of the desert can get on. It is the place which embraces all places and is all places embraced. It is a belonging to all that can be belonged to and all that can be belonged to belongs to it. We must keep in mind that this is the mind's discovery. Geographically it is nonsense. The belongings, the property, of which it speaks, are not like those occasional possessions which pass from hand to hand. Although the mind borrows its words from geography and getting and spending, it has discovered something else. It has discovered order, connection, interdependence, integrity, completeness, perfection. It has discovered essence, existence, idea and power. These do not define something to be found on a map or dated in a calendar. They define something without which nothing can be nor be conceived. Without it there could be no sands of the desert and no man to discover it. Put it into a definition with words which philosophers use, it turns out to be the definition of that which theologians name God. To belong to nature is to belong to what nature *is*, to belong to that without which neither the sands of the desert nor the people of New York could be at all. Spinoza is convinced of this. In the light of this conviction, he was convinced that that true good he sought could be found, that object which could evoke a changeless love for ever, the mind's love of God which is God's love itself.

Such were Spinoza's convictions. They were not the result of his writing his book, but the reason why he wrote it. By that I mean that his book does not represent the way he arrived at his convictions, but the way he expressed them. He was convinced himself and sought to convince others. He tries to convince them, not by persuasion, but by demonstration; not by having the sounds of great words impose upon the heart, but by having a rigorous proof control the mind by its necessity. He seems to have thought that there was but one possible way of doing this and risked it, even if he made it very difficult to follow. It was the way of geometry, that science which, ever since its exaltation by Plato and its demonstration by Euclid, has exerted supremely the force of conviction over the human mind. Spinoza chose it and tried to cast the substance of what he had to say in geometrical form. He begins with definitions which are to identify for himself and the reader the objects of his demonstrations, definitions of what he means by such terms as "substance," "attribute," "mode," "God." He follows these with axioms or propositions which are not themselves proved, but are to be accepted for the proof of other propositions, as, for example, "Whatever can be conceived as non-existent, its essence does not involve existence." Then he proceeds to propositions about substance and God with the demonstrations of them. For example: Prop. I. "Substance is by nature prior to its modes." Demonstration: "This is evident from definitions 3 and 5." And so on through his five books, adding here and there explanations in discursive form for the assistance of the reader. In this way, with the force of geometry, he tried to convince others that his convictions were demonstrable.

I have always seen in Spinoza's use of the geometrical method something more than a technique of demonstration. The pattern which the propositions of geometry weave is like the pattern which Spinoza's convictions weave. It is a pattern which the eye does not see, but which the mind embraces and comprehends. You can not spread the pattern out and make a map of it, yet you deal with figures, like triangles and circles, which you draw and which the eye does see, but which without the pattern could neither be nor be conceived, as figures of just that kind, as circles and triangles. The pattern is not stretched out in time, yet proposition follows proposition. Among them there is before and after, and they exemplify themselves in the fleeting figures which you draw. But the pattern — the mind discovers that, and once discovered, it discloses that no single proposition can be true unless all the others are true, and they can not be true unless it is true. They belong to it and it belongs to them. Their place in the pattern is its place also. There is no choice place, nor any chosen figure. There is only perfection, the perfection of the pattern, shared equally by everything that falls under it. Apart from that falling under, the figures are inaccurately drawn triangles and untrue circles. Apart from the pattern, they are imperfect. Acknowledging their places in the pattern, they are perfect. It all sounds like Spinoza's convictions in geometrical terms — anxious man and desert sands transformed through the recognition of their place.

I turn again to the book. It is about ethics and ethics for Spinoza is the study of the life of freedom. In this study he puts God first, for God is not the last resort of desperation, but the first resort of understanding. It may sound strange to many ears, to hear that of all objects of knowledge, God is the best and readiest known. It sounds strange because the ears have habitually heard that God is the God of Abraham, Isaac and Jacob, and of the Christian Church. He is, but not as he is said to be. He is the God of creation or of nature, first, and, consequently, might be the God of Christian and of Jew. When the consequence alone is remembered and the fact that it is a consequence forgotten, then God is a last resort and quite impossible to understand. He behaves in an astonishing manner. When, however, it is remembered that he is the God of creation or of nature, then there lies nature before us like an open book to be read. We may be puzzled about details and let them confuse our understanding, but when we consider the matter carefully, we are not confused at all because then we see that nature is the order and connection of things and that the mind is engaged with and is in that order and connection. We need not be ignorant, because we really are not, that this order and connection is the way that things and the mind are held together and that without it, things and the mind would not be at all. This knowledge, simple as it is, is profound. Philosophers have turned it into a doctrine of substance. They explain to us how we are forced to say that substance is in all ways self-sufficient. It needs nothing outside itself and is nothing outside itself. It is perfect, complete, infinite, with infinite attributes, its essence, existence, idea, and power are all identical each with each. Because of it whatever is, follows. Whatever is, is in it and without it nothing can be or be conceived. This is what philosophers say substance is. It is also what they say nature is. When they forget Christians and Jews or ask what God is before he is the God of people, they say that God is substance. Integrated order and connection, substance, nature, ultimate essence, existence, idea, and power, God — these are all only different expressions for that in which everything that is, *is* and without which nothing can be nor be conceived. Of nothing else, thinks Spinoza, have we more immediate or more certain knowledge. On it knowledge of everything else depends. Into it our knowledge of everything else must be fitted, our knowledge of the nature and origin of the mind, of the origin and nature of the affections, of human slavery and the forces of the affections, of human freedom and intellectual power. Then ethics has rounded out its study of the life of freedom.

The first part of the *Ethics* is a demonstration complete in itself, and, technically considered, is the most perfect of all the parts. It controls the others. By that I mean that the others are fitted into it, and that is what Spinoza would have. We may study the mind independently if we want to, as the psychologist does. We may study our emotional and affectionate life in a similar way. So also we may study human morals and institutions, as instrumentalities of better living. We may consider independently how we are let and hindered and how free we are to do what we would. Such studies, pursued in this independent way, fall short. They leave us without foundations. They bewilder and disorganize the mind. They leave us in ultimate ignorance and perplexity. There is war, not peace, in the camps of the learned. *Perturbationes mentis*, mental disturbances, find their home in schools. The reason is the attempt at independence of approach. This will not do for Ethics. It will not do for those who want a life of freedom or a life of love. For such and for Ethics, all knowledge must be seen in its relation to knowledge of substance, of nature, of God. It must be seen geometrically as one sees circles and triangles, not as individuals in their isolation and imperfection, but in their order and connection, having their place in the perfect. If we begin with God, thinks Spinoza, we shall not cease to be men, we shall not cease to work hard or to have troubles and pains, but our attitude of mind will be changed. We shall not go through life crying, complaining, and afraid. We shall not be docile, submissive, dissolute, or resolute. We shall be something quite different. We shall be like one who has found an object which creates an irresistible love which can not be lost, or taken away, or impaired should others love it too.

Did Spinoza really prove all this? I wonder if that is an important or even a decent question to ask. If we must answer it, the answer seems to be "No" because serious students have repeatedly found that his argument in its own terms is not convincing. But how much has an argument to do with a man's convictions? It may clarify them to himself and others whether it is sound or not. The convictions and their power are far more important than the argument. It is very important to discover what living in this world does do and can do to a man. It generates convictions. What are they? What are they worth? What is their power? These are better questions than, Is the argument sound? I have tried to exhibit what the convictions of Spinoza were and to indicate how he supported them argumentatively. The question of their power, I leave him to answer in his own concluding words if you will let me imagine him to be speaking English instead of Latin.

"I have now finished what I wished to show about the power of the mind over the affections and about the freedom of the mind. From it all it is clear how much stronger and more powerful the wise man is than a fool who is moved by impulse alone. For the fool is not only agitated in many ways by external causes and has no real peace of mind, but he lives ignorant of himself and of God, and of things; as soon as he ceases to suffer, he ceases to be. But the wise man, in so far as he is considered wise, has a mind hard to disturb; conscious by an eternal necessity of himself and of God and of things, he never ceases to be and is always possessed of a mind truly at peace. If the way which I have shown leads to this, seems to be very difficult, yet it can be found. And surely it must be difficult, because it is so rarely found. For if deliverance were impromptu and could be had without great labor, how could it happen that almost everybody misses it? But all excellent things are as difficult as they are rare."

SELECTED BIBLIOGRAPHY

In addition to the works presented in this volume, Spinoza's writings include his *Short Treatise on God, Man and His Well-Being* (translated by A. Wolf, London, 1910), his *Tractatus theologico-politicus* and his *Tractatus politicus* (translated by R. H. M. Elwes, London, 1905–1906). Students are also urged to read Spinoza's *Correspondence* (translated by A. Wolf, London, 1928).

Alexander, Samuel, *Spinoza and Time.* London, 1927.

Brunschwicg, Léon, *Spinoza et ses contemporains.* Paris, 1923.

Caird, John, *Spinoza.* Edinburgh, 1899.

Duff, R. A., *Spinoza's Political and Ethical Philosophy.* Glasgow, 1903.

Fischer, Kuno, *Spinozas Leben, Werke und Lehre.* Heidelberg, 1909.

Friedländer, M. H., *Spinoza, His Life and Philosophy.* London, 1887.

Hallett, H. F., *Aeternitas.* Oxford, 1930.

Joachim, H. H., *A Study of the Ethics of Spinoza.* Oxford, 1901.

Martineau, James, *A Study of Spinoza.* London, 1882.

McKeon, Richard, *The Philosophy of Spinoza.* New York, 1928.

Pollock, Frederick, *Spinoza, His Life and Philosophy.* London, 1889.

—— *Spinoza.* London, 1935.

Roth, Leon, *Spinoza, Descartes, and Maimonides.* Oxford, 1924.

—— *Spinoza.* London, 1935.

Wolf, Abraham, *The Oldest Biography of Spinoza.* New York, 1927.

Wolfson, H. A., *The Philosophy of Spinoza.* Cambridge, 1934.

Various Authors, *Septimana Spinozana.* The Hague, 1933.

ON THE IMPROVEMENT
OF THE UNDERSTANDING

Treatise on the Correction of the Understanding and
on the Way in Which It May Be Directed toward
a True Knowledge of Things

On the Improvement of the Understanding

AFTER experience had taught me that all the usual surroundings of social life are vain and futile; seeing that none of the objects of my fears contained in themselves anything either good or bad, except in so far as the mind is affected by them, I finally resolved to inquire whether there might be some real good having power to communicate itself, which would affect the mind singly, to the exclusion of all else: whether, in fact, there might be anything of which the discovery and attainment would enable me to enjoy continuous, supreme, and unending happiness. I say "I *finally* resolved," for at first sight it seemed unwise willingly to lose hold on what was sure for the sake of something then uncertain. I could see the benefits which are acquired through fame and riches, and that I should be obliged to abandon the quest of such objects, if I seriously devoted myself to the search for something different and new. I perceived that if true happiness chanced to be placed in the former I should necessarily miss it; while if, on the other hand, it were not so placed, and I gave them my whole attention, I should equally fail.

I therefore debated whether it would not be possible to arrive at the new principle, or at any rate at a certainty concerning its existence, without changing the conduct and usual plan of my life; with this end in view I made many efforts, but in vain. For the ordinary surroundings of life which are esteemed by men (as their actions testify) to be the highest good, may be classed under the three heads — Riches, Fame, and the Pleasures of Sense: with these three the mind is so absorbed that it has little power to reflect on any different good. By sensual pleasure the mind is enthralled to the extent of quiescence, as if the supreme good were actually attained, so that it is quite incapable of thinking of any other object; when such pleasure has been gratified it is followed by extreme melancholy, whereby the mind, though not enthralled, is disturbed and dulled.

The pursuit of honors and riches is likewise very absorbing, especially if such objects be sought simply for their own sake,[1] inasmuch as they

[1] This might be explained more at large and more clearly: I mean, by distinguishing riches according as they are pursued for their own sake, or in furtherance of fame,

are then supposed to constitute the highest good. In the case of fame the mind is still more absorbed, for fame is conceived as always good for its own sake, and as the ultimate end to which all actions are directed. Further, the attainment of riches and fame is not followed as in the case of sensual pleasures by repentance, but, the more we acquire, the greater is our delight, and, consequently, the more we are incited to increase both the one and the other; on the other hand, if our hopes happen to be frustrated we are plunged into the deepest sadness. Fame has the further drawback that it compels its votaries to order their lives according to the opinions of their fellow-men, shunning what they usually shun, and seeking what they usually seek.

When I saw that all these ordinary objects of desire would be obstacles in the way of a search for something different and new — nay, that they were so opposed thereto, that either they or it would have to be abandoned, I was forced to inquire which would prove the most useful to me: for, as I say, I seemed to be willingly losing hold on a sure good for the sake of something uncertain. However, after I had reflected on the matter, I came in the first place to the conclusion that by abandoning the ordinary objects of pursuit, and betaking myself to a new quest, I should be leaving a good, uncertain by reason of its own nature, as may be gathered from what has been said, for the sake of a good not uncertain in its nature (for I sought for a fixed good), but only in the possibility of its attainment.

Further reflection convinced me that if I could really get to the root of the matter, I should be leaving certain evils for a certain good. I thus perceived that I was in a state of great peril, and I compelled myself to seek with all my strength for a remedy, however uncertain it might be—as a sick man struggling with a deadly disease, when he sees that death will surely be upon him unless a remedy be found, is compelled to seek such a remedy with all his strength, inasmuch as his whole hope lies therein. All the objects pursued by the multitude, not only bring no remedy that tends to preserve our being, but even act as hindrances, causing the death not seldom of those who possess them, and always of those who are possessed by them.[2] There are

or sensual pleasure, or the advancement of science and art. But this subject is reserved to its own place, for it is not here proper to investigate the matter more accurately.

[2]These considerations should be set forth more precisely.

many examples of men who have suffered persecution even to death for the sake of their riches, and of men who in pursuit of wealth have exposed themselves to so many dangers that they have paid away their life as a penalty for their folly. Examples are no less numerous of men, who have endured the utmost wretchedness for the sake of gaining or preserving their reputation. Lastly, there are innumerable cases of men who have hastened their death through over-indulgence in sensual pleasure. All these evils seem to have arisen from the fact that happiness or unhappiness is made wholly to depend on the quality of the object which we love. When a thing is not loved, no quarrels will arise concerning it — no sadness will be felt if it perishes — no envy if it is possessed by another — no fear, no hatred, in short no disturbances of the mind. All these arise from the love of what is perishable, such as the objects already mentioned. But love toward a thing eternal and infinite feeds the mind wholly with joy, and is itself unmingled with any sadness, wherefore it is greatly to be desired and sought for with all our strength. Yet it was not at random that I used the words, "If I could go to the root of the matter," for, though what I have urged was perfectly clear to my mind, I could not forthwith lay aside all love of riches, sensual enjoyment, and fame. One thing was evident, namely, that while my mind was employed with these thoughts it turned away from its former objects of desire, and seriously considered the search for a new principle; this state of things was a great comfort to me, for I perceived that the evils were not such as to resist all remedies. Although these intervals were at first rare, and of very short duration, yet afterwards, as the true good became more and more discernible to me, they became more frequent and more lasting; especially after I had recognized that the acquisition of wealth, sensual pleasure, or fame, is only a hindrance, so long as they are sought as ends, not as means; if they be sought as means, they will be under restraint, and, far from being hindrances, will further not a little the end for which they are sought, as I will show in due time.

I will here only briefly state what I mean by true good, and also what is the nature of the highest good. In order that this may be rightly understood, we must bear in mind that the terms good and evil are only applied relatively, so that the same thing may be called both good and bad, according to the relations in view, in the same way as it may be called perfect or imperfect. Nothing regarded in its own nature can be called perfect or imperfect; especially when we are aware that all things which come to pass, come to pass according to the eternal order and fixed laws of Nature. However, human weakness cannot attain to this order in its own thoughts, but meanwhile man conceives a human character much more stable than his own, and sees that there is no reason why he should not himself acquire such a character. Thus he is led to seek for means which will bring him to this pitch of perfection, and calls everything which will serve as such means a true good. The chief good is that he should arrive, together with other individuals if possible, at the possession of the aforesaid character. What that character is we shall show in due time, namely, that it is the knowledge of the union existing between the mind and the whole of Nature.[3] This, then, is the end for which I strive: to attain to such a character myself, and to endeavor that many should attain to it with me. In other words, it is part of my happiness to lend a helping hand, that many others may understand even as I do, so that their understanding and desire may entirely agree with my own. In order to bring this about, it is necessary to understand as much of Nature as will enable us to attain to the aforesaid character, and also to form a social order such as is most conducive to the attainment of this character by the greatest number with the least difficulty and danger. We must seek the assistance of Moral Philosophy[4] and the Theory of Education; further, as health is no insignificant means for attaining our end, we must also include the whole science of Medicine, and, as many difficult things are by contrivance rendered easy, and we can in this way gain much time and convenience, the science of Mechanics must in no way be despised. But, before all things, a means must be devised for improving the understanding and purifying it, as far as may be at the outset, so that it may apprehend things without error, and in the best possible way.

Thus it is apparent to every one that I wish to direct all sciences to one end and aim,[5] so that we may attain to the supreme human perfection which we have named; and, therefore, whatsoever in the

[3]These matters are explained more at length elsewhere.
[4]N.B. I do no more here than enumerate the sciences necessary for our purpose; I lay no stress on their order.
[5]There is for the sciences but one end, to which they should all be directed.

sciences does not serve to promote our object will have to be rejected as useless. To sum up the matter in a word, all our actions and thoughts must be directed to this one end. Yet, as it is necessary that while we are endeavoring to attain our purpose, and bring the understanding into the right path, we should carry on our life, we are compelled first of all to lay down certain rules of life as provisionally good, to wit, the following:

I. To speak in a manner intelligible to the multitude, and to comply with every general custom that does not hinder the attainment of our purpose. For we can gain from the multitude no small advantages, provided that we strive to accommodate ourselves to its understanding as far as possible; moreover, we shall in this way gain a friendly audience for the reception of the truth.

II. To indulge ourselves with pleasures only in so far as they are necessary for preserving health.

III. Lastly, to endeavor to obtain only sufficient money or other commodities to enable us to preserve our life and health, and to follow such general customs as are consistent with our purpose.

Having laid down these preliminary rules, I will betake myself to the first and most important task, namely, the amendment of the understanding, and the rendering it capable of understanding things in the manner necessary for attaining our end.

In order to bring this about, the natural order demands that I should here recapitulate all the modes of perception, which I have hitherto employed for affirming or denying anything with certainty, so that I may choose the best, and at the same time begin to know my own powers and the nature which I wish to perfect.

Reflection shows that all modes of perception or knowledge may be reduced to four:

I. Perception arising from hearsay or from some sign which everyone may name as he pleases.

II. Perception arising from mere experience — that is, from experience not yet classified by the intellect, and only so called because the given event has happened to take place, and because we have no contradictory fact to set against it, so that it therefore remains unassailed in our mind.

III. Perception arising when the essence of one thing is inferred from another thing, but not adequately; this comes[6] when from some effect we gather its cause, or when it is inferred from some general proposition that some property is always present.

IV. Lastly, there is the perception arising when a thing is perceived solely through its essence, or through the knowledge of its proximate cause.

All these kinds of perception I will illustrate by examples. By hearsay I know the day of my birth, my parentage, and other matters about which I have never felt any doubt. By mere experience I know that I shall die, for this I can affirm from having seen that others like myself have died, though all did not live for the same period, or die by the same disease. I know by mere experience that oil has the property of feeding fire, and water of extinguishing it. In the same way I know that a dog is a barking animal, man a rational animal, and in fact nearly all the practical knowledge of life.

We deduce one thing from another as follows: when we clearly perceive that we feel a certain body and no other, we thence clearly infer that the mind is united to the body,[7] and that their union is the cause of the given sensation; but we cannot thence absolutely understand the nature of the sensation and the union.[8] Or, after I have become acquainted with the nature of vision, and know that it has

[6]In this case we do not understand anything of the cause from the consideration of it in the effect. This is sufficiently evident from the fact that the cause is only spoken of in very general terms, such as — there exists then something; there exists then some power, etc.; or from the fact that we only express it in a negative manner — it is not this or that, etc. In the second case something is ascribed to the cause because of the effect, as we shall show in an example, but only a property, never the essence.

[7]From this example may be clearly seen what I have just drawn attention to. For through this union we understand nothing beyond the sensation, the effect, to wit, from which we inferred the cause of which we understand nothing.

[8]A conclusion of this sort, though it be certain, is yet not to be relied on without great caution; for unless we are exceedingly careful we shall forthwith fall into error. When things are conceived thus abstractedly, and not through their true essence, they are apt to be confused by the imagination. For that which is in itself one, men imagine to be multiplex. To those things which are conceived abstractedly, apart, and confusedly, terms are applied which are apt to become wrested from their strict meaning and bestowed on things more familiar; whence it results that these latter are imagined in the same way as the former to which the terms were originally given.

the property of making one and the same thing appear smaller when far off than when near, I can infer that the sun is larger than it appears, and can draw other conclusions of the same kind.

Lastly, a thing may be perceived solely through its essence: when, from the fact of knowing something, I know what it is to know that thing, or when, from knowing the essence of the mind, I know that it is united to the body. By the same kind of knowledge we know that two and three make five, or that two lines each parallel to a third, are parallel to one another, etc. The things which I have been able to know by this kind of knowledge are as yet very few.

In order that the whole matter may be put in a clearer light, I will make use of a single illustration as follows. Three numbers are given — it is required to find a fourth, which shall be to the third as the second is to the first. Tradesmen will at once tell us that they know what is required to find the fourth number, for they have not yet forgotten the rule which was given to them arbitrarily without proof by their masters; others construct a universal axiom from their experience with simple numbers, where the fourth number is self-evident, as in the case of 2, 4, 3, 6; here it is evident that if the second number be multiplied by the third, and the product divided by the first, the quotient is 6; when they see that by this process the number is produced which they knew beforehand to be the proportional, they infer that the process always holds good for finding a fourth number proportional. Mathematicians, however, know by the proof of the nineteenth proposition of the seventh book of Euclid, what numbers are proportionals, namely, from the nature and property of proportion it follows that the product of the first and fourth will be equal to the product of the second and third; still they do not see the adequate proportionality of the given numbers or, if they do see it, they see it not by virtue of Euclid's proposition, but intuitively, without going through any process.

In order that from these modes of perception the best may be selected, it is well that we should briefly enumerate the means necessary for attaining our end.

I. To have an exact knowledge of our nature which we desire to perfect, and to know as much as is needful of Nature in general.

II. To collect in this way the differences, the agreements, and the oppositions of things.

III. To learn thus exactly how far they can or cannot be modified.

IV. To compare this result with the nature and power of man. We shall thus discern the highest degree of perfection to which man is capable of attaining. We shall then be in a position to see which mode of perception we ought to choose.

As to the first mode, it is evident that from hearsay our knowledge must always be uncertain, and, moreover, can give us no insight into the essence of a thing, as is manifest in our illustration; now one can only arrive at knowledge of a thing through knowledge of its essence, as will hereafter appear. We may, therefore, clearly conclude that the certainty arising from hearsay cannot be scientific in its character. For simple hearsay cannot affect anyone whose understanding does not, so to speak, meet it half way.

The second mode of perception[9] cannot be said to give us the idea of the proportion of which we are in search. Moreover its results are very uncertain and indefinite, for we shall never discover anything in natural phenomena by its means, except accidental properties, which are never clearly understood, unless the essence of the things in question be known first. Wherefore this mode also must be rejected.

Of the third mode of perception we may say in a manner that it gives us the idea of the thing sought, and that it enables us to draw conclusions without risk of error; yet it is not by itself sufficient to put us in possession of the perfection we aim at.

The fourth mode alone apprehends the adequate essence of a thing without danger of error. This mode, therefore, must be the one which we chiefly employ. How, then, should we avail ourselves of it so as to gain the fourth kind of knowledge with the least delay concerning things previously unknown? I will proceed to explain.

Now that we know what kind of knowledge is necessary for us, we must indicate the way and the method whereby we may gain the said knowledge concerning the things needful to be known. In order to accomplish this, we must first take care not to commit ourselves to a search, going back to infinity — that is, in order to discover the best method for finding out the truth, there is no need of another method to discover such method; nor of a third method for discovering

[9] I shall here treat a little more in detail of experience, and shall examine the method adopted by the Empirics, and by recent philosophers.

the second, and so on to infinity. By such proceedings, we should never arrive at the knowledge of the truth, or, indeed, at any knowledge at all. The matter stands on the same footing as the making of material tools, which might be argued about in a similar way. For, in order to work iron, a hammer is needed, and the hammer cannot be forthcoming unless it has been made; but, in order to make it, there was need of another hammer and other tools, and so on to infinity. We might thus vainly endeavor to prove that men have no power of working iron. But as men at first made use of the instruments supplied by nature to accomplish very easy pieces of workmanship, laboriously and imperfectly, and then, when these were finished, wrought other things more difficult with less labor and greater perfection; and so gradually mounted from the simplest operations to the making of tools, and from the making of tools to the making of more complex tools, and fresh feats of workmanship, till they arrived at making, with small expenditure of labor, the vast number of complicated mechanisms which they now possess. So, in like manner, the intellect, by its native strength,[10] makes for itself intellectual instruments, whereby it acquires strength for performing other intellectual operations,[11] and from these operations gets again fresh instruments, or the power of pushing its investigations further, and thus gradually proceeds till it reaches the summit of wisdom.

That this is the path pursued by the understanding may be readily seen when we understand the nature of the method for finding out the truth, and of the natural instruments so necessary for the construction of more complex instruments, and for the progress of investigation. I thus proceed with my demonstration.

A true idea[12] (for we possess a true idea) is something different from its correlate (*idealum*); thus a circle is different from the idea of a circle. The idea of a circle is not something having a circumference and a center, as a circle has; nor is the idea of a body that body itself. Now, as it is something different from its correlate, it is capable of being understood through itself; in other words, the idea,

---

[10]By native strength, I mean that not bestowed on us by external causes, as I shall afterwards explain in my philosophy.

[11]I here term them operations: I shall explain their nature in my philosophy.

[12]I shall take care not only to demonstrate what I have just advanced, but also that we have hitherto proceeded rightly, and other things needful to be known.

in so far as its actual essence (*essentia formalis*) is concerned, may be the subject of another subjective essence (*essentia objectiva*).[13]   And, again, this second subjective essence will, regarded in itself, be something real, and capable of being understood; and so on, indefinitely. For instance, the man Peter is something real; the true idea of Peter is the reality of Peter represented subjectively, and is in itself something real, and quite distinct from the actual Peter.   Now, as this true idea of Peter is in itself something real, and has its own individual existence, it will also be capable of being understood — that is, of being the subject of another idea, which will contain by representation (*objective*) all that the idea of Peter contains actually (*formaliter*). And, again, this idea of the idea of Peter has its own individuality, which may become the subject of yet another idea; and so on, indefinitely.   This every one may make trial of for himself, by reflecting that he knows what Peter is, and also knows that he knows, and further knows that he knows that he knows, etc.   Hence it is plain that, in order to understand the actual Peter, it is not necessary first to understand the idea of Peter, and still less the idea of the idea of Peter.   This is the same as saying that, in order to know, there is no need to know that we know, much less to know that we know that we know.   This is no more necessary than to know the nature of a circle before knowing the nature of a triangle.[14]   But, with these ideas, the contrary is the case: for, in order to know that I know, I must first know.   Hence it is clear that certainty is nothing else than the subjective essence of a thing: in other words, the mode in which we perceive an actual reality is certainty.   Further, it is also evident that, for the certitude of truth, no further sign is necessary beyond the possession of a true idea: for, as I have shown, it is not necessary to know that we know that we know.   Hence, again, it is clear that no one can know the nature of the highest certainty, unless he possesses an adequate idea, or the subjective essence of a thing: for certainty is

[13]In modern language, "the idea may become the subject of another representation." *Objectivus* generally corresponds to the modern "subjective," *formalis* to the modern "objective." — Tr.

[14]Observe that we are not here inquiring how this first subjective essence is innate in us. This belongs to an investigation into Nature, where all these matters are amply explained, and it is shown that without ideas neither affirmation nor negation nor volition are possible.

identical with such subjective essence. Thus, as the truth needs no sign — it being sufficient to possess the subjective essence of things, or, in other words, the ideas of them, in order that all doubts may be removed — it follows that the true method does not consist in seeking for the signs of truth after the acquisition of the idea, but that the true method teaches us the order in which we should seek for truth itself,[15] or the subjective essences of things, or ideas, for all these expressions are synonymous. Again, method must necessarily be concerned with reasoning or understanding — I mean, method is not identical with reasoning in the search for causes, still less is it the comprehension of the causes of things: it is the discernment of a true idea, by distinguishing it from other perceptions and by investigating its nature in order that we may thus know our power of understanding, and may so train our mind that it may, by a given standard, comprehend whatsoever is intelligible, by laying down certain rules as aids and by avoiding useless mental exertion.

Whence we may gather that method is nothing else than reflective knowledge, or the idea of an idea; and that as there can be no idea of an idea — unless an idea exists previously — there can be no method without a pre-existent idea. Therefore, that will be a good method which shows us how the mind should be directed according to the standard of the given true idea.

Again, seeing that the ratio existing between two ideas is the same as the ratio between the actual realities corresponding to those ideas, it follows that the reflective knowledge which has for its object the most perfect being is more excellent than reflective knowledge concerning other objects — in other words, that method will be most perfect which affords the standard of the given idea of the most perfect being whereby we may direct our mind. We thus easily understand how, in proportion as it acquires new ideas, the mind simultaneously acquires fresh instruments for pursuing its inquiries further. For we may gather from what has been said, that a true idea must necessarily first of all exist in us as a natural instrument; and that when this idea is apprehended by the mind, it enables us to understand the difference existing between itself and all other perceptions. In this, one part of the method consists.

Now it is clear that the mind apprehends itself better in proportion

[15]The nature of mental search is explained in my philosophy.

as it understands a greater number of natural objects; it follows, therefore, that this portion of the method will be more perfect in proportion as the mind attains to the comprehension of a greater number of objects, and that it will be absolutely perfect when the mind gains a knowledge of the absolutely perfect Being or becomes conscious thereof. Again, the more things the mind knows, the better does it understand its own strength and the order of Nature; by increased self-knowledge it can direct itself more easily, and lay down rules for its own guidance; and, by increased knowledge of Nature, it can more easily avoid what is useless.

And this is the sum total of method, as we have already stated. We may add that the idea in the world of thought is in the same case as its correlate in the world of reality. If, therefore, there be anything in Nature which is without connection[16] with any other thing, and if we assign to it a subjective essence, which would in every way correspond to the objective reality, the subjective essence would have no connection with any other ideas — in other words, we could not draw any conclusion with regard to it. On the other hand, those things which are connected with others — as all things that exist in Nature — will be understood by the mind, and their subjective essences will maintain the same mutual relations as their objective realities — that is to say, we shall infer from these ideas other ideas, which will in turn be connected with others, and thus our instruments for proceeding with our investigation will increase. This is what we are endeavoring to prove. Further, from what has just been said — namely, that an idea must, in all respects, correspond to its correlate in the world of reality — it is evident that, in order to reproduce in every respect the faithful image of Nature, our mind must deduce all its ideas from the idea which represents the origin and source of the whole of Nature, so that it may itself become the source of other ideas.

It may, perhaps, provoke astonishment that, after having said that the good method is that which teaches us to direct our mind according to the standard of the given true idea, we should prove our point by reasoning, which would seem to indicate that it is not self-evident. We may, therefore, be questioned as to the validity of our reasoning. If our reasoning be sound, we must take as a starting point a true idea.

[16]To be connected with other things is to be produced by them, or to produce them.

Now, to be certain that our starting point is really a true idea, we need a proof. This first course of reasoning must be supported by a second, the second by a third, and so on to infinity. To this I make answer that, if by some happy chance anyone had adopted this method in his investigations of Nature — that is, if he had acquired new ideas in the proper order, according to the standard of the original true idea, he would never have doubted of the truth of his knowledge,[17] inasmuch as truth, as we have shown, makes itself manifest, and all things would flow, as it were, spontaneously towards him. But as this never, or rarely, happens, I have been forced so to arrange my proceedings that we may acquire by reflection and forethought what we cannot acquire by chance, and that it may at the same time appear that, for proving the truth, and for valid reasoning, we need no other means than the truth and valid reasoning themselves: for by valid reasoning I have established valid reasoning, and, in like measure, I seek still to establish it. Moreover, this is the order of thinking adopted by men in their inward meditations. The reasons for its rare employment in investigations of Nature are to be found in current misconceptions, whereof we shall examine the causes hereafter in our philosophy. Moreover, it demands, as we shall show, a keen and accurate discernment. Lastly, it is hindered by the conditions of human life, which are, as we have already pointed out, extremely changeable. There are also other obstacles, which we will not here inquire into.

If any one asks why I have not at the starting point set forth all the truths of Nature in their due order, inasmuch as truth is self-evident, I reply by warning him not to reject as false any paradoxes he may find here, but to take the trouble to reflect on the chain of reasoning by which they are supported; he will then be no longer in doubt that we have attained to the truth. This is why I have begun as above.

If there yet remains some sceptic, who doubts of our primary truth, and of all deductions we make, taking such truth as our standard, he must either be arguing in bad faith, or we must confess that there are men in complete mental blindness, either innate or due to misconceptions — that is, to some external influence.

Such persons are not conscious of themselves. If they affirm or doubt anything, they know not that they affirm or doubt: they say

[17] In the same way as we have here no doubt of the truth of our knowledge.

that they know nothing, and they say that they are ignorant of the very fact of their knowing nothing. Even this they do not affirm absolutely; they are afraid of confessing that they exist, so long as they know nothing; in fact, they ought to remain dumb, for fear of haply supposing something which should smack of truth. Lastly, with such persons, one should not speak of sciences: for, in what relates to life and conduct, they are compelled by necessity to suppose that they exist, and seek their own advantage, and often affirm and deny, even with an oath. If they deny, grant, or gainsay, they know not that they deny, grant, or gainsay, so that they ought to be regarded as automata, utterly devoid of intelligence.

Let us now return to our proposition. Up to the present, we have, first, defined the end to which we desire to direct all our thoughts; second, we have determined the mode of perception best adapted to aid us in attaining our perfection; third, we have discovered the way which our mind should take, in order to make a good beginning — namely, that it should use every true idea as a standard in pursuing its inquiries according to fixed rules. Now, in order that it may thus proceed, our method must furnish us, first, with a means of distinguishing a true idea from all other perceptions, and enabling the mind to avoid the latter; second, with rules for perceiving unknown things according to the standard of the true idea; third, with an order which enables us to avoid useless labor. When we became acquainted with this method, we saw that, fourth, it would be perfect when we had attained to the idea of the absolutely perfect Being. This is an observation which should be made at the outset, in order that we may arrive at the knowledge of such a being more quickly.

Let us then make a beginning with the first part of the method, which is, as we have said, to distinguish and separate the true idea from other perceptions, and to keep the mind from confusing with true ideas those which are false, fictitious, and doubtful. I intend to dwell on this point at length, partly to keep a distinction so necessary before the reader's mind, and also because there are some who doubt of true ideas, through not having attended to the distinction between a true perception and all others. Such persons are like men who, while they are awake, doubt not that they are awake, but, afterward in a dream, as often happens, thinking that they are surely awake and then finding that they were in error, become doubtful even of being awake. This state of mind arises through neglect of the distinction between sleeping and waking.

Meanwhile, I give warning that I shall not here give the essence of every perception, and explain it through its proximate cause. Such work lies in the province of philosophy. I shall confine myself to what concerns method — that is, to the character of fictitious, false, and doubtful perception, and the means of freeing ourselves therefrom. Let us then first inquire into the nature of a fictitious idea.

Every perception has for its object either a thing considered as existing, or solely the essence of a thing. Now "fiction" is chiefly occupied with things considered as existing. I will, therefore, consider these first — I mean cases where only the existence of an object is feigned, and the thing thus feigned is understood, or assumed to be understood. For instance, I feign that Peter, whom I know to have gone home, is gone to see me,[18] or something of that kind. With what is such an idea concerned? It is concerned with things possible, and not with things necessary or impossible. I call a thing *impossible*, when its existence would imply a contradiction; *necessary*, when its non-existence would imply a contradiction; *possible*, when neither its existence nor its non-existence imply a contradiction, but when the necessity or impossibility of its nature depends on causes unknown to us, while we feign that it exists. If the necessity or impossibility of its existence depending on external causes were known to us, we could not form any fictitious hypothesis about it; whence it follows that if there be a God, or omniscient Being, such an one cannot form fictitious hypotheses. For, as regards ourselves, when I know that I exist, I cannot hypothesize that I exist or do not exist,[19] any more than I can hypothesize an elephant that can go through the eye of a needle; nor when I know the nature of God, can I hypothesize that He exists or does not exist.[20] The same thing must be said of the Chimera, whereof

[18]See below the note on hypotheses, whereof we have a clear understanding; the fiction consists in saying that such hypotheses exist in heavenly bodies.

[19]As a thing, when once it is understood, manifests itself, we have need only of an example without further proof. In the same way the contrary has only to be presented to our minds to be recognized as false, as will forthwith appear when we come to discuss fiction concerning essences.

[20]Observe, that although many assert that they doubt whether God exists, they have nought but his name in their minds, or else some fiction which they call God: this fiction is not in harmony with God's real nature, as we will duly show,

the nature implies a contradiction. From these considerations, it is plain, as I have already stated, that fiction cannot be concerned with eternal truths.[21]

But before proceeding further, I must remark, in passing, that the difference between the essence of one thing and the essence of another thing is the same as that which exists between the reality or existence of one thing and the reality or existence of another; therefore, if we wished to conceive the existence, for example, of Adam, simply by means of existence in general, it would be the same as if, in order to conceive his existence, we went back to the nature of being, so as to define Adam as a being. Thus, the more existence is conceived generally, the more is it conceived confusedly, and the more easily can it be ascribed to a given object. Contrariwise, the more it is conceived particularly, the more is it understood clearly, and the less liable is it to be ascribed, through negligence of Nature's order, to anything save its proper object. This is worthy of remark.

We now proceed to consider those cases which are commonly called fictions, though we clearly understand that the thing is not as we imagine it. For instance, I know that the earth is round, but nothing prevents my telling people that it is a hemisphere, and that it is like a half apple carved in relief on a dish; or, that the sun moves round the earth, and so on. However, examination will show us that there is nothing here inconsistent with what has been said, provided we first admit that we may have made mistakes, and be now conscious of them; and, further, that we can hypothesize, or at least suppose, that others are under the same mistake as ourselves, or can, like us, fall under it. We can, I repeat, thus hypothesize so long as we see no impossibility. Thus, when I tell anyone that the earth is not round, etc., I merely recall the error which I perhaps made myself, or which I might have fallen into, and afterward I hypothesize that the person to whom I tell it is still, or may still fall under the same mistake. This I say, I can feign so long as I do not perceive any impossibility or necessity; if I truly understood either one or the other

---

[21] I shall presently show that no fiction can concern eternal truths. By an eternal truth, I mean that which being positive could never become negative. Thus it is a primary and eternal truth that *God exists*, but it is not an eternal truth that *Adam thinks*. That the *Chimera does not exist* is an eternal truth, that *Adam does not think* is not so.

I should not be able to feign, and I should be reduced to saying that I had made the attempt.

It remains for us to consider hypotheses made in problems, which sometimes involve impossibilities. For instance, when we say: let us assume that this burning candle is not burning, or, let us assume that it burns in some imaginary space, or where there are no physical objects. Such assumptions are freely made, though the last is clearly seen to be impossible. But, though this be so, there is no fiction in the case. For, in the first case, I have merely recalled to memory another candle[22] not burning, or conceived the candle before me as without a flame, and then I understand as applying to the latter, leaving its flame out of the question, all that I think of the former. In the second case, I have merely to abstract my thoughts from the objects surrounding the candle, for the mind to devote itself to the contemplation of the candle singly looked at in itself only; I can then draw the conclusion that the candle contains in itself no cause for its own destruction, so that if there were no physical objects the candle, and even the flame, would remain unchangeable, and so on. Thus there is here no fiction, but true and bare assertions.[23]

Let us now pass on to the fictions concerned with essences only, or with some reality or existence simultaneously. Of these we must specially observe that in proportion as the mind's understanding is smaller, and its experience multiplex, so will its power of coining fictions be larger, whereas, as its understanding increases, its capacity for entertaining fictitious ideas becomes less. For instance, in the same way as we are unable, while we are thinking, to feign that we

[22]Afterwards, when we come to speak of fiction that is concerned with essences, it will be evident that fiction never creates or furnishes the mind with anything new; only such things as are already in the brain or imagination are recalled to the memory when the attention is directed to them confusedly and all at once. For instance, we have remembrance of spoken words and of a tree; when the mind directs itself to them confusedly, it forms the notion of a tree speaking. The same may be said of existence, especially when it is conceived quite generally as entity; it is then readily applied to all things occurring together in the memory. This is specially worthy of remark.

[23]We must understand as much in the case of hypotheses put forward to explain certain movements accompanying celestial phenomena; but from these, when applied to the celestial motions, we may draw conclusions as to the nature of the heavens, whereas this last may be quite different, especially as many other causes are conceivable which would account for such motions.

are thinking or not thinking, so, also, when we know the nature of body we cannot imagine an infinite fly; or, when we know the nature of the soul,[24] we cannot imagine it as square, though anything may be expressed verbally. But, as we said above, the less men know of Nature, the more easily can they coin fictitious ideas, such as trees speaking, men instantly changed into stones or into fountains, ghosts appearing in mirrors, something issuing from nothing, even gods changed into beasts and men, and infinite other absurdities of the same kind.

Some persons think, perhaps, that fiction is limited by fiction, and not by understanding; in other words, after I have formed some fictitious idea, and have affirmed of my own free will that it exists under a certain form in nature, I am thereby precluded from thinking of it under any other form. For instance, when I have feigned (to repeat their argument) that the nature of body is of a certain kind, and have of my own free will desired to convince myself that it actually exists under this form, I am no longer able to hypothesize that a fly, for example, is infinite; so, when I have hypothesized the essence of the soul, I am not able to think of it as square, etc. But these arguments demand further inquiry. First, their upholders must either grant or deny that we can understand anything. If they grant it, then necessarily the same must be said of understanding, as is said of fiction. If they deny it, let us, who know that we do know something, see what they mean. They assert that the soul can be conscious of, and perceive in a variety of ways, not itself nor things which exist, but only things which are neither in itself nor anywhere else, in other words, that the soul can, by its unaided power, create sensations or ideas unconnected with things. In fact, they regard the soul as a sort of god. Further, they assert that we or our soul have such freedom that we can constrain ourselves, or our soul, or even our soul's freedom. For, after it has formed a fictitious idea, and has given its assent thereto, it cannot think or feign it in any other manner, but is constrained by the first fictitious idea to keep all its other thoughts in

[24] It often happens that a man recalls to mind this word *soul*, and forms at the same time some corporeal image: as the two representations are simultaneous, he easily thinks that he imagines and feigns a corporeal soul: thus confusing the name with the thing itself. I here beg that my readers will not be in a hurry to refute this proposition; they will, I hope, have no mind to do so, if they pay close attention to the examples given and to what follows.

harmony therewith. Our opponents are thus driven to admit, in support of their fiction, the absurdities which I have just enumerated; and which are not worthy of rational refutation.[25]

While leaving such persons in their error, we will take care to derive from our argument with them a truth serviceable for our purpose, namely, that the mind, in paying attention to a thing hypothetical or false, so as to meditate upon it and understand it, and derive the proper conclusions in due order therefrom, will readily discover its falsity; and if the thing hypothetical be in its nature true, and the mind pays attention to it, so as to understand it, and deduce the truths which are derivable from it, the mind will proceed with an uninterrupted series of apt conclusions; in the same way as it would at once discover (as we showed just now) the absurdity of a false hypothesis, and of the conclusions drawn from it.

We need, therefore, be in no fear of forming hypotheses, so long as we have a clear and distinct perception of what is involved. For, if we were to assert, haply, that men are suddenly turned into beasts, the statement would be extremely general, so general that there would be no conception, that is, no idea or connection of subject and predicate, in our mind. If there were such a conception we should at the same time be aware of the means and the causes whereby the event took place. Moreover, we pay no attention to the nature of the subject and the predicate. Now, if the first idea be not fictitious, and if all the other ideas be deduced therefrom, our hurry to form fictitious ideas will gradually subside. Further, as a fictitious idea cannot be clear and distinct, but is necessarily confused, and as all confusion arises from the fact that the mind has only partial knowledge of a thing either simple or complex, and does not distinguish between the known and the unknown, and, again, that it directs its attention promiscuously to all parts of an object at once without making distinctions, it follows, *first*, that if the idea be of something very simple, it must necessarily be clear and distinct. For a very simple object

[25]Though I seem to deduce this from experience, some may deny its cogency because I have given no formal proof. I therefore append the following for those who may desire it. As there can be nothing in Nature contrary to Nature's laws since all things come to pass by fixed laws, so that each thing must irrefragably produce its own proper effect, it follows that the soul, as soon as it possesses the true conception of a thing, proceeds to reproduce in thought that thing's effects. See below, where I speak of the false idea.

cannot be known in part; it must either be known altogether or not at all. *Secondly*, it follows that if a complex object be divided by thought into a number of simple component parts, and if each part be regarded separately, all confusion will disappear. *Thirdly*, it follows that fiction cannot be simple, but is made up of the blending of several confused ideas of diverse objects or actions existent in nature, or rather is composed of attention[26] directed to all such ideas at once, and unaccompanied by any mental assent.

Now a fiction that was simple would be clear and distinct, and therefore true; also a fiction composed only of distinct ideas would be clear and distinct, and therefore true. For instance, when we know the nature of the circle and the square, it is impossible for us to blend together these two figures, and to hypothesize a square circle, any more than a square soul, or things of that kind. Let us shortly come to our conclusion, and again repeat that we need have no fear of confusing with true ideas that which is only a fiction. As for the first sort of fiction of which we have already spoken, when a thing is clearly conceived, we saw that if the existence of that thing is in itself an eternal truth, fiction can have no part in it; but if the existence of the thing conceived be not an eternal truth, we have only to be careful that such existence be compared to the thing's essence, and to consider the order of Nature. As for the second sort of fiction, which we stated to be the result of simultaneously directing the attention, without the assent of the intellect, to different confused ideas representing different things and actions existing in Nature, we have seen that an absolutely simple thing cannot be feigned, but must be understood, and that a complex thing is in the same case if we regard separately the simple parts whereof it is composed; we shall not even be able to hypothesize any untrue action concerning such objects, for we shall be obliged to consider at the same time the causes and the manner of such action.

These matters being thus understood, let us pass on to consider the false idea observing the objects with which it is concerned and

---

[26]Observe that fiction regarded in itself, only differs from dreams in that in the latter we do not perceive the external causes which we perceive through the senses while awake. It has hence been inferred that representations occurring in sleep have no connection with objects external to us. We shall presently see that error is the dreaming of a waking man: if it reaches a certain pitch it becomes delirium.

the means of guarding ourselves from falling into false perceptions. Neither of these tasks will present much difficulty, after our inquiry concerning fictitious ideas. The false idea only differs from the fictitious idea in the fact of implying a mental assent — that is, as we have already remarked, while the representations are occurring, there are no causes present to us wherefrom, as in fiction, we can conclude that such representations do not arise from external objects: in fact, it is much the same as dreaming with our eyes open, or while awake. Thus a false idea is concerned with, or (to speak more correctly) attributable to, the existence of a thing whereof the essence is known, or the essence itself, in the same way as a fictitious idea. If attributable to the existence of the thing, it is corrected in the same way as a fictitious idea under similar circumstances. If attributable to the essence, it is likewise corrected in the same way as a fictitious idea. For if the nature of the thing known implies necessary existence, we cannot possibly be in error with regard to its existence; but if the nature of the thing be not an eternal truth, like its essence, but contrariwise the necessity or impossibility of its existence depends on external causes, then we must follow the same course as we adopted in the case of fiction, for it is corrected in the same manner. As for false ideas concerned with essences, or even with actions, such perceptions are necessarily always confused, being compounded of different confused perceptions of things existing in Nature, as, for instance, when men are persuaded that deities are present in woods, in statues, in brute beasts, and the like; that there are bodies which, by their composition alone, give rise to intellect; that corpses reason, walk about and speak; that God is deceived, and so on. But ideas which are clear and distinct can never be false: for ideas of things clearly and distinctly conceived are either very simple themselves, or are compounded from very simple ideas — that is, are deduced therefrom. The impossibility of a very simple idea being false is evident to every one who understands the nature of truth or understanding and of falsehood.

As regards that which constitutes the reality of truth, it is certain that a true idea is distinguished from a false one, not so much by its extrinsic object as by its intrinsic nature. If an architect conceives a building properly constructed, though such a building may never have existed, and may never exist, nevertheless the idea is true; and the idea remains the same, whether it be put into execution or not. On the other hand, if any one asserts, for instance, that Peter exists, without knowing whether Peter really exists or not, the assertion, as far as its asserter is concerned, is false, or not true, even though Peter actually does exist. The assertion that Peter exists is true only with regard to him who knows for certain that Peter does exist. Whence it follows that there is in ideas something real, whereby the true are distinguished from the false. This reality must be inquired into if we are to find the best standard of truth (we have said that we ought to determine our thoughts by the given standard of a true idea, and that method is reflective knowledge) and are to know the properties of our understanding. Neither must we say that the difference between true and false arises from the fact that true knowledge consists in knowing things through their primary causes, wherein it is totally different from false knowledge, as I have just explained it: for thought is said to be true, if it involves subjectively the essence of any principle which has no cause, and is known through itself and in itself. Wherefore the reality (*forma*) of true thought must exist in the thought itself, without reference to other thoughts; it does not acknowledge the object as its cause, but must depend on the actual power and nature of the understanding. For, if we suppose that the understanding has perceived some new entity which has never existed, as some conceive the understanding of God before He created things (a perception which certainly could not arise from any object), and has legitimately deduced other thoughts from the said perception, all such thoughts would be true, without being determined by any external object; they would depend solely on the power and nature of the understanding. Thus, that which constitutes the reality of a true thought must be sought in the thought itself, and deduced from the nature of the understanding. In order to pursue our investigation, let us confront ourselves with some *true* idea, whose object we know for certain to be dependent on our power of thinking, and to have nothing corresponding to it in Nature. With an idea of this kind before us, we shall, as appears from what has just been said, be more easily able to carry on the research we have in view. For instance, in order to form the conception of a sphere, I invent a cause at my pleasure — namely, a semicircle revolving round its centre, and thus producing a sphere. This is indisputably a true idea; and, although we know that no sphere in nature has ever actually been so formed, the perception remains true, and is the easiest manner of conceiving a sphere. We must observe that this perception asserts the rotation of a semicircle — which assertion would be false if it were not associated with the conception of a sphere or of a cause determining a motion of the kind, or absolutely, if the assertion were isolated. The mind would then only tend to the affirmation of the sole motion of a semicircle, which is not contained in the conception of a semicircle, and does not arise from the conception of any cause capable of producing such motion.

Thus *falsity* consists only in this, that something is affirmed of a thing, which is not contained in the conception we have formed of that thing, as motion or rest of a semicircle. Whence it follows that simple ideas cannot be other than *true* — e.g., the simple idea of a semicircle, of motion, of rest, of quantity, etc.

Whatsoever affirmation such ideas contain is equal to the concept formed, and does not extend further. Wherefore we may form as many simple ideas as we please, without any fear of error. It only remains for us to inquire by what power our mind can form true ideas, and how far such power extends. It is certain that such power cannot extend itself infinitely. For when we affirm somewhat of a thing, which is not contained in the concept we have formed of that thing, such an affirmation shows a defect of our perception, or that we have formed fragmentary or mutilated ideas. Thus we have seen that the motion of a semicircle is false when it is isolated in the mind, but true when it is associated with the concept of a sphere, or of some cause determining such a motion. But if it be the nature of a thinking being, as seems, *prima facie*, to be the case, to form true or adequate thoughts, it is plain that inadequate ideas arise in us only because we are parts of a thinking being, whose thoughts — some in their entirety, others in fragments only — constitute our mind.

But there is another point to be considered, which was not worth raising in the case of fiction, but which gives rise to complete deception — namely, that certain things presented to the imagination also exist in the understanding — in other words, are conceived clearly and distinctly. Hence, so long as we do not separate that which is distinct from that which is confused, certainty, or the true idea, becomes mixed with indistinct ideas. For instance, certain Stoics heard, perhaps, the term "soul," and also that the soul is immortal, yet imagined it only confusedly; they imagined, also, and understood that very subtle bodies penetrate all others, and are penetrated by none. By combining these ideas, and being at the same time certain of the truth of the axiom, they forthwith became convinced that the mind consists of very subtle bodies; that these very subtle bodies cannot be divided, etc. But we are freed from mistakes of this kind, so long as we endeavor to examine all our perceptions by the standard of the given true idea. We must take care, as has been said, to separate such perceptions from all those which arise from hearsay or unclassified experience.

Moreover, such mistakes arise from things being conceived too much in the abstract; for it is sufficiently self-evident that what I conceive as in its true object I cannot apply to anything else. Lastly, they arise from a want of understanding of the primary elements of Nature as a whole; whence we proceed without due order, and confound Nature with abstract rules, which, although they be true enough in their sphere, yet, when misapplied, confound themselves, and pervert the order of Nature. However, if we proceed with as little abstraction as possible, and begin from primary elements — that is, from the source and origin of Nature, as far back as we can reach — we need not fear any deceptions of this kind. As far as the knowledge of the origin of Nature is concerned, there is no danger of our confounding it with abstractions. For when a thing is conceived in the abstract, as are all universal notions, the said universal notions are always more extensive in the mind than the number of individuals forming their contents really existing in Nature.

Again, there are many things in Nature, the difference between which is so slight as to be hardly perceptible to the understanding; so that it may readily happen that such things are confounded together, if they be conceived abstractedly. But since the first principle of Nature cannot (as we shall see hereafter) be conceived abstractedly or universally, and cannot extend further in the understanding than it does in reality, and has no likeness to mutable things, no confusion need be feared in respect to the idea of it, provided (as before shown) that we possess a standard of truth. This is, in fact, a being single[27] and infinite; in other words, it is the sum total of being,[28] beyond which there is no being found.

[27]These are not attributes of God displaying His essence, as I will show in my philosophy.

[28]This has been shown already. For if such a being did not exist it would never

Thus far we have treated of the false idea. We have now to investigate the doubtful idea — that is, to inquire what can cause us to doubt, and how doubt may be removed. I speak of real doubt existing in the mind, not of such doubt as we see exemplified when a man says that he doubts, though his mind does not really hesitate. The cure of the latter does not fall within the province of method, it belongs rather to inquiries concerning obstinacy and its cure. Real doubt is never produced in the mind by the thing doubted of. In other words, if there were only one idea in the mind, whether that idea were true or false, there would be no doubt or certainty present, only a certain sensation. For an idea is in itself nothing else than a certain sensation; but doubt will arise through another idea, not clear and distinct enough for us to be able to draw any certain conclusion with regard to the matter under consideration; that is, the idea which causes us to doubt is not clear and distinct. To take an example: Supposing that a man has never reflected, or been taught by experience or by any other means, that our senses sometimes deceive us, he will never doubt whether the sun be greater or less than it appears. Thus rustics are generally astonished when they hear that the sun is much larger than the earth. But from reflection on the deceitfulness of the senses[29] doubt arises, and if, after doubting, we acquire a true knowledge of the senses, and how things at a distance are represented through their instrumentality, doubt is again removed. Hence we cannot cast doubt on true ideas by the supposition that there is a deceitful Deity who leads us astray even in what is most certain. We can only hold such an hypothesis so long as we have no clear and distinct idea — in other words, until we reflect on the knowledge which we have of the first principle of all things, and find that which teaches us that God is not a deceiver, and until we know this with the same certainty as we know from reflecting on the nature of a triangle that its three angles are equal to two right angles. But if we have a knowledge of God equal to that which we have of a triangle, all doubt is removed. In the same way as we can arrive at the said knowledge of a triangle, though not absolutely sure that there is not some archdeceiver leading us astray, so can we come to a like knowledge of God under the like condition, and when we have

be produced: therefore the mind would be able to understand more than Nature could furnish; and this has been shown above to be false.

[29]That is, it is known that the senses sometimes deceive us. But it is only known confusedly, for it is not known how they deceive us.

attained to it, it is sufficient, as I said before, to remove every doubt which we can possess concerning clear and distinct ideas. Thus, if a man proceeded with our investigations in due order, inquiring first into those things which should first be inquired into, never passing over a link in the chain of association, and with knowledge how to define his questions before seeking to answer them, he will never have any ideas save such as are very certain, or, in other words, clear and distinct; for doubt is only a suspension of the spirit concerning some affirmation or negation which it would pronounce upon unhesitatingly if it were not in ignorance of something, without which the knowledge of the matter in hand must needs be imperfect. We may, therefore, conclude that doubt always proceeds from want of due order in investigation.

These are the points I promised to discuss in this first part of my treatise on method. However, in order not to omit anything which can conduce to the knowledge of the understanding and its faculties, I will add a few words on the subject of memory and forgetfulness.

The point most worthy of attention is that memory is strengthened both with and without the aid of the understanding. For the more intelligible a thing is, the more easily is it remembered; and the less intelligible it is, the more easily do we forget it. For instance, a number of unconnected words is much more difficult to remember than the same number in the form of a narration. The memory is also strengthened without the aid of the understanding by means of the power wherewith the imagination or the sense called common is affected by some particular physical object. I say *particular*, for the imagination is only affected by particular objects. If we read, for instance, a single romantic comedy, we shall remember it very well, so long as we do not read many others of the same kind, for it will reign alone in the memory. If, however, we read several others of the same kind, we shall think of them altogether, and easily confuse one with another. I say, also *physical*, for the imagination is only affected by physical objects. As, then, the memory is strengthened both with and without the aid of the understanding, we may conclude that it is different from the understanding, and that in the latter considered in itself there is neither memory nor forgetfulness. What, then, is memory? It is nothing else than the actual sensation of impressions on the brain, accompanied with the thought of a definite duration of the sensation.[30] This is also shown by reminiscence. For then we think of the sensation, but without the notion of continuous duration; thus the idea of that sensation is not the actual duration of the sensation or actual memory. Whether ideas are or are not subject to corruption will be seen in my philosophy. If this seems too absurd to any one, it will be sufficient for our purpose if he reflect on the fact that a thing is more easily remembered in proportion to its singularity, as appears from the example of the comedy just cited. Further, a thing is remembered more easily in proportion to its intelligibility; therefore we cannot help remembering that which is extremely singular and sufficiently intelligible.

Thus, then, we have distinguished between a true idea and other perceptions, and shown that ideas fictitious, false, and the rest, originate in the imagination — that is, in certain sensations fortuitous (so to speak) and disconnected, arising not from the power of the mind, but from external causes, according as the body, sleeping or waking, receives various motions.

But one may take any view one likes of the imagination so long as one acknowledges that it is different from the understanding, and that the soul is passive with regard to it. The view taken is immaterial, if we know that the imagination is something indefinite, with regard to which the soul is passive, and that we can by some means or other free ourselves therefrom with the help of the understanding. Let no one then be astonished that before proving the existence of body, and other necessary things, I speak of imagination of body, and of its composition. The view taken is, I repeat, immaterial, so long as we know that imagination is something indefinite, etc. As regards a true idea, we have shown that it is simple or compounded of simple ideas; that it shows how and why something is or has been made; and that its subjective effects in the soul correspond to the actual reality of its object. This conclusion is identical with the saying of the ancients,

[30] If the duration be indefinite, the recollection is imperfect; this everyone seems to have learnt from Nature. For we often ask, to strengthen our belief in something we hear of, when and where it happened; though ideas themselves have their own duration in the mind, yet, as we are wont to determine duration by the aid of some measure of motion which, again, takes place by aid of the imagination, we preserve no memory connected with pure intellect.

that true science proceeds from cause to effect; though the ancients, so far as I know, never formed the conception put forward here that the soul acts according to fixed laws; and is, as it were, an immaterial automaton. Hence, as far as is possible at the outset, we have acquired a knowledge of our understanding, and such a standard of a true idea that we need no longer fear confounding truth with falsehood and fiction. Neither shall we wonder why we understand some things which in nowise fall within the scope of the imagination, while other things are in the imagination but wholly opposed to the understanding, or others, again, which agree therewith. We now know that the operations, whereby the effects of imagination are produced, take place under other laws quite different from the laws of the understanding, and that the mind is entirely passive with regard to them. Whence we may also see how easily men may fall into grave errors through not distinguishing accurately between the imagination and the understanding, such as believing that extension must be localized, that it must be finite, that its parts are really distinct one from the other, that it is the primary and single foundation of all things, that it occupies more space at one time than at another, and other similar doctrines, all entirely opposed to truth, as we shall duly show.

Again, since words are a part of the imagination — that is, since we form many conceptions in accordance with confused arrangements of words in the memory, dependent on particular bodily conditions — there is no doubt that words may, equally with the imagination, be the cause of many and great errors, unless we keep strictly on our guard. Moreover, words are formed according to popular fancy and intelligence, and are, therefore, signs of things as existing in the imagination, not as existing in the understanding. This is evident from the fact that to all such things as exist only in the understanding, not in the imagination, negative names are often given, such as incorporeal, infinite, etc. So, also, many conceptions really affirmative are expressed negatively, and *vice versa*, such as uncreate, independent, infinite, immortal, etc., inasmuch as their contraries are much more easily imagined, and, therefore, occurred first to men, and usurped positive names. Many things we affirm and deny, because the nature of words allows us to do so, though the nature of things does not. While we remain unaware of this fact, we may easily mistake falsehood for truth.

Let us also beware of another great cause of confusion, which prevents the understanding from reflecting on itself. Sometimes, while making no distinction between the imagination and the intellect, we think that what we more readily imagine is clearer to us; and also we think that what we imagine we understand. Thus, we put first that which should be last: the true order of progression is reversed, and no legitimate conclusion is drawn.

Now, in order at length to pass on to the second part of this method,[31] I shall first set forth the object aimed at, and next the means for its attainment. The object aimed at is the acquisition of clear and distinct ideas, such as are produced by the pure intellect, and not by chance physical motions. In order that all ideas may be reduced to unity, we shall endeavor so to associate and arrange them that our mind may, as far as possible, reflect subjectively the reality of Nature, both as a whole and as parts.

As for the first point, it is necessary (as we have said) for our purpose that everything should be conceived, either *solely through its essence,* or *through its proximate cause.* If the thing be self-existent, or as is commonly said, the cause of itself, it must be understood through its essence only; if it be not self-existent, but requires a cause for its existence, it must be understood through its proximate cause. For, in reality, the knowledge of an effect is nothing else than the acquisition of more perfect knowledge of its cause.[32] Therefore, we may never, while we are concerned with inquiries into actual things, draw any conclusions from abstractions; we shall be extremely careful not to confound that which is only in the understanding with that which is in the thing itself. The best basis for drawing a conclusion will be either some particular affirmative essence, or a true and legitimate definition. For the understanding can not descend from universal axioms by themselves to particular things, since axioms are of infinite extent, and do not determine the understanding to contemplate one particular thing more than another. Thus the true method of discovery is to form thoughts from some given definition. This process

---

[31]The chief rule of this part is, as appears from the first part, to review all the ideas coming to us through pure intellect, so as to distinguish them from such as we imagine; the distinction will be shown through the properties of each, namely, of the imagination and of the understanding.

[32]Observe that it is hereby manifest that we cannot understand anything of ature without at the same time increasing our knowledge of the first cause, or God.

will be the more fruitful and easy in proportion as the thing given be better defined. Wherefore, the cardinal point of all this second part of method consists in the knowledge of the conditions of good definition, and the means of finding them. I will first treat of the conditions of definition.

A definition, if it is to be called perfect, must explain the inmost essence of a thing, and must take care not to substitute for this any of its properties. In order to illustrate my meaning, without taking an example which would seem to show a desire to expose other people's errors, I will choose the case of something abstract, the definition of which is of little moment. Such is a circle. If a circle be defined as a figure, such that all straight lines drawn from the center to the circumference are equal, every one can see that such a definition does not in the least explain the essence of a circle, but solely one of its properties. Though, as I have said, this is of no importance in the case of figures and other abstractions, it is of great importance in the case of physical beings and realities: for the properties of things are not understood so long as their essences are unknown. If the latter be passed over, there is necessarily a perversion of the succession of ideas which should reflect the succession of Nature, and we go far astray from our object.

In order to be free from this fault, the following rules should be observed in definition:

I. If the thing in question be created, the definition must (as we have said) comprehend the proximate cause. For instance, a circle should, according to this rule, be defined as follows: the figure described by any line whereof one end is fixed and the other free. This definition clearly comprehends the proximate cause.

II. A conception or definition of a thing should be such that all the properties of that thing, in so far as it is considered by itself, and not in conjunction with other things, can be deduced from it, as may be seen in the definition given of a circle: for from that it clearly follows that all straight lines drawn from the center to the circumference are equal. That this is a necessary characteristic of a definition is so clear to any one who reflects on the matter that there is no need to spend time in proving it, or in showing that, owing to this second condition, every definition should be affirmative. I speak of intellectual affirmation, giving little thought to verbal affirmations which, owing to the poverty of the language, must sometimes, perhaps, be expressed negatively, though the idea contained is affirmative.

The rules for the definition of an uncreated thing are as follows:

I. The exclusion of all idea of cause — that is, the thing must not need explanation by anything outside itself.

II. When the definition of the thing has been given, there must be no room for doubt as to whether the thing exists or not.

III. It must contain, as far as the mind is concerned, no substantives which could be put into an adjectival form; in other words, the object defined must not be explained through abstractions.

IV. Lastly, though this is not absolutely necessary, it should be possible to deduce from the definition all the properties of the thing defined.

All these rules become obvious to any one giving strict attention to the matter.

I have also stated that the best basis for drawing a conclusion is a particular affirmative essence. The more specialized the idea is, the more is it distinct, and therefore clear. Wherefore a knowledge of particular things should be sought for as diligently as possible.

As regards the order of our perceptions, and the manner in which they should be arranged and united, it is necessary that, as soon as is possible and rational, we should inquire whether there be any being (and, if so, what being) that is the cause of all things, so that its essence, represented in thought, may be the cause of all our ideas, and then our mind will to the utmost possible extent reflect Nature. For it will possess, subjectively, Nature's essence, order, and union. Thus we can see that it is before all things necessary for us to deduce all our ideas from physical things — that is, from real entities, proceeding, as far as may be, according to the series of causes, from one real entity to another real entity, never passing to universals and abstractions for the purpose of either deducing some real entity from them or deducing them from some real entity. Either of these processes interrupts the true progress of the understanding. But it must be observed that, by the series of causes and real entities, I do not here mean the series of particular and mutable things, but only the series of fixed and eternal things. It would be impossible for human infirmity to follow up the series of particular mutable things, both on account of their multitude, surpassing all calculation, and on account of the infinitely diverse circumstances surrounding one and the same thing, any one of which may be the cause for its existence or non-existence. Indeed, their existence has no connection with their essence, or (as we have said already) is not an eternal truth. Neither is there any need that we should understand their series, for the essences of particular mutable things are not to be gathered from their series or order of existence, which would furnish us with nothing beyond their extrinsic denominations, their relations, or, at most, their circumstances, all of which are very different from their inmost essence. This inmost essence must be sought solely from fixed and eternal things, and from the laws, inscribed (so to speak) in those things as in their true codes, according to which all particular things take place and are arranged; nay, these mutable particular things depend so intimately and essentially (so to phrase it) upon the fixed things that they cannot either be or be conceived without them.

Whence these fixed and eternal things, though they are themselves particular, will nevertheless, owing to their presence and power everywhere, be to us as universals, or genera of definitions of particular mutable things, and as the proximate causes of all things.

But, though this be so, there seems to be no small difficulty in arriving at the knowledge of these particular things, for to conceive them all at once would far surpass the powers of the human understanding. The arrangement whereby one thing is understood before another, as we have stated, should not be sought from their series of existence, nor from eternal things. For the latter are all by nature simultaneous. Other aids are therefore needed besides those employed for understanding eternal things and their laws; however, this is not the place to recount such aids, nor is there any need to do so, until we have acquired a sufficient knowledge of eternal things and their infallible laws, and until the nature of our senses has become plain to us.

Before betaking ourselves to seek knowledge of particular things, it will be seasonable to speak of such aids, as all tend to teach us the mode of employing our senses, and to make certain experiments under fixed rules and arrangement which may suffice to determine the object of our inquiry, so that we may therefrom infer what laws of eternal things it has been produced under, and may gain an insight into its inmost nature, as I will duly show. Here, to return to my purpose, I will only endeavor to set forth what seems necessary for enabling us to attain to knowledge of eternal things, and to define them under the conditions laid down above.

With this end, we must bear in mind what has already been stated, namely, that when the mind devotes itself to any thought, so as to examine it and to deduce therefrom in due order all the legitimate conclusions possible, any falsehood which may lurk in the thought will be detected; but if the thought be true, the mind will readily proceed without interruption to deduce truths from it. This, I say, is necessary for our purpose, for our thoughts may be brought to a close by the absence of a foundation. If, therefore, we wish to investigate the first thing of all, it will be necessary to supply some foundation which may direct our thoughts thither. Further, since method is reflective knowledge, the foundation which must direct our thoughts can be nothing else than the knowledge of that which constitutes the reality of truth, and the knowledge of the understanding, its properties, and powers. When this has been acquired we shall possess a foundation wherefrom we can deduce our thoughts, and a path whereby the intellect, according to its capacity, may attain the knowledge of eternal things, allowance being made for the extent of the intellectual powers.

If, as I stated in the first part, it belongs to the nature of thought to form true ideas, we must here inquire what is meant by the faculties and power of the understanding. The chief part of our method is to understand as well as possible the powers of the intellect, and its nature; we are, therefore, compelled (by the considerations advanced in the second part of the method) necessarily to draw these conclusions from the definition itself of thought and understanding. But, so far, we have not got any rules for finding definitions, and, as we cannot set forth such rules without a previous knowledge of Nature, that is without a definition of the understanding and its power, it follows either that the definition of the understanding must be clear in itself, or that we can understand nothing. Nevertheless this definition is not absolutely clear in itself; however, since its properties, like all things that we possess through the understanding, cannot be known clearly and distinctly, unless its nature be known previously, the definition of the understanding makes itself manifest, if we pay attention to its properties, which we know clearly and distinctly. Let us, then, enumerate here the properties of the understanding, let us examine them, and begin by discussing the instruments for research which we find innate in us.

The properties of the understanding which I have chiefly remarked, and which I clearly understand, are the following:

I. It involves certainty — in other words, it knows that a thing exists in reality as it is reflected subjectively.

II. That it perceives certain things, or forms some ideas absolutely, some ideas from others. Thus it forms the idea of quantity absolutely, without reference to any other thoughts; but ideas of motion it only forms after taking into consideration the idea of quantity.

III. Those ideas which the understanding forms absolutely express infinity; determinate ideas are derived from other ideas. Thus in the idea of quantity, perceived by means of a cause, the quantity is determined, as when a body is perceived to be formed by the motion of a plane, a plane by the motion of a line, or, again, a line by the motion of a point. All these are perceptions which do not serve towards understanding quantity, but only towards determining it. This is proved by the fact that we conceive them as formed as it were by motion, yet this motion is not perceived unless the quantity be perceived also; we can even prolong the motion so as to form an infinite line, which we certainly could not do unless we had an idea of infinite quantity.

IV. The understanding forms positive ideas before forming negative ideas.

V. It perceives things not so much under the condition of duration as under a certain form of eternity, and in an infinite number; or rather in perceiving things it does not consider either their number or duration, whereas, in imagining them, it perceives them in a determinate number, duration, and quantity.

VI. The ideas which we form as clear and distinct seem so to follow from the sole necessity of our nature, that they appear to depend absolutely on our sole power; with confused ideas the contrary is the case. They are often formed against our will.

VII. The mind can determine in many ways the ideas of things which the understanding forms from other ideas: thus, for instance, in order to define the plane of an ellipse, it supposes a point adhering to a cord to be moved round two centres, or, again, it conceives an infinity of points, always in the same fixed relation to a given straight line, or a cone cut in an oblique plane, so that the angle of inclination is greater than the angle of the vertex of the cone, or in an infinity of other ways.

VIII. The more ideas express perfection of any object, the more perfect are they themselves; for we do not admire the architect who has planned a chapel so much as the architect who has planned a splendid temple.

I do not stop to consider the rest of what is referred to thought, such as love, joy, etc. They are nothing to our present purpose, and cannot even be conceived unless the understanding be perceived previously. When perception is removed, all these go with it.

False and fictitious ideas have nothing positive about them (as we have abundantly shown), which causes them to be called false or fictitious; they are only considered as such through the defectiveness of knowledge. Therefore, false and fictitious ideas as such can teach us nothing concerning the essence of thought; this must be sought from the positive properties just enumerated; in other words, we must lay down some common basis from which these properties necessarily follow, so that when this is given, the properties are necessarily given also, and when it is removed, they too vanish with it.

[*The rest of the treatise is wanting.*]

ETHICS

Demonstrated in Geometrical Order and Divided into Five Parts Which Treat (1) of God; (2) of the Nature and Origin of the Mind; (3) on the Nature and Origin of the Emotions; (4) of Human Bondage; or of the Strength of the Emotions; (5) of the Power of the Intellect; or of Human Liberty

PART ONE
Of God

DEFINITIONS

I. By cause of itself I understand that whose essence involves existence, or that whose nature cannot be conceived unless existing.

II. That thing is called finite in its own kind (*in suo genere*) which can be limited by another thing of the same nature. For example, a body is called finite because we always conceive another which is greater. So a thought is limited by another thought; but a body is not limited by a thought, nor a thought by a body.

III. By substance I understand that which is in itself and is conceived through itself; in other words, that the conception of which does not need the conception of another thing from which it must be formed.

IV. By attribute I understand that which the intellect perceives of substance as constituting its essence.

V. By mode I understand the modifications of substance, or that which is in another thing through which also it is conceived.

VI. By God I understand Being absolutely infinite, that is to say, substance consisting of infinite attributes, each one of which expresses eternal and infinite essence.

Explanation. I say absolutely infinite but not infinite in its own kind (*in suo genere*), for of whatever is infinite only in its own kind (*in suo genere*), we can deny infinite attributes; but to the essence of that which is absolutely infinite pertains whatever expresses essence and involves no negation.

VII. That thing is called free which exists from the necessity of its own nature alone and is determined to action by itself alone. That thing, on the other hand, is called necessary or rather compelled which by another is determined to existence and action in a fixed and prescribed manner.

VIII. By eternity I understand existence itself, so far as it is conceived necessarily to follow from the definition alone of the eternal thing.

Explanation. For such existence, like the essence of the thing, is conceived as an eternal truth. It cannot therefore be explained by duration or time, even if the duration be conceived without beginning or end.

AXIOMS

I. Everything which is, is either in itself or in another.

II. That which cannot be conceived through another must be conceived through itself.

III. From a given determinate cause an effect necessarily follows; and, on the other hand, if no determinate cause be given it is impossible that an effect can follow.

IV. The knowledge (*cognitio*) of an effect depends upon and involves the knowledge of the cause.

V. Those things which have nothing mutually in common with one another cannot through one another be mutually understood, that is to say, the conception of the one does not involve the conception of the other.

VI. A true idea must agree with that of which it is the idea (*cum suo ideato*).

VII. The essence of that thing which can be conceived as not existing does not involve existence.

PROPOSITIONS

PROPOSITION I. *Substance is by its nature prior to its modifications.*

Demonstration. This is evident from Defs. 3 and 5.

PROPOSITION II. *Two substances having different attributes have nothing in common with one another.*

Demonstration. This is also evident from Def. 3. For each substance must be in itself and must be conceived through itself, that is to say, the conception of one does not involve the conception of the other. — Q.E.D.

PROPOSITION III. *If two things have nothing in common with one another, one cannot be the cause of the other.*

Demonstration. If they have nothing mutually in common with one another, they cannot (Ax. 5) through one another be mutually understood, and therefore (Ax. 4) one cannot be the cause of the other. — Q.E.D.

PROPOSITION IV. *Two or more distinct things are distinguished from one another, either by the difference of the attributes of the substances or by the difference of their modifications.*

Demonstration. Everything which is, is either in itself or in another (Ax. 1), that is to say (Defs. 3 and 5), outside the intellect there is nothing but substances and their modifications. There is nothing therefore outside the intellect by which a number of things can be distinguished one from another, but substances or (which is the same thing by Def. 4) their attributes and their modifications.—Q. E. D.

PROPOSITION V. *In nature there cannot be two or more substances of the same nature or attribute.*

Demonstration. If there were two or more distinct substances, they must be distinguished one from the other by difference of attributes or difference of modifications (Prop. 4). If they are distinguished only by difference of attributes, it will be granted that there is but one substance of the same attribute. But if they are distinguished by difference of modifications, since substance is prior by nature to its modifications (Prop. 1), the modifications therefore being placed on one side, and the substance being considered in itself, or, in other words (Def. 3 and Ax. 6), truly considered, it cannot be conceived as distinguished from another substance, that is to say (Prop. 4), there cannot be two or more substances, but only one possessing the same nature or attribute. — Q.E.D.

PROPOSITION VI. *One substance cannot be produced by another substance.*

Demonstration. There cannot in nature be two substances of the same attribute (Prop. 5), that is to say (Prop. 2), two which have anything in common with one another. And therefore (Prop. 3), one cannot be the cause of the other, that is to say, one cannot be produced by the other. — Q.E.D.

Corollary. Hence it follows that there is nothing by which substance can be produced, for in Nature there is nothing but substances and their modifications (as is evident from Ax. 1 and Defs. 3 and 5). But substance cannot be produced by substance (Prop. 6). Therefore absolutely there is nothing by which substance can be produced. — Q.E.D.

Another Demonstration. This corollary is demonstrated more easily by the *reductio ad absurdum.* For if there were anything by which substance could be produced, the knowledge of substance would be dependent upon the knowledge of its cause (Ax. 4), and therefore (Def. 3) it would not be substance.

PROPOSITION VII. *It pertains to the nature of substance to exist.*

Demonstration. There is nothing by which substance can be produced (Corol. Prop. 6). It will therefore be the cause of itself, that is to say (Def. 1), its essence necessarily involves existence, or, in other words, it pertains to its nature to exist. — Q.E.D.

PROPOSITION VIII. *Every substance is necessarily infinite.*

Demonstration. Substance which has only one attribute cannot exist except as one substance (Prop. 5), and to the nature of this one substance it pertains to exist (Prop. 7). It must therefore from its nature exist as finite or infinite. But it cannot exist as finite substance, for (Def. 2) it must (if finite) be limited by another substance of the same nature, which also must necessarily exist (Prop. 7), and therefore there would be two substances of the same attribute, which is absurd (Prop. 5). It exists therefore as infinite substance. — Q.E.D.

Note 1. Since finiteness is in truth partly negation, and infinitude absolute affirmation of existence of some kind, it follows from Prop. 7 alone that all substance must be infinite.

Note 2. I fully expect that those who judge things confusedly, and who have not been accustomed to cognize things through their first causes, will find it difficult to comprehend the demonstration of the seventh Proposition, since they do not distinguish between the modifications of substances and substances themselves, and are ignorant of the manner in which things are produced. Hence it comes to pass that they erroneously ascribe to substances a beginning like that which they see belongs to natural things; for those who are ignorant of the true causes of things confound everything, and without any mental repugnance represent trees speaking like men, or imagine that men are made out of stones as well as begotten from seed, and that all forms can be changed the one into the other. So also those who confound human nature with the divine readily attribute to God human emotions, especially so long as they are ignorant of the manner in which emotions are produced in the mind. But if men would attend to the nature of substance, they could not entertain a single doubt of the truth of Proposition 7; indeed this proposition would be considered by all to be axiomatic, and reckoned amongst common notions. For by "substance" would be understood that which is in itself and is conceived through itself, or, in other words, that the knowledge of which does not need the knowledge of another thing. But by "modifications" would be understood those things which are in another thing — those things the conception of which is formed from the conception of the thing in which they are. Hence we can have true ideas of non-existent modifications, since, although they may not actually exist outside the intellect, their essence nevertheless is so comprehended in something else that they may be conceived through it. But the truth of substances is not outside the intellect unless in the substances themselves, because they are conceived through themselves. If anyone, therefore, were to say that he possessed a clear and distinct, that is to say, a true idea of substance, and that he nevertheless doubted whether such a substance exists, he would forsooth be in the same position as if he were to say that he had a true idea and nevertheless doubted whether or not it was false (as is evident to anyone who pays a little attention). Similarly if anyone were to affirm that substance is created, he would affirm at the same time that a false idea had become true, and this is a greater absurdity than can be conceived. It is therefore necessary to admit that the existence of substance, like its essence, is an eternal truth. Hence a demonstration (which I have thought worth while to append) by a different method is possible, showing that there are not two substances possessing the same nature. But in order to prove this methodically it is to be noted, first, that the true definition of any one thing neither involves nor expresses anything except the nature of the thing defined. From which it follows, secondly, that a definition does not involve or express any certain number of individuals, since it expresses nothing but the nature of the thing defined. For example, the definition of a triangle expresses nothing but the simple nature of a triangle, and not any certain number of triangles. Thirdly, it is to be observed that of every existing thing there is some certain cause by reason of which it exists. Fourthly and finally, it is to be observed that this cause by reason of which a thing exists must either be contained in the nature itself and definition of the existing thing (simply because it pertains to the nature of the thing to exist), or it must exist outside the thing. This being granted, it follows that if a certain number of individuals exist in nature there must necessarily be a cause why those individuals, and neither more nor fewer, exist. If, for example, there are twenty men in existence (whom, for the sake of greater clearness, I suppose existing at the same time, and that no others existed before them), it will not be sufficient, in order that we may give a reason why twenty men exist, to give a cause for human nature generally; but it will be necessary, in addition, to give a reason why neither more nor fewer than twenty exist, since, as we have already observed under the third head, there must necessarily be a cause why each exists. But this cause (as we have shown under the second and third heads) cannot be contained in human nature itself, since the true definition of a man does not involve the number twenty, and therefore (by the fourth head) the cause why these twenty men exist, and consequently the cause why each exists, must necessarily lie outside each one; and therefore we must conclude generally that whenever it is possible for several individuals of the same nature to exist, there must necessarily be an external cause for their existence.

Since now it pertains to the nature of substance to exist (as we have shown in this note), its definition must involve necessary existence, and consequently from its definition alone its existence must be concluded. But from its definition (as we have already shown under the second and third heads) the existence of more substances than one cannot be deduced. It follows, therefore, from this definition necessarily that there cannot be two substances possessing the same nature.

PROPOSITION IX. *The more reality or being a thing possesses, the more attributes belong to it.*

Demonstration. This is evident from Def. 4.

PROPOSITION X. *Each attribute of a substance must be conceived through itself.*

Demonstration. For an attribute is that which the intellect perceives of substance, as if constituting its essence (Def. 4), and therefore (Def. 3) it must be conceived through itself. — Q.E.D.

Note. From this it is apparent that although two attributes may be conceived as really distinct — that is to say, one without the assistance of the other — we cannot nevertheless thence conclude that they constitute two beings or two different substances; for this is the nature of substance that each of its attributes is conceived through itself, since all the attributes which substance possesses were always in it together, nor could one be produced by another; but each expresses the reality or being of substance. It is very far from being absurd, therefore, to ascribe to one substance a number of attributes, since nothing in Nature is clearer than that each being must be conceived under some attribute, and the more reality or being it has, the more attributes it possesses expressing necessity or eternity and infinity. Nothing consequently is clearer than that Being absolutely infinite is necessarily defined, as we have shown (Def. 6), as Being which consists of infinite attributes, each one of which expresses a certain essence, eternal and infinite. But if anyone now asks by what sign, therefore, we may distinguish between substances, let him read the following propositions, which show that in Nature only one substance exists, and that it is absolutely infinite. For this reason that sign would be sought for in vain.

PROPOSITION XI. *God or substance consisting of infinite attributes, each one of which expresses eternal and infinite essence, necessarily exists.*

Demonstration. If this be denied, conceive, if it be possible, that God does not exist. Then it follows (Ax. 7) that His essence does not involve existence. But this (Prop. 7) is absurd. Therefore God necessarily exists. — Q.E.D.

Another demonstration. For the existence or non-existence of everything there must be a reason or cause. For example, if a triangle exists there must be a reason or cause why it exists; and if it does not exist there must be a reason or cause which hinders its existence or which negates it. But this reason or cause must either be contained in the nature of the thing or lie outside it. For example, the nature of the thing itself shows the reason why a square circle does not exist, the reason being that a square circle involves a contradiction. And the reason, on the other hand, why substance exists follows from its nature alone, which involves existence (see Prop. 7). But the reason why a circle or triangle exists or does not exist is not drawn from their nature, but from the order of corporeal nature generally; for from that it must follow either that a triangle necessarily exists or that it is impossible for it to exist. But this is self-evident. Therefore it follows that if there be no cause nor reason which hinders a thing from existing it exists necessarily. If, therefore, there be no reason nor cause which hinders God from existing or which negates His existence, we must conclude absolutely that He necessarily exists. But if there be such a reason or cause it must be either in the nature itself of God or must lie outside it, that is to say, in another substance of another nature. For if the reason lay in a substance of the same nature, the existence of God would be by this very fact admitted. But substance possessing another nature could have nothing in common with God (Prop. 2), and therefore could not give Him existence nor negate it. Since, therefore, the reason or cause which could negate the divine existence cannot be outside the divine nature, it will necessarily, supposing that the divine nature does not exist, be in His nature itself, which would therefore involve a contradiction. But to affirm this of the Being absolutely infinite and consummately perfect is absurd. Therefore, neither in God nor outside God is there any cause or reason which can negate His existence, and therefore God necessarily exists. — Q.E.D.

Another demonstration. Inability to exist is impotence, and, on the other hand, ability to exist is power, as is self-evident. If, therefore, there is nothing which necessarily exists except things finite, it follows that things finite are more powerful than the absolutely infinite Being, and this (as is self-evident) is absurd; therefore, either nothing exists or Being absolutely infinite also necessarily exists. But we ourselves exist, either in ourselves or in something else which necessarily exists (Ax. I and Prop. 7). Therefore, the Being absolutely infinite — that is to say (Def. 6), God — necessarily exists. — Q.E.D.

Note. In this last demonstration I wished to prove the existence of God *a posteriori*, in order that the demonstration might be the more easily understood, and not because the existence of God does not follow *a priori* from the same grounds. For since ability to exist is power, it follows that the more reality belongs to the nature of anything, the greater is the power for existence it derives from itself; and it also follows, therefore, that the Being absolutely infinite, or God, has from Himself an absolutely infinite power of existence, and that He therefore necessarily exists. Many persons, nevertheless, will perhaps not be able easily to see the force of this demonstration, because they have been accustomed to contemplate those things alone which flow from external causes, and they see also that those things which are quickly produced from these causes, that is to say, which easily exist easily perish, whilst, on the other hand, they adjudge those things to be more difficult to produce, that is to say, not so easy to bring into existence, to which they conceive more properties pertain. In order that these prejudices may be removed I do not need here to show in what respect this saying, "What is quickly made quickly perishes," is true, nor to inquire whether, looking at the whole of Nature, all things are or are not equally easy. But this only it will be sufficient for me to observe: that I do not speak of things which are produced by external causes, but that I speak of substances alone which (Prop. 6) can be produced by no external cause. For whatever perfection or reality those things may have which are produced by external causes, whether they consist of many parts or of few, they owe it all to the virtue of an external cause, and therefore their existence springs from the perfection of an external cause alone and not from their own. On the other hand, whatever perfection substance has is due to no external cause. Therefore, its existence must follow from its nature alone, and is, therefore, nothing else than its essence. Perfection consequently does not prevent the existence of a thing but establishes it; imperfection, on the other hand, prevents existence, and so of no existence can we be more sure than of the existence of the Being absolutely infinite or perfect, that is to say, God. For since His essence shuts out all imperfection and involves absolute perfection, for this very reason all cause of doubt concerning His existence is taken away, and the highest certainty concerning it is given — a truth which I trust will be evident to anyone who bestows only moderate attention.

PROPOSITION XII. *No attribute of substance can be truly conceived from which it follows that substance can be divided.*

Demonstration. For the parts into which substance thus conceived would be divided will or will not retain the nature of substance. If they retain it, then (Prop. 8) each part will be infinite, and (Prop. 6) the cause of itself, and will consist of an attribute differing from that of any other part (Prop. 5), so that from one substance more substances could be formed, which (Prop. 6) is absurd. Moreover, the parts (Prop. 2) would have nothing in common with their whole, and the whole (Def. 4 and Prop. 10) could be and could be conceived without its parts, which no one will doubt to be an absurdity. But if the second case be supposed, namely, that the parts will not retain the nature of substance, then, since the whole substance might be divided into equal parts, it would lose the nature of substance and cease to be, which (Prop. 7) is absurd.

PROPOSITION XIII. *Substance absolutely infinite is indivisible.*

Demonstration. For if it were divisible, the parts into which it would be divided will or will not retain the nature of substance absolutely infinite. If they retain it there will be a plurality of substances possessing the same nature, which (Prop. 5) is absurd. If the second case be supposed, then (as above) substance absolutely infinite can cease to be, which (Prop. 11) is also absurd.

Corollary. Hence it follows that no substance, and consequently no bodily substance in so far as it is substance, is divisible.

Note. That substance is indivisible is more easily to be understood from this consideration alone — that the nature of substance cannot be conceived unless as infinite, and that by a part of substance nothing else can be understood than finite substance, which (Prop. 8) involves a manifest contradiction.

PROPOSITION XIV. *Besides God no substance can be nor can be conceived.*

Demonstration. Since God is Being absolutely infinite, of whom no attribute can be denied which expresses the essence of substance (Def. 6), and since He necessarily exists (Prop. 11), it follows that if there were any substance besides God, it would have to be explained by some attribute of God, and thus two substances would exist possessing the same attribute, which (Prop. 5) is absurd; and therefore there cannot be any substance except God, and consequently none other can be conceived. For if any other could be conceived, it would necessarily be conceived as existing, and this (by the first part of this demonstration) is absurd. Therefore, besides God no substance can be nor can be conceived. — Q.E.D.

Corollary 1. Hence it follows with the greatest clearness, firstly, that God is one, that is to say (Def. 6), in Nature there is but one substance, and it is absolutely infinite, as (Note, Prop. 10) we have already intimated.

Corollary 2. It follows, secondly, that the thing extended (*rem extensam*) **and the** thing thinking (*rem cogitantem*) are either attributes of God or (**Ax.** 1) modifications of the attributes of God.

PROPOSITION XV. *Whatever is, is in God, and nothing can either be or be conceived without God.*

Demonstration. Besides God there is no substance, nor can any be conceived (Prop. 14), that is to say (Def. 3), nothing which is in itself and is conceived through itself. But modes (Def. 5) can neither be nor be conceived without substance; therefore in the divine nature only can they be, and through it alone can they be conceived. But besides substances and modes nothing is assumed (Ax. 1). Therefore, nothing can be or be conceived without God. — Q.E.D.

Note. There are those who imagine God to be like a man, composed of body and soul and subject to passions; but it is clear enough from what has already been demonstrated how far off men who believe this are from the true knowledge of God. But these I dismiss, for all men who have in any way looked into the divine nature deny that God is corporeal. That He cannot be so they conclusively prove by showing that by "body" we understand a certain quantity possessing length, breadth, and depth, limited by some fixed form; and that to attribute these to God, a being absolutely infinite, is the greatest absurdity. But yet at the same time, from other arguments by which they endeavor to confirm their proof, they clearly show that they remove altogether from the divine nature substance itself corporeal or extended, affirming that it was created by God. By what divine power, however, it could have been created they are altogether ignorant, so that it is clear they do not understand what they themselves say. But I have demonstrated, at least in my own opinion, with sufficient clearness (see Corol. Prop. 6 and Note 2, Prop. 8), that no substance can be produced or created by another being (*ab alio*). Moreover (Prop. 14), we have shown that besides God no substance can be nor can be conceived; and hence we have concluded that extended substance is one of the infinite attributes of God. But for the sake of a fuller explanation I will refute my adversaries' arguments, which, taken altogether, come to this: first, that corporeal substance, in so far as it is substance, consists, as they suppose, of parts, and therefore they deny that it can be infinite, and consequently that it can pertain to God. This they illustrate by many examples, one or two of which I will adduce. If corporeal substance, they say, be infinite, let us conceive it to be divided into two parts; each part, therefore, will be either finite or infinite. If each part be finite, then the infinite is composed of two finite parts, which is absurd. If each part be infinite, there is then an infinite twice as great as another infinite, which is also absurd. Again, if infinite quantity be measured by equal parts of a foot each, it must contain an infinite number of such parts, and similarly if it be measured by equal parts of an inch each; and therefore one infinite number will be twelve times greater than another infinite number. Lastly, if from one point of any infinite quantity it be imagined that two lines, AB, AC, which at first are at a certain and determinate distance from one another, be infinitely extended, it is plain that the distance between B and C will be continually increased, and at length from being determinate will be indeterminable. Since therefore these absurdities follow, as they think, from supposing quantity to be infinite, they conclude that corporeal substance must be finite, and consequently cannot pertain to the essence of God. A second argument is assumed from the absolute perfection of God. For God, they say, since He is a being absolutely perfect, cannot suffer; but corporeal substance, since it is divisible, can suffer; it follows, therefore, that it does not pertain to God's essence. These are the arguments which I find in authors, by which they endeavor to show that corporeal substance is unworthy of the divine nature and cannot pertain to it. But anyone who will properly attend will discover that I have already answered these arguments, since the sole foundation of them is the supposition that bodily substance consists of parts — a supposition which (Prop. 12 and Corol. Prop. 13) I have shown to be absurd. Moreover, if anyone will rightly consider the matter, he will see that all these absurdities (supposing that they are all absurdities — a point which I will now take for granted), from which these authors attempt to draw the conclusion that substance extended is finite, do not by any means follow from the supposition that quantity is infinite, but from the supposition that infinite quantity is measurable, and that it is made up of finite parts. Therefore, from the

absurdities to which this leads nothing can be concluded except that
infinite quantity is not measurable, and that it cannot be composed
of finite parts. But this is what we have already demonstrated (Prop.
12 etc.), and the shaft therefore which is aimed at us turns against
those who cast it. If, therefore, from these absurdities anyone should
attempt to conclude that substance extended must be finite, he would,
forsooth, be in the position of the man who supposes a circle to have
the properties of a square, and then concludes that it has no centre,
such that all the lines drawn from it to the circumference are equal.
For corporeal substance, which cannot be conceived except as infinite,
one and indivisible (Props. 8, 5, and 12), is conceived by those against
whom I argue to be composed of finite parts, and to be multiplex and
divisible, in order that they may prove it finite. Just in the same way
others, after they have imagined a line to consist of points, know how
to discover many arguments by which they show that a line cannot be
divided *ad infinitum;* and indeed it is not less absurd to suppose that
corporeal substance is composed of bodies or parts than to suppose
that a body is composed of surfaces, surfaces of lines, and that lines,
finally, are composed of points. Every one who knows that clear
reason is infallible ought to admit this, and especially those who deny
that a vacuum can exist. For if corporeal substance could be so
divided that its parts could be really distinct, why could not one part
be annihilated, the rest remaining, as before, connected with one
another? And why must all be so fitted together that there can be
no vacuum? For of things which are really distinct the one from the
other, one can be and remain in its own position without the other.
Since, therefore, it is supposed that there is no vacuum in Nature
(about which I will speak at another time), but that all the parts must
be united so that no vacuum can exist, it follows that they cannot
be really separated, that is to say, that corporeal substance, in so far
as it is substance, cannot be divided. If, nevertheless, anyone should
now ask why there is a natural tendency to consider quantity as
capable of division, I reply that quantity is conceived by us in two
ways: either abstractly or superficially, that is to say, as we imagine
it, or else as substance, in which way it is conceived by the intellect
alone. If, therefore, we regard quantity (as we do very often and
easily) as it exists in the imagination, we find it to be finite, divisible,
and composed of parts; but if we regard it as it exists in the intellect,

and conceive it in so far as it is substance, which is very difficult, then, as we have already sufficiently demonstrated, we find it to be infinite, one, and indivisible. This will be plain enough to all who know how to distinguish between the imagination and the intellect, and more especially if we remember that matter is everywhere the same, and that, except in so far as we regard it as affected in different ways, parts are not distinguished in it, that is to say, they are distinguished with regard to mode, but not with regard to reality. For example, we conceive water as being divided, in so far as it is water, and that its parts are separated from one another; but in so far as it is corporeal substance we cannot thus conceive it, for as such it is neither separated nor divided. Moreover, water, in so far as it is water, is originated and destroyed; but in so far as it is substance, it is neither originated nor destroyed. By this reasoning I think that I have also answered the second argument, since that, too, is based upon the assumption that matter, considered as substance, is divisible and composed of parts. And even if what I have urged were not true, I do not know why matter should be unworthy of the divine nature, since (Prop. 14) outside God no substance can exist from which the divine nature could suffer. All things, I say, are in God, and everything which takes place takes place by the laws alone of the infinite nature of God, and follows (as I shall presently show) from the necessity of His essence. Therefore, in no way whatever can it be asserted that God suffers from anything, or that substance extended, even if it be supposed divisible, is unworthy of the divine nature, provided only it be allowed that it is eternal and infinite. But enough on this point for the present.

PROPOSITION XVI. *From the necessity of the divine nature infinite numbers of things in infinite ways (that is to say, all things which can be conceived by the infinite intellect) must follow.*

Demonstration. This proposition must be plain to every one who considers that from the given definition of anything a number of properties necessarily following from it (that is to say, following from the essence of the thing itself) are inferred by the intellect, and just in proportion as the definition of the thing expresses a greater reality, that is to say, just in proportion as the essence of the thing defined involves a greater reality, will more properties be inferred. But the divine nature possesses absolutely infinite attributes (Def. 6), each one of which expresses infinite essence in its own kind (*in suo genere*), and therefore, from the necessity of the divine nature, infinite numbers of things in infinite ways (that is to say, all things which can be conceived by the infinite intellect) must necessarily follow. — Q.E.D.

Corollary 1. Hence it follows that God is the efficient cause of all things which can fall under the infinite intellect.

Corollary 2. It follows, secondly, that God is cause through Himself, and not through that which is contingent (*per accidens*).

Corollary 3. It follows, thirdly, that God is absolutely the first cause.

PROPOSITION XVII. *God acts from the laws of His own nature only, and is compelled by no one.*

Demonstration. We have just shown (Prop. 16) that from the necessity, or (which is the same thing) from the laws only of the divine nature, infinite numbers of things absolutely follow; and we have demonstrated (Prop. 15) that nothing can be nor can be conceived without God, but that all things are in God. Therefore, outside Himself, there can be nothing by which He may be determined or compelled to act; and therefore He acts from the laws of His own nature only, and is compelled by no one. — Q.E.D.

Corollary 1. Hence it follows, firstly, that there is no cause, either external to God or within Him, which can excite Him to act except the perfection of His own nature.

Corollary 2. It follows, secondly, that God alone is a free cause; for God alone exists from the necessity alone of His own nature (Prop. 11, and Corol. 1, Prop. 14), and acts from the necessity alone of His own nature (Prop. 17). Therefore (Def. 7), He alone is a free cause. — Q.E.D.

Note. There are some who think that God is a free cause because He can, as they think, bring about that those things which we have said follow from His nature — that is to say, those things which are in His power — should not be or should not be produced by Him. But this is simply saying that God could bring about that it should not follow from the nature of a triangle that its three angles should be equal to two right angles, or that from a given cause an effect should not follow, which is absurd. But I shall show further on, without the help of this proposition, that neither intellect nor will pertain to the nature of God.

I know, indeed, that there are many who think themselves able to demonstrate that intellect of the highest order and freedom of will both pertain to the nature of God, for they say that they know nothing more perfect which they can attribute to Him than that which is the chief perfection in ourselves. But although they conceive God as actually possessing the highest intellect, they nevertheless do not believe that He can bring about that all those things should exist which are actually in His intellect, for they think that by such a supposition they would destroy His power. If He had created, they say, all things which are in His intellect, He could have created nothing more, and this, they believe, does not accord with God's omnipotence; so then they prefer to consider God as indifferent to all things, and creating nothing except that which He has decreed to create by a certain absolute will. But I think that I have shown with sufficient clearness (Prop. 16) that from the supreme power of God, or from His infinite nature, infinite things in infinite ways, that is to say, all things, have necessarily flowed, or continually follow by the same necessity, in the same way as it follows from the nature of a triangle, from eternity and to eternity, that its three angles are equal to two right angles. The omnipotence of God has therefore been actual from eternity, and in the same actuality will remain to eternity. In this way the omnipotence of God, in my opinion, is far more firmly established. My adversaries, indeed (if I may be permitted to speak plainly), seem to deny the omnipotence of God, inasmuch as they are forced to admit that He has in His mind an infinite number of things which might be created, but which, nevertheless, He will never be able to create, for if He were to create all things which He has in His mind, He would, according to them, exhaust His omnipotence and make Himself imperfect. Therefore, in order to make a perfect God, they are compelled to make Him incapable of doing all those things to which His power extends, and anything more absurd than this, or more opposed to God's omnipotence, I do not think can be imagined. Moreover — to say a word, too, here about the intellect and will which we commonly attribute to God — if intellect and will pertain to His eternal essence, these attributes cannot be understood in the sense in which men generally use them, for the intellect and will which could constitute His essence would have to differ entirely from our intellect and will, and could resemble ours in nothing except in name. There could be no further likeness than that between the celestial constellation of the Dog and the animal which barks. This I will demonstrate as follows. If intellect pertains to the divine nature, it cannot, like our intellect, follow the things which are its object (as many suppose), nor can it be simultaneous in its nature with them, since God is prior to all things in causality (Corol. 1, Prop. 16); but, on the contrary, the truth and formal essence of things is what it is, because as such it exists objectively in God's intellect. Therefore, the intellect of God, in so far as it is conceived to constitute His essence, is in truth the cause of things, both of their essence and of their existence — a truth which seems to have been understood by those who have maintained that God's intellect, will, and power are one and the same thing. Since, therefore, God's intellect is the sole cause of things, both of their essence and of their existence (as we have already shown), it must necessarily differ from them with regard both to its essence and existence; for an effect differs from its cause precisely in that which it has from its cause. For example, one man is the cause of the existence but not of the essence of another, for the essence is an eternal truth; and therefore, with regard to essence, the two men may exactly resemble one another, but, with regard to existence, they must differ. Consequently, if the existence of one should perish, that of the other will not therefore perish; but if the essence of one could be destroyed and become false, the essence of the other would be likewise destroyed. Therefore a thing which is the cause both of the essence and of the existence of any effect must differ from that effect both with regard to its essence and with regard to its existence. But the intellect of God is the cause both of the essence and existence of our intellect; therefore the intellect of God, so far as it is conceived to constitute the divine essence, differs from our intellect both with regard to its essence and its existence, nor can it coincide with our intellect in anything except the name, which is what we essayed to prove. The same demonstration may be applied to the will, as anyone may easily see for himself.

PROPOSITION XVIII. *God is the immanent and not the transient cause of all things.*

Demonstration. All things which are, are in God and must be conceived through Him (Prop. 15), and therefore (Corol. 1, Prop. 16) He is the cause of the things which are in Himself. This is the first thing which was to be proved. Moreover, outside God there can be no substance (Prop. 14), that is to say (Def. 3), outside Him nothing can exist which is in itself. This was the second thing to be proved. God, therefore, is the immanent, but not the transient, cause of all things. — Q.E.D.

PROPOSITION XIX. *God is eternal, or, in other words, all His attributes are eternal.*

Demonstration. For God (Def. 6) is substance which (Prop. 11) necessarily exists, that is to say (Prop. 7), a substance to whose nature it pertains to exist, or (which is the same thing) a substance from the definition of which it follows that it exists, and therefore (Def. 8) He is eternal. Again, by the attributes of God is to be understood that which (Def. 4) expresses the essence of the divine substance, that is to say, that which pertains to substance. It is this, I say, which the attributes themselves must involve. But eternity pertains to the nature of substance (Prop. 7). Therefore, each of the attributes must involve eternity, and therefore all are eternal. — Q.E.D.

Note. This proposition is as clear as possible, too, from the manner in which (Prop. 11) I have demonstrated the existence of God. From that demonstration I say it is plain that the existence of God, like His essence, is an eternal truth. Moreover (Prop. 19 of the *Principles of the Cartesian Philosophy*), I have demonstrated by another method the eternity of God, and there is no need to repeat the demonstration here.

PROPOSITION XX. *The existence of God and His essence are one and the same thing.*

Demonstration. God (Prop. 19) and all His attributes are eternal, that is to say (Def. 8), each one of His attributes expresses existence. The same attributes of God, therefore, which (Def. 4) manifest the eternal essence of God, at the same time manifest His eternal existence, that is to say, the very same thing which constitutes the essence of God constitutes at the same time His existence, and therefore His existence and His essence are one and the same thing. — Q.E.D.

Corollary 1. Hence it follows, first, that the existence of God, like His essence, is an eternal truth.

Corollary 2. It follows, secondly, that God is immutable, or (which is the same thing) all His attributes are immutable; for if they were changed as regards their existence, they must be changed also as regards their essence (Prop. 20), that is to say (as is self-evident), from being true, they would become false, which is absurd.

PROPOSITION XXI. *All things which follow from the absolute nature of any attribute of God must forever exist, and must be infinite, that is to say, through that same attribute they are eternal and infinite.*

Demonstration. Conceive, if possible (supposing that the truth of the proposition is denied), that in some attribute of God something which is finite and has a determinate existence or duration follows from the absolute nature of that attribute — for example, an idea of God in thought.[2] But thought, since it is admitted to be an attribute of God, is necessarily (Prop. 11) in its nature infinite. But so far as it has the idea of God it is by supposition finite. But (Def. 2) it cannot be conceived as finite unless it be determined by thought itself. But it cannot be determined by thought itself so far as it constitutes the idea of God, for so far by supposition it is finite. Therefore it must be determined by thought so far as it does not constitute the idea of God, but which, nevertheless (Prop. 11), necessarily exists. Thought,

²Not the idea which man forms of God, but rather one of God's ideas. The original *idea Dei* admits either interpretation when taken without the context. — TR.

therefore, exists which does not form the idea of God, and therefore from its nature, in so far as it is absolute thought, the idea of God does not necessarily follow (for it is conceived as forming and as not forming the idea of God), which is contrary to the hypothesis. Therefore, if an idea of God in thought or anything else in any attribute of God follow from the necessity of the absolute nature of that attribute (for the demonstration being universal will apply in every case), that thing must necessarily be infinite, which was the first thing to be proved.

Again, that which thus follows from the necessity of the nature of any attribute cannot have a determinate duration. For, if the truth of this be denied, let it be supposed that in some attribute of God a thing exists which follows from the necessity of the nature of the attribute — for example, an idea of God in thought — and let it be supposed that at some time it has either not existed or will not exist. But since thought is supposed to be an attribute of God, it must exist both necessarily and unchangeably (Prop. 11, and Corol. 2, Prop. 20). Therefore, beyond the limits of the duration of the idea of God (for it is supposed that at some time it has either not existed or will not exist), thought must exist without the idea of God; but this is contrary to hypothesis, for the supposition is that thought being given, the idea of God necessarily follows. Therefore, neither an idea of God in thought, nor anything else which necessarily follows from the absolute nature of any attribute of God, can have a determinate duration, but through the same attribute is eternal; which was the second thing to be proved. Observe that what we have affirmed here is true of everything which in any attribute of God necessarily follows from the absolute nature of God. — Q.E.D.

PROPOSITION XXII. *Whatever follows from any attribute of God, in so far as it is modified by a modification which through the same attribute exists necessarily and infinitely, must also exist necessarily and infinitely.*

Demonstration. This proposition is demonstrated in the same manner as the preceding proposition.

PROPOSITION XXIII. *Every mode which exists necessarily and infinitely must necessarily follow either from the absolute nature of some attribute of God or from some attribute modified by a modification which exists necessarily and infinitely.*

Demonstration. Mode is that which is in something else through which it must be conceived (Def. 5), that is to say (Prop. 15), it is in God alone and through God alone can it be conceived. If a mode, therefore, be conceived to exist necessarily and to be infinite, its necessary existence and infinitude must be concluded from some attribute of God or perceived through it, in so far as it is conceived to express infinitude and necessity of existence, that is to say (Def. 8), eternity, or, in other words (Def. 6 and Prop. 19), in so far as it is considered absolutely. A mode, therefore, which exists necessarily and infinitely must follow from the absolute nature of some attribute of God, either immediately (Prop. 21) or mediately through some modification following from His absolute nature, that is to say (Prop. 22), a modification which necessarily and infinitely exists. — Q.E.D.

PROPOSITION XXIV. *The essence of things produced by God does not involve existence.*

Demonstration. This is evident from the first Definition, for that thing whose nature (considered, that is to say, in itself) involves existence is the cause of itself and exists from the necessity of its own nature alone.

Corollary. Hence it follows that God is not only the cause of the commencement of the existence of things, but also of their continuance in existence, or, in other words (to use scholastic phraseology), God is the *causa essendi rerum*. For if we consider the essence of things, whether existing or non-existing, we discover that it neither involves existence nor duration, and therefore the essence of existing things cannot be the cause of their existence nor of their duration, but God only is the cause, to whose nature alone existence pertains (Corol. 1, Prop. 14).

PROPOSITION XXV. *God is not only the efficient cause of the existence of things, but also of their essence.*

Demonstration. Suppose that God is not the cause of the essence of things, then (Ax. 4) the essence of things can be conceived without God, which (Prop. 15) is absurd. Therefore, God is the cause of the essence of things. — Q.E.D.

Note. This proposition more clearly follows from Prop. 16. For from this proposition it follows that, from the existence of the divine nature, both the essence of things and their existence must necessarily be concluded, or, in a word, in the same sense in which God is said to be the cause of Himself He must be called the cause of all things. This will appear still more clearly from the following corollary.

Corollary. Individual things are nothing but modifications or modes of God's attributes, expressing those attributes in a certain and determinate manner. This is evident from Prop. 15 and Def. 5.

PROPOSITION XXVI. *A thing which has been determined to any action was necessarily so determined by God, and that which has not been thus determined by God cannot determine itself to action.*

Demonstration. That by which things are said to be determined to any action is necessarily something positive (as is self-evident); and therefore God, from the necessity of His nature, is the efficient cause both of its essence and of its existence (Props. 25 and 16), which was the first thing to be proved. From this also the second part of the proposition follows most clearly. For if a thing which has not been determined by God could determine itself, the first part of the proposition would be false, and to suppose this possible is an absurdity, as we have shown. — Q.E.D.

PROPOSITION XXVII. *A thing which has been determined by God to any action cannot render itself indeterminate.*

Demonstration. This proposition is evident from the third Axiom.

PROPOSITION XXVIII. *An individual thing, or a thing which is finite and which has a determinate existence, cannot exist nor be determined to action unless it be determined to existence and action by another cause which is also finite and has a determinate existence; and again, this cause cannot exist nor be determined to action unless by another cause which is also finite and determined to existence and action, and so on* ad infinitum.

Demonstration. Whatever is determined to existence and action is thus determined by God (Prop. 26 and Corol. Prop. 24). But that which is finite and which has a determinate existence could not be produced by the absolute nature of any attribute of God, for whatever follows from the absolute nature of any attribute of God is infinite and eternal (Prop. 21). The finite and determinate must therefore follow from God, or from some attribute of God, in so far as the latter is considered to be affected by some mode, for besides substance and modes nothing exists (Ax. 1, and Defs. 3 and 5), and modes (Corol. Prop. 25) are nothing but modifications of God's attributes. But the finite and determinate could not follow from God, or from any one of His attributes so far as that attribute is modified by a modification which is eternal and infinite (Prop. 22). It must, therefore, follow or be determined to existence and action by God or by some attribute of God, in so far as the attribute is modified by a modification which is finite, and which has a determinate existence. This was the first thing to be proved. Again, this cause or this mode (by the same reasoning by which we have already demonstrated the first part of this proposition) must be determined by another cause which is also finite, and which has a determinate existence, and this last cause (by the same reasoning) must, in its turn, be determined by another cause, and so on continually (by the same reasoning) *ad infinitum.* — Q.E.D.

Note. Since certain things must have been immediately produced by God, that is to say, those which necessarily follow from His absolute nature — these primary products being the mediating cause for those things which, nevertheless, without God can neither be nor can be conceived — it follows, firstly, that of things immediately produced by God He is the proximate cause absolutely, and not in their own kind (*in suo genere*), as we say, for effects of God can neither be nor be conceived without their cause (Prop. 15, and Corol. Prop. 24).

It follows, secondly, that God cannot be properly called the remote cause of individual things unless for the sake of distinguishing them from the things which He has immediately produced, or rather which follow from His absolute nature. For by a "remote cause" we understand that which is in no way joined to its effect. But all things which are, are in God, and so depend upon Him that without Him they can neither be nor be conceived.

PROPOSITION XXIX. *In Nature there is nothing contingent, but all things are determined from the necessity of the divine nature to exist and act in a certain manner.*

Demonstration. Whatever is, is in God (Prop. 15); but God cannot be called a contingent thing, for (Prop. 11) He exists necessarily and not contingently. Moreover, the modes of the divine nature have followed from it necessarily and not contingently (Prop. 16), and that, too, whether it be considered absolutely (Prop. 21), or as determined to action in a certain manner (Prop. 27). But God is the cause of these modes, not only in so far as they simply exist (Corol. Prop. 24), but also (Prop. 26) in so far as they are considered as determined to any action. And if they are not determined by God (by the same proposition), it is an impossibility and not a contingency that they should determine themselves; and, on the other hand (Prop. 27), if they are determined by God, it is an impossibility and not a contingency that they should render themselves indeterminate. Wherefore all things are determined from a necessity of the divine nature, not only to exist, but to exist and act in a certain manner, and there is nothing contingent. — Q.E.D.

Note. Before I go any further, I wish here to explain or rather to recall to recollection what we mean by *natura naturans* and what by *natura naturata.*[3] For, from what has gone before, I think it is plain that by *natura naturans* we are to understand that which is in itself and is conceived through itself, or those attributes of substance which express eternal and infinite essence, that is to say (Corol. 1, Prop. 14,

[3]These are two expressions derived from a scholastic philosophy which strove to signify by the same verb the oneness of God and the world, and yet at the same time to mark by a difference of inflexion that there was not absolute identity. — TR.

and Corol. 2, Prop. 17), God in so far as He is considered as a free
cause. But by *natura naturata* I understand everything which follows
from the necessity of the nature of God or of any one of God's attributes, that is to say, all the modes of God's attributes in so far as they
are considered as things which are in God, and which without God
can neither be nor can be conceived.

PROPOSITION XXX. *The actual intellect,[4] whether finite or infinite,
must comprehend the attributes of God and the modifications of
God, and nothing else.*

Demonstration. A true idea must agree with that of which it is the
idea (Ax. 6), that is to say (as is self-evident), that which is objectively
contained in the intellect must necessarily exist in nature. But in
nature (Corol. 1, Prop. 14) only one substance exists, namely, God,
and no modifications (Prop. 15) except those which are in God, and
which (by the same proposition) can neither be nor be conceived
without God. Therefore, the actual intellect, whether finite or infinite,
must comprehend the attributes of God and the modifications of God,
and nothing else. — Q.E.D.

PROPOSITION XXXI. *The actual intellect, whether it be finite or infinite,
together with the will, desire, love, etc., must be referred to the "natura
naturata" and not to the "natura naturans."*

Demonstration. For by the intellect (as is self-evident) we do not
understand absolute thought, but only a certain mode of thought,
which mode differs from other modes, such as desire, love, etc., and
therefore (Def. 5) must be conceived through absolute thought, that
is to say (Prop. 15 and Def. 6), it must be conceived through some
attribute of God which expresses the eternal and infinite essence of
thought in such a manner that without that attribute it can neither
be nor can be conceived. Therefore (Note, Prop. 29), the actual
intellect, etc., must be referred to the *natura naturata*, and not to the

⁴Distinguished from potential intellect (Note, Prop. 31). — TR.

natura naturans, in the same manner as all other modes of thought. — Q.E.D.

Note. I do not here speak of the *actual* intellect because I admit that any intellect *potentially* exists, but because I wish, in order that there may be no confusion, to speak of nothing except of that which we perceive with the utmost clearness, that is to say, the understanding itself, which we perceive as clearly as we perceive anything. For we can understand nothing through the intellect which does not lead to a more perfect knowledge of the understanding.

PROPOSITION XXXII. *The will cannot be called a free cause, but can only be called necessary.*

Demonstration. The will is only a certain mode of thought, like the intellect, and therefore (Prop. 28) no volition can exist or be determined to action unless it be determined by another cause, and this again by another, and so on *ad infinitum.* And if the will be supposed infinite, it must be determined to existence and action by God, not in so far as He is substance absolutely infinite, but in so far as He possesses an attribute which expresses the infinite and eternal essence of thought (Prop. 23). In whatever way, therefore, the will be conceived, whether as finite or infinite, it requires a cause by which it may be determined to existence and action, and therefore (Def. 7) it cannot be called a free cause, but only necessary or compelled. — Q.E.D.

Corollary. 1. Hence it follows, first, that God does not act from freedom of the will.

Corollary. 2. It follows, secondly, that will and intellect are related to the nature of God as motion and rest, and absolutely as all natural things, which (Prop. 29) must be determined by God to existence and action in a certain manner. For the will, like all other things, needs a cause by which it may be determined to existence and action in a certain manner, and although from a given will or intellect infinite things may follow, God cannot on this account be said to act from freedom of will, any more than He can be said to act from freedom of motion and rest by reason of the things which follow from motion and rest (for from motion and rest infinite numbers of things follow). Therefore, will does not appertain to the nature of God more than other natural things, but is related to it as motion and rest and all other things are related to it — these all following, as we have shown, from the necessity of the divine nature, and being determined to existence and action in a certain manner.

PROPOSITION XXXIII. *Things could have been produced by God in no other manner and in no other order than that in which they have been produced.*

Demonstration. All things have necessarily followed from the given nature of God (Prop. 16), and from the necessity of His nature have been determined to existence and action in a certain manner (Prop. 29). If, therefore, things could have been of another nature or could have been determined in another manner to action, so that the order of nature would have been different, the nature of God might then be different to that which it now is, and hence (Prop. 11) that different nature would necessarily exist, and there might consequently be two or more Gods, which (Corol. 1, Prop. 14) is absurd. Therefore, things could be produced by God in no other manner and in no other order than that in which they have been produced. — Q.E.D.

Note 1. Since I have thus shown, with greater clearness than that of noonday light, that in things there is absolutely nothing by virtue of which they can be called contingent, I wish now to explain in a few words what is to be understood by "contingent," but firstly, what is to be understood by "necessary" and "impossible." A thing is called necessary either in reference to its essence or its cause. For the existence of a thing necessarily follows either from the essence and definition of the thing itself or from a given efficient cause. In the same way a thing is said to be impossible either because the essence of the thing itself or its definition involves a contradiction, or because no external cause exists determinate to the production of such a thing. But a thing cannot be called contingent unless with reference to a deficiency in our knowledge. For if we do not know that the essence of a thing involves a contradiction, or if we actually know that it involves no contradiction, and nevertheless we can affirm nothing with certainty about its existence because the order of causes is concealed from us, that thing can never appear to us either as necessary or impossible, and therefore we call it either contingent or possible. *Note 2.* From what has gone before it clearly follows that things have been produced by God in the highest degree of perfection, since they have necessarily followed from the existence of a most perfect nature. Nor does this doctrine accuse God of any imperfection, but, on the contrary, His perfection has compelled us to affirm it. Indeed, from its contrary would clearly follow, as I have shown above, that God is not absolutely perfect, since, if things had been produced in any other fashion, another nature would have had to be assigned to Him, different from that which the consideration of the most perfect Being compels us to assign to Him. I do not doubt that many will reject this opinion as ridiculous, nor will they care to apply themselves to its consideration, and this from no other reason than that they have been in the habit of assigning to God another liberty widely different from that absolute will which (Def. 7) we have taught. On the other hand, I do not doubt, if they were willing to study the matter and properly to consider the series of our demonstrations, that they would altogether reject this liberty which they now assign to God, not only as of no value, but as a great obstacle to knowledge. Neither is there any need that I should here repeat those things which are said in the Note to Prop. 17. But for the sake of those who differ from me, I will here show that, although it be granted that will pertains to God's essence, it follows nevertheless from His perfection that things could be created in no other mode or order by Him. This it will be easy to show if we first consider that which my opponents themselves admit — that it depends upon the decree and will of God alone that each thing should be what it is, for otherwise God would not be the cause of all things. It is also admitted that all God's decrees were decreed by God Himself from all eternity, for otherwise imperfection and inconstancy would be proved against Him. But since in eternity there is no *when* nor *before* nor *after*, it follows from the perfection of God alone that He neither can decree nor could ever have decreed anything else than that which He has decreed, that is to say, God has not existed before His decrees, and can never exist without them. But it is said that although it be supposed that God had made the nature of things different from that which it is, or that from eternity He had decreed something else about Nature and her order, it would not thence follow that any imperfection exists in God. But if this be said, it must at the same time be allowed that God can change His decrees. For if God had decreed something about Nature and her order other than that which He has decreed — that is to say, if He had willed and conceived something else about Nature — He would necessarily have had an intellect and a will different from those which He now has. And if it be allowed to assign to God another intellect and another will without any change of His essence and of His perfections, what is the reason why He cannot now change His decrees about creation and nevertheless remain equally perfect? For His intellect and will regarding created things and their order remain the same in relationship to His essence and perfection in whatever manner His intellect and will are conceived. Moreover, all the philosophers whom I have seen admit that there is no such thing as an intellect existing potentially in God, but only an intellect existing actually. But since His intellect and His will are not distinguishable from His essence, as all admit, it follows from this also that if God had had another intellect actually and another will, His essence would have been necessarily different, and hence, as I showed at the beginning, if things had been produced by God in a manner different from that in which they now exist, God's intellect and will, that is to say, His essence (as has been granted), must have been different, which is absurd.

Since, therefore, things could have been produced by God in no other manner or order, this being a truth which follows from His absolute perfection, there is no sound reasoning which can persuade us to believe that God was unwilling to create all things which are in His intellect with the same perfection as that in which they exist in His intellect. But we shall be told that there is no perfection nor imperfection in things, but that that which is in them by reason of which they are perfect or imperfect and are said to be good or evil depends upon the will of God alone, and therefore, if God had willed He could have effected that that which is now perfection should have been the extreme of imperfection, and *vice versa*. But what else would this be than openly to affirm that God, who necessarily understands what He wills, is able by His will to understand things in a manner different from that in which He understands them, which, as I have just shown, is a great absurdity? I can therefore turn the argument on my opponents in this way: all things depend upon the power of God. In order that things may be differently constituted, it would be necessary that God's will should be differently constituted; but God's will cannot be other than it is, as we have lately most clearly deduced from His perfection. Things therefore cannot be differently constituted. I confess that this opinion, which subjects all things to a certain indifferent God's will, and affirms that all things depend upon God's good pleasure, is at a less distance from the truth than the opinion of those who affirm that God does everything for the sake of the Good. For these seem to place something outside of God which is independent of Him, to which He looks while He is at work as to a model, or at which He aims as if at a certain mark. This is indeed nothing else than to subject God to fate, the most absurd thing which can be affirmed of Him whom we have shown to be the first and only free cause of the essence of all things as well as of their existence. Therefore it is not worth while that I should waste time in refuting this absurdity.

PROPOSITION XXXIV. *The power of God is His essence itself.*

Demonstration. From the necessity alone of the essence of God it follows that God is the cause of Himself (Prop. 11), and (Prop. 16 and its Corol.) the cause of all things. Therefore, the power of God by which He Himself and all things are and act is His essence itself. — Q.E.D.

PROPOSITION XXXV. *Whatever we conceive to be in God's power necessarily exists.*

Demonstration. For whatever is in God's power must (Prop. 34) be so comprehended in His essence that it necessarily follows from it, and consequently exists necessarily. — Q.E.D.

PROPOSITION XXXVI. *Nothing exists from whose nature an effect does not follow.*

Demonstration. Whatever exists expresses the nature or the essence of God in a certain and determinate manner (Corol. Prop. 25), that is to say (Prop. 34), whatever exists expresses the power of God, which is the cause of all things, in a certain and determinate manner, and therefore (Prop. 16) some effect must follow from it. — Q. E. D.

APPENDIX

I have now explained the nature of God and its properties. I have shown that He necessarily exists; that He is one God; that from the necessity alone of His own nature He is and acts; that He is, and in what way He is, the free cause of all things; that all things are in Him, and so depend upon Him that without Him they can neither be nor can be conceived; and, finally, that all things have been predetermined by Him, not indeed from freedom of will or from absolute good pleasure, but from His absolute nature or infinite power.

Moreover, wherever an opportunity was afforded, I have endeavored to remove prejudices which might hinder the perception of the truth of what I have demonstrated; but because not a few still remain which have been and are now sufficient to prove a very great hindrance to the comprehension of the connection of things in the manner in which I have explained it, I have thought it worth while to call them up to be examined by reason. But all these prejudices which I here undertake to point out depend upon this solely: that it is commonly supposed that all things in Nature, like men, work to some end; and, indeed, it is thought to be certain that God Himself directs all things to some sure end, for it is said that God has made all things for man, and man that he may worship God. This, therefore, I will first investigate by inquiring, first, why so many rest in this prejudice, and why all are so naturally inclined to embrace it. I shall then show its falsity, and, finally, the manner in which there have arisen from it prejudices concerning *good* and *evil*, *merit* and *sin*, *praise* and *blame*, *order* and *disorder*, *beauty* and *deformity*, and so forth. This, however, is not the place to deduce these things from the nature of the human mind. It will be sufficient if I here take as an axiom that which no one ought to dispute, namely, that man is born ignorant of the causes of things, and that he has a desire, of which he is conscious, to seek that which is profitable to him. From this it follows, first, that he thinks himself free because he is conscious of his wishes and appetites, whilst at the same time he is ignorant of the causes by which he is led to wish and desire, not dreaming what they are; and, secondly, it follows that man does everything for an end, namely, for that which is profitable to him, which is what he seeks. Hence it happens that he attempts to discover merely the final causes of that which has happened; and when he has heard them he is satisfied, because there is no longer any cause for further uncertainty. But if he cannot hear from another what these final causes are, nothing remains but to turn to himself and reflect upon the ends which usually determine him to the like actions, and thus by his own mind he necessarily judges that of another. Moreover, since he discovers, both within and without himself, a multitude of means which contribute not a little to the attainment of what is profitable to himself — for example, the eyes, which are useful for seeing, the teeth for mastication, plants and animals for nourishment, the sun for giving light, the sea for feeding fish, etc. — it comes to pass that all natural objects are considered as means for obtaining what is profitable. These, too, being evidently discovered and not created by man, hence he has a cause for believing that some other person exists who has prepared them for man's use. For having considered them as means it was impossible to believe that they had created themselves, and so he was obliged to infer from the means which he was in the habit of providing for himself that some ruler or rulers of Nature exist, endowed with human liberty, who have taken care of all things for him, and have made all things for his use. Since he never heard anything about the mind of these rulers, he was compelled to judge of it from his own, and hence he affirmed that the gods direct everything for his advantage in order that he may be bound to them and hold them in the highest honor. This is the reason why each man has devised for himself, out of his own brain, a different mode of worshipping God, so that God might love him above others, and direct all Nature to the service of his blind cupidity and insatiable avarice.

Thus has this prejudice been turned into a superstition and has driven deep roots into the mind — a prejudice which was the reason why everyone has so eagerly tried to discover and explain the final causes of things. The attempt, however, to show that Nature does nothing in vain (that is to say, nothing which is not profitable to man) seems to end in showing that Nature, the gods, and man are alike mad.

Do but see, I pray, to what all this has led. Amidst so much in Nature that is beneficial, not a few things must have been observed which are injurious, such as storms, earthquakes, diseases, and it was affirmed that these things happened either because the gods were angry because of wrongs which had been inflicted on them by man, or because of sins committed in the method of worshipping them; and although experience daily contradicted this, and showed by an infinity of examples that both the beneficial and the injurious were indiscriminately bestowed on the pious and the impious, the inveterate prejudices on this point have not therefore been abandoned. For it was much easier for a man to place these things aside with others of the use of which he was ignorant, and thus retain his present and inborn state of ignorance, than to destroy the whole superstructure and think out a new one. Hence it was looked upon as indisputable that the judgments of the gods far surpass our comprehension; and this opinion alone would have been sufficient to keep the human race in darkness to all eternity if mathematics, which does not deal with ends but with the essences and properties of forms, had not placed before us another rule of truth. In addition to mathematics, other causes also might be assigned, which it is superfluous here to enumerate, tending to make men reflect upon these universal prejudices, and leading them to a true knowledge of things.

I have thus sufficiently explained what I promised in the first place to explain. There will now be no need of many words to show that Nature has set no end before herself, and that all final causes are nothing but human fictions. For I believe that this is sufficiently evident both from the foundations and causes of this prejudice, and from Prop. 16 and Corol. Prop. 32, as well as from all those propositions in which I have shown that all things are begotten by a certain eternal necessity of Nature and in absolute perfection. This much, nevertheless, I will add, that this doctrine concerning an end altogether overturns Nature. For that which is in truth the cause it considers as the effect, and *vice versâ*. Again, that which is first in Nature it puts last; and, finally, that which is supreme and most perfect it makes the most imperfect. For (passing by the first two assertions as self-evident) it is plain from Props. 21, 22, and 23, that that effect is the most perfect which is immediately produced by God, and in proportion as intermediate causes are necessary for the production of a thing is it imperfect. But if things which are immediately produced by God were made in order that He might obtain the end He had in view, then the last things for the sake of which the first exist must be the most perfect of all. Again, this doctrine does away with God's perfection. For if God works to obtain an end, He necessarily seeks something of which he stands in need. And although theologians and metaphysicians distinguish between the end of want and the end of assimilation (*finem indigentiæ et finem assimilationis*), they confess that God has done all things for His own sake, and not for the sake of the things to be created, because before the creation they can assign nothing except God for the sake of which God could do anything, and, therefore, they are necessarily compelled to admit that God stood in need of and desired those things for which He determined to prepare means. This is self-evident. Nor is it here to be overlooked that the adherents of this doctrine, who have found a pleasure in displaying their ingenuity in assigning the ends of things, have introduced a new species of argument, not the *reductio ad impossibile*, but the *reductio ad ignorantiam*, to prove their position which shows that it had no other method of defense left. For, by way of example, if a stone has fallen from some roof on somebody's head and killed him, they will demonstrate in this manner that the stone has fallen in order to kill the man. For if it did not fall for that purpose by the will of God, how could so many circumstances concur through chance (and a number often simultaneously do concur)? You will answer, perhaps, that the event happened because the wind blew and the man was passing that way. But, they will urge, why did the wind blow at that time, and why did the man pass that way precisely at the same moment? If you again reply that the wind rose then because the sea on the preceding day began to be stormy, the weather hitherto having been calm, and that the man had been invited by a friend, they will urge again — because there is no end of questioning — But why was the sea agitated, why was the man invited at that time? And so they will not cease from asking the causes of causes until at last you fly to the will of God — the refuge for ignorance.

So, also, when they behold the structure of the human body, they are amazed; and because they are ignorant of the causes of such art, they conclude that the body was made not by mechanical but by a supernatural or divine art, and has been formed in such a way so that the one part may not injure the other. Hence it happens that the man who endeavors to find out the true causes of miracles, and who desires as a wise man to understand Nature, and not to gape at it like a fool, is generally considered and proclaimed to be a heretic and impious by those whom the vulgar worship as the interpreters both of Nature and the gods. For these know that if ignorance be removed, amazed stupidity — the sole ground on which they rely in arguing or in defending their authority — is taken away also. But these things I leave and pass on to that which I determined to do in the third place.

After man has persuaded himself that all things which exist are made for him, he must in everything adjudge that to be of the greatest importance which is most useful to him, and he must esteem that to be of surpassing worth by which he is most beneficially affected. In this way he is compelled to form those notions by which he explains Nature, such, for instance, as *good, evil, order, confusion, heat, cold, beauty,* and *deformity*, etc.; and because he supposes himself to be free, notions like those of *praise* and *blame, sin* and *merit*, have arisen. These latter I shall hereafter explain when I have treated of human nature; the former I will here briefly unfold.

It is to be observed that man has given the name "good" to everything which leads to health and the worship of God; on the contrary, everything which does not lead thereto he calls "evil." But because those who do not understand Nature affirm nothing about things themselves, but only imagine them and take the imagination to be understanding, they therefore, ignorant of things and their nature, firmly believe an *order* to be in things; for when things are so placed that, if they are represented to us through the senses, we can easily imagine them and, consequently, easily remember them, we call them well arranged; but if they are not placed so that we can imagine and remember them, we call them badly arranged or "confused." Moreover, since those things are more especially pleasing to us which we can easily imagine, men therefore prefer order to confusion, as if order were something in Nature apart from our own imagination; and they say that God has created everything in order, and in this manner they ignorantly attribute imagination to God unless they mean perhaps that God, out of consideration for the human imagination, has disposed things in the manner in which they can most easily be imagined. No hesitation either seems to be caused by the fact that an infinite number of things are discovered which far surpass our imagination, and very many which confound it through its weakness. But enough of this. The other notions which I have mentioned are nothing but modes in which the imagination is affected in different ways, and, nevertheless, they are regarded by the ignorant as being specially attributes of things because, as we have remarked, men consider all things as made for themselves, and call the nature of a thing good, evil, sound, putrid, or corrupt, just as they are affected by it. For example, if the motion by which the nerves are affected by means of objects represented to the eye conduces to well-being, the objects by which it is caused are called "beautiful"; while those exciting a contrary motion are called "deformed." Those things, too, which stimulate the senses through the nostrils are called sweet-smelling or stinking; those which act through the taste are called sweet or bitter, full-flavoured or insipid; those which act through the touch, hard or soft, heavy or light; those, lastly, which act through the ears are said to make a noise, sound, or harmony, the last having caused men to lose their senses to such a degree that they have believed that God even is delighted with it. Indeed, philosophers may be found who have persuaded themselves that the celestial motions beget a harmony. All these things sufficiently show that everyone judges things by the constitution of his brain, or rather accepts the modifications of his imagination in the place of things. It is not, therefore, to be wondered at, as we may observe in passing, that all those controversies which we see have arisen amongst men, so that at last scepticism has been the result. For although human bodies agree in many things, they differ in more, and therefore that which to one person is good will appear to another evil, that which to one is well arranged to another is confused, that which pleases one will displease another, and so on in other cases which I pass by both because we cannot notice them at length here, and because they are within the experience of everyone. For everyone has heard the expressions: So many heads, so many ways of thinking; everyone is satisfied with his own way of thinking; differences of brains are not less common than differences of taste — all which maxims show that men decide upon matters according to the constitution of their brains, and imagine rather than understand things. If men understood things, they would, as mathematics prove, at least be all alike convinced if they were not all alike attracted. We see, therefore, that all those methods by which the common people are in the habit of explaining Nature are only different sorts of imaginations, and do not reveal the nature of anything in itself, but only the constitution of the imagination; and because they have names as if they were entities existing apart from the imagination, I call them entities not of the reason but of the imagination. All argument, therefore, urged against us based upon such notions can be easily refuted. Many people, for instance, are accustomed to argue thus: If all things have followed from the necessity of the most perfect nature of God, how is it that so many imperfections have arisen in Nature — corruption, for instance, of things till they stink; deformity, exciting disgust; confusion, evil, crime, etc.? But, as I have just observed, all this is easily answered. For the perfection of things is to be judged by their nature and power alone; nor are they more or less perfect because they delight or offend the human senses, or because they are beneficial or prejudicial to human nature. But to those who ask why God has not created all men in such a manner that they might be controlled by the dictates of reason alone, I give but this answer: because to Him material was not wanting for the creation of everything, from the highest down to the very lowest grade of perfection; or, to speak more properly, because the laws of His nature were so ample that they sufficed for the production of everything which can be conceived by an infinite intellect, as I have demonstrated in Prop. 16.

These are the prejudices which I undertook to notice here. If any others of a similar character remain, they can easily be rectified with a little thought by anyone.

PART TWO

Of the Nature and Origin of the Mind

I PASS on now to explain those things which must necessarily follow from the essence of God or the Being eternal and infinite — not, indeed, to explain all these things, for we have demonstrated (Prop. 16, pt. 1) that an infinitude of things must follow in an infinite number of ways, but to consider those things only which may conduct us, as it were by the hand, to a knowledge of the human mind and its highest happiness.

DEFINITIONS

I. By body I understand a mode which expresses in a certain and determinate manner the essence of God in so far as He is considered as the thing extended. (See Corol. Prop. 25, pt. 1.)

II. I say that to the essence of anything pertains that, which being given, the thing itself is necessarily posited, and, being taken away, the thing is necessarily taken; or, in other words, that without which the thing can neither be nor be conceived, and which in its turn cannot be nor be conceived without the thing.

III. By idea I understand a conception of the mind which the mind forms because it is a thinking thing.

Explanation. I use the word "conception" rather than "perception" because the name perception seems to indicate that the mind is passive in its relation to the object. But the word conception seems to express the action of the mind.

IV. By adequate idea I understand an idea which, in so far as it is considered in itself, without reference to the object, has all the properties or internal signs (*denominationes intrinsecas*) of a true idea.

Explanation. I say internal, so as to exclude that which is external, the agreement, namely, of the idea with its object.

V. Duration is the indefinite continuation of existence.

Explanation. I call it indefinite because it cannot be determined by the nature itself of the existing thing nor by the efficient cause,

79

which necessarily posits the existence of the thing but does not take it away.

VI. By reality and perfection I understand the same thing.

VII. By individual things I understand things which are finite an l which have a determinate existence; and if a number of individuals so unite in one action that they are all simultaneously the cause of one effect, I consider them all, so far, as a one individual thing.

AXIOMS

I. The essence of man does not involve necessary existence; that is to say, the existence as well as the non-existence of this or that man may or may not follow from the order of nature.

II. Man thinks.

III. Modes of thought, such as love, desire, or the emotions of the mind, by whatever name they may be called, do not exist unless in the same individual exists the idea of a thing loved, desired, etc. But the idea may exist although no other mode of thinking exist.

IV. We perceive that a certain body is affected in many ways.

V. No individual things are felt or perceived by us except bodies and modes of thought.

The postulates will be found after Proposition 13.

PROPOSITIONS

PROPOSITION I. *Thought is an attribute of God, or God is a thinking thing.*

Demonstration. Individual thoughts, or this and that thought, are modes which express the nature of God in a certain and determinate manner (Corol. Prop. 25, pt. 1). God therefore possesses an attribute (Def. 5, pt. 1) the conception of which is involved in all individual thoughts, and through which they are conceived. Thought, therefore, is one of the infinite attributes of God which expresses the eternal and infinite essence of God (Def. 6, pt. 1), or, in other words, God is a thinking thing. — Q.E.D.

Note. This proposition is plain from the fact that we can conceive an infinite thinking Being. For the more things a thinking being can think, the more reality or perfection we conceive it to possess, and therefore the being which can think an infinitude of things in infinite ways is necessarily infinite by his power of thinking. Since, therefore, we can conceive an infinite Being by attending to thought alone, thought is necessarily one of the infinite attributes of God (Defs. 4 and 6, pt. 1), which is the proposition we wished to prove.

PROPOSITION II. *Extension is an attribute of God, or God is an extended thing.*

Demonstration. The demonstration of this proposition is of the same character as that of the last.

PROPOSITION III. *In God there necessarily exists the idea of His essence and of all things which necessarily follow from His essence.*

Demonstration. For God (Prop. 1, pt. 2) can think an infinitude of things in infinite ways, or (which is the same thing, by Prop. 16, pt. 1) can form an idea of His essence and of all the things which necessarily follow from it. But everything which is in the power of God is necessary (Prop. 35, pt. 1), and therefore this idea necessarily exists, and (Prop. 15, pt. 1) it cannot exist unless in God. — Q.E.D.

Note. The common people understand by God's power His free will and right over all existing things, which are therefore commonly looked upon as contingent; for they say that God has the power of destroying everything and reducing it to nothing. They very frequently, too, compare God's power with the power of kings. That there is any similarity between the two we have disproved in the first and second Corollaries of Prop. 32, pt. 1; and in Prop. 16, pt. 1, we have shown that God does everything with that necessity with which He understands Himself, that is to say, as it follows from the necessity of the divine nature that God understands Himself (a truth admitted by all), so by the same necessity it follows that God does an infinitude of things in infinite ways. Moreover, in Prop. 34, pt. 1, we have shown that the power of God is nothing but the active essence of God, and therefore it is as impossible for us to conceive that God does not act as that He does not exist. If it pleased me to go further, I could show besides that the power which the common people ascribe to God is not only a human power (which shows that they look upon God as a man or as being like a man), but that it also involves weakness. But I do not care to talk so much upon the same subject. Again and again I ask the reader to consider and reconsider what is said upon this subject in the first part, from Prop. 16 to the end. For it is not possible for anyone properly to understand the things which I wish to prove unless he takes great care not to confound the power of God with the human power and right of kings.

PROPOSITION IV. *The idea of God,[1] from which infinite numbers of things follow in infinite ways, can be one only.*

Demonstration. The infinite intellect comprehends nothing but the attributes of God and His modifications (Prop. 30, pt. 1). But God is one (Corol. 1, Prop. 14, pt. 1). Therefore the idea of God, from which infinite numbers of things follow in infinite ways, can be one only. — Q.E.D.

PROPOSITION V. *The formal[2] being of ideas recognizes God for its cause in so far only as He is considered as a thinking thing, and not in so far as He is manifested by any other attribute; that is to say, the ideas both of God's attributes and of individual things do not recognize as their efficient cause the objects of the ideas or the things which are perceived, but God Himself in so far as He is a thinking thing.*

Demonstration. This is plain, from Prop. 3, pt. 2; for we there demonstrated that God can form an idea of His own essence, and of all things which necessarily follow from it, solely because He is a thinking thing, and not because He is the object of His idea. Therefore, the formal being of ideas recognizes God as its cause in so far as He is a thinking thing. But the proposition can be proved in another

[1]Or God's idea (*Idea Dei*), see p. 60. — TR.

[2]"Formal" = "objective," as now understood, but it does not necessarily mean materially objective. The "formal being of ideas" = the mind. — TR.

way. The formal being of ideas is a mode of thought (as is self-evident), that is to say, (Corol. Prop. 25, pt. 1), a mode which expresses in a certain manner the nature of God in so far as He is a thinking thing. It is a mode, therefore (Prop. 10, pt. 1), that involves the conception of no other attribute of God, and consequently is the effect (Ax. 4, pt. 1) of no other attribute except that of thought; therefore the formal Being of ideas, etc. — Q.E.D.

PROPOSITION VI. *The modes of any attribute have God for a cause only in so far as He is considered under that attribute of which they are modes, and not in so far as He is considered under any other attribute.*

Demonstration. Each attribute is conceived by itself and without any other (Prop. 10, pt. 1). Therefore the modes of any attribute involve the conception of that attribute and of no other, and therefore (Ax. 4, pt. 1) have God for a cause in so far as He is considered under that attribute of which they are modes, and not so far as He is considered under any other attribute. — Q.E.D.

Corollary. Hence it follows that the formal being of things which are not modes of thought does not follow from the divine nature because of His prior knowledge of these things, but, as we have shown, just as ideas follow from the attribute of thought, in the same manner and with the same necessity the objects of ideas follow and are concluded from their attributes.

PROPOSITION VII. *The order and connection of ideas is the same as the order and connection of things.*

This is evident from Ax. 4, pt. 1. For the idea of anything caused depends upon a knowledge of the cause of which the thing caused is the effect.

Corollary. Hence it follows that God's power of thinking is equal to His actual power of acting, that is to say, whatever follows *formally* from the infinite nature of God, follows from the idea of God [*idea Dei*], in the same order and in the same connection *objectively* in God.

Note. Before we go any further, we must here recall to our memory what we have already demonstrated — that everything which can be perceived by the infinite intellect as constituting the essence of substance pertains entirely to the one sole substance only, and consequently that substance thinking and substance extended are one and the same substance, which is now comprehended under this attribute and now under that. Thus, also, a mode of extension and the idea of that mode are one and the same thing expressed in two different ways — a truth which some of the Hebrews appear to have seen as if through a cloud, since they say that God, the intellect of God, and the things which are the objects of that intellect are one and the same thing. For example, the circle existing in Nature and the idea that is in God of an existing circle are one and the same thing which is manifested through different attributes; and, therefore, whether we think of Nature under the attribute of extension or under the attribute of thought or under any other attribute whatever, we shall discover one and the same order or one and the same connection of causes, that is to say, in every case the same sequence of things. Nor have I had any other reason for saying that God is the cause of the idea, for example, of the circle in so far only as He is a thinking thing, and of the circle itself in so far as He is an extended thing, but this, that the formal being of the idea of a circle can only be perceived through another mode of thought, as its proximate cause, and this again must be perceived through another, and so on *ad infinitum*. So that when things are considered as modes of thought we must explain the order of the whole of Nature or the connection of causes by the attribute of thought alone, and when things are considered as modes of extension, the order of the whole of Nature must be explained through the attribute of extension alone, and so with other attributes. Therefore, God is in truth the cause of things as they are in themselves, in so far as He consists of infinite attributes, nor for the present can I explain the matter more clearly.

PROPOSITION VIII. *The ideas of non-existent individual things or modes are comprehended in the infinite idea of God, in the same way that the formal essences of individual things or modes are contained in the attributes of God.*

Demonstration. This proposition is evident from the preceding proposition, but is to be understood more clearly from the preceding Note.

Corollary. Hence it follows that when individual things do not exist unless in so far as they are comprehended in the attributes of God, their objective being or ideas do not exist unless in so far as the infinite idea of God exists; and when individual things are said to exist, not only in so far as they are included in God's attributes, but in so far as they are said to have duration, their ideas involve the existence through which they are said to have duration.

Note. If any one desires an instance in order that what I have said may be more fully understood, I cannot give one which will adequately explain what I have been saying, since an exact parallel does not exist; nevertheless, I will endeavor to give as good an illustration as can be found.

The circle, for example, possesses this property that the rectangles contained by the segments of all straight lines cutting one another in the same circle are equal; therefore in a circle there is contained an infinite number of rectangles equal to one another, but none of them can be said to exist unless in so far as the circle exists, nor can the idea of any one of these rectangles be said to exist unless in so far as it is comprehended in the idea of the circle. Out of this infinite number of rectangles, let two only, E and D, be conceived to exist. The ideas of these two rectangles do not now exist merely in so far as they are comprehended in the idea of the circle, 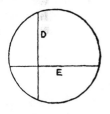 but because they involve the existence of their rectangles, and it is this which distinguishes them from the other ideas of the other rectangles.

PROPOSITION IX. *The idea of an individual thing actually existing has God for a cause, not in so far as He is infinite, but in so far as He is considered to be affected by another idea of an individual thing actually existing, of which idea also He is the cause in so far as He is affected by a third, and so on* ad infinitum.

Demonstration. The idea of any individual thing actually existing is an individual mode of thought, and is distinct from other modes of thought (Corol. and Note, Prop. 8, pt. 2), and therefore (Prop. 6, pt. 2) has God for a cause in so far only as He is a thinking thing; not indeed as a thinking thing absolutely (Prop. 28, pt. 1), but in so far as He is considered as affected by another mode of thought. Again, He is the cause of this latter mode of thought in so far as He is considered as affected by another, and so on *ad infinitum.* But the order and connection of ideas (Prop. 7, pt. 2) is the same as the order and connection of causes; therefore every individual idea has for its cause another idea, that is to say, God in so far as He is affected by another idea, while of this second idea God is again the cause in the same way, and so on *ad infinitum.* — Q.E.D.

Corollary. A knowledge of everything which happens in the individual object of any idea exists in God in so far only as He possesses the idea of that object.

Demonstration. The idea of everything which happens in the object of any idea exists in God (Prop. 3, pt. 2), not in so far as He is infinite, but in so far as He is considered as affected by another idea of an individual thing (Prop. 9, pt. 2); but (Prop. 7, pt. 2) the order and connection of ideas is the same as the order and connection of things, and therefore the knowledge of that which happens in any individual object will exist in God in so far only as He has the idea of that object. — Q.E.D.

PROPOSITION X. *The being of substance does not pertain to the essence of man, or, in other words, substance does not constitute the form of man.*

Demonstration. The being of substance involves necessary existence (Prop. 7, pt. 1). If, therefore, the being of substance pertained to the essence of man, the existence of man would necessarily follow from the existence of substance (Def. 2, pt. 2), and consequently he would necessarily exist, which (Ax. 1, pt. 2) is an absurdity. Therefore the being of substance does not pertain, etc. — Q.E.D.

Note. This proposition may be demonstrated from Prop. 5, pt. 1, which proves that there are not two substances of the same nature.

For since it is possible for more men than one to exist, therefore that which constitutes the form of man is not the being of substance. This proposition is evident also from the other properties of substance, as, for example, that it is by its nature infinite, immutable, indivisible, etc., as anyone may easily see.

Corollary. Hence it follows that the essence of man consists of certain modifications of the attributes of God; for the being of substance does not pertain to the essence of man (Prop. 10, pt. 2). It is therefore something (Prop. 15, pt. 1) which is in God, and which without God can neither be nor be conceived, or (Corol. Prop. 25, pt. 1) a modification or mode which expresses the nature of God in a certain and determinate manner.

Note. Everyone must admit that without God nothing can be nor can be conceived; for everyone admits that God is the sole cause both of the essence and of the existence of all things, that is to say, God is not only the cause of things, to use a common expression, *secundum fieri*, but also *secundum esse*. But many people say that that pertains to the essence of a thing without which the thing can neither be nor can be conceived, and they therefore believe either that the nature of God belongs to the essence of created things or that created things can be or can be conceived without God; or, which is more probable, there is no consistency in their thought. I believe that the cause of this confusion is that they have not observed a proper order of philosophic study. For although the divine nature ought to be studied first, because it is first in the order of knowledge and in the order of things, they think it last, while, on the other hand, those things which are called objects of the senses are believed to stand before everything else. Hence it has come to pass that there was nothing of which men thought less than the divine nature while they have been studying natural objects, and when they afterwards applied themselves to think about God, there was nothing of which they could think less than those prior fictions upon which they had built their knowledge of natural things, for these fictions could in no way help to the knowledge of the divine nature. It is no wonder, therefore, if we find them continually contradicting themselves. But this I pass by. For my only purpose was to give a reason why I did not say that that pertains to the essence of a thing without which the thing can neither be nor can be conceived; and my reason is that individual things cannot be nor be conceived without God, and yet God does not pertain to their essence. I have rather, therefore, said that the essence of a thing is necessarily that, which being given, the thing is posited, and being taken away, the thing is taken away, or that without which the thing can neither be nor be conceived, and which in its turn cannot be nor be conceived without the thing.

PROPOSITION XI. *The first thing which forms the actual being of the human mind is nothing else than the idea of an individual thing actually existing.*

Demonstration. The essence of man is formed (Corol. Prop. 10, pt. 2) by certain modes of the attributes of God, that is to say (Ax. 2, pt. 2), modes of thought, the idea of all of them being prior by nature to the modes of thought themselves (Ax. 3, pt. 2); and if this idea exists, other modes (which also have an idea in nature prior to them) must exist in the same individual likewise (Ax. 3, pt. 2). Therefore an idea is the first thing which forms the being of the human mind. But it is not the idea of a non-existent thing, for then the idea itself (Corol. Prop. 8, pt. 2) could not be said to exist. It will, therefore, be the idea of something actually existing. Neither will it be the idea of an infinite thing, for an infinite thing must always necessarily exist (Props. 21 and 22, pt. 1), and this (Ax. 1, pt. 2) is absurd. Therefore, the first thing which forms the actual being of the human mind is the idea of an individual thing actually existing. — Q.E.D.

Corollary. Hence it follows that the human mind is a part of the infinite intellect of God, and therefore, when we say that the human mind perceives this or that thing, we say nothing else than that God has this or that idea; not indeed in so far as He is infinite, but in so far as He is manifested through the nature of the human mind, or in so far as He forms the essence of the human mind; and when we say that God has this or that idea, not merely in so far as He forms the nature of the human mind, but in so far as He has at the same time with the human mind the idea also of another thing, then we say that the human mind perceives the thing partially or inadequately.

Note. At this point many of my readers will no doubt stick fast, and will think of many things which will cause delay; and I therefore beg of them to advance slowly, step by step, with me, and not to pronounce judgment until they shall have read everything which I have to say.

PROPOSITION XII. *Whatever happens in the object of the idea constituting the human mind must be perceived by the human mind; or, in other words, an idea of that thing will necessarily exist in the human mind. That is to say, if the object of the idea constituting the human mind be a body, nothing can happen in that body which is not perceived by the mind.*

Demonstration. The knowledge of everything which happens in the object of any idea necessarily exists in God (Corol. Prop. 9, pt. 2), in so far as He is considered as affected with the idea of that object; that is to say (Prop. 11, pt. 2), in so far as He forms the mind of any being. The knowledge, therefore, necessarily exists in God of everything which happens in the object of the idea constituting the human mind, that is to say, it exists in Him in so far as He forms the nature of the human mind; or, in other words (Corol. Prop. 11, pt. 2), the knowledge of this thing will necessarily be in the mind, or the mind perceives it. — Q.E.D.

Note. This proposition is plainly deducible and more easily to be understood from Note, Prop. 7, pt. 2, to which the reader is referred.

PROPOSITION XIII. *The object of the idea constituting the human mind is a body, or a certain mode of extension actually existing, and nothing else.*

Demonstration. For if the body were not the object of the human mind, the ideas of the modifications of the body would not be in God (Corol. Prop. 9, pt. 2) in so far as He has formed our mind, but would be in Him in so far as He has formed the mind of another thing; that is to say (Corol. Prop. 11, pt. 2), the ideas of the modifications of the body would not be in our mind. But (Ax. 4, pt. 2) we have ideas of the modifications of a body, therefore, the object of the idea constituting the human mind is a body, and that, too, (Prop. 11, pt. 2) actually existing. Again, if there were also any other object of the mind besides a body, since nothing exists from which some effect does not follow (Prop. 36, pt. 1), the idea of some effect produced by this object would necessarily exist in our mind (Prop. 11, pt. 2). But (Ax. 5, pt. 2) there is no such idea, and therefore the object of our mind is a body existing, and nothing else. — Q.E.D.

Corollary. Hence it follows that man is composed of mind and body, and that the human body exists as we perceive it.

Note. Hence we see not only that the human mind is united to the body, but also what is to be understood by the union of the mind and body. But no one can understand it adequately or distinctly without knowing adequately beforehand the nature of our body; for those things which we have proved hitherto are altogether general, nor do they refer more to man than to other individuals, all of which are animate, although in different degrees. For of everything there necessarily exists in God an idea of which He is the cause, in the same way as the idea of the human body exists in Him; and therefore everything that we have said of the idea of the human body is necessarily true of the idea of any other thing. We cannot, however, deny that ideas, like objects themselves, differ from one another, and that one is more excellent and contains more reality than another, just as the object of one idea is more excellent and contains more reality than another. Therefore, in order to determine the difference between the human mind and other things and its superiority over them, we must first know, as we have said, the nature of its object, that is to say, the nature of the human body. I am not able to explain it here, nor is such an explanation necessary for what I wish to demonstrate.

Thus much, nevertheless, I will say generally — that in proportion as one body is better adapted than another to do or suffer many things, in the same proportion will the mind at the same time be better adapted to perceive many things, and the more the actions of a body depend upon itself alone, and the less other bodies co-operate with it in action, the better adapted will the mind be for distinctly understanding. We can thus determine the superiority of one mind to another; we can also see the reason why we have only a very confused knowledge of our body, together with many other things which I shall deduce in what follows. For this reason I have thought it worth while more accurately to explain and demonstrate the truths just mentioned, to which end it is necessary for me to say beforehand a few words upon the nature of bodies.

AXIOM 1. All bodies are either in a state of motion or rest.

AXIOM 2. Every body moves, sometimes slowly, sometimes quickly.

LEMMA I. *Bodies are distinguished from one another in respect of motion and rest, quickness and slowness, and not in respect of substance.*

Demonstration. I suppose the first part of this proposition to be self-evident. But it is plain that bodies are not distinguished in respect of substance, both from Prop. 5, pt. 1, and Prop. 8, pt. 1, and still more plainly from what I have said in the Note to Prop. 15, pt. 1.

LEMMA II. *All bodies agree in some respects.*

Demonstration. For all bodies agree in this that they involve the conception of one and the same attribute (Def. 1, pt. 2). They have, moreover, this in common that they are capable generally of motion and of rest, and of motion at one time quicker, and at another slower.

LEMMA III. *A body in motion or at rest must be determined to motion or rest by another body, which was also determined to motion or rest by another, and that in its turn by another, and so on* ad infinitum.

Demonstration. Bodies (Def. 1, pt. 2) are individual things, which (Lem. 1) are distinguished from one another in respect of motion and rest, and therefore (Prop. 28, pt. 1) each one must necessarily be determined to motion or rest by another individual thing, that is to say (Prop. 6, pt. 1), by another body which (Ax. 1) is also either in motion or at rest. But this body, by the same reasoning, could not be in motion or at rest unless it had been determined to motion or rest by another body, and this again, by the same reasoning, must have been determined by a third, and so on *ad infinitum.* — Q.E.D.

Corollary. Hence it follows that a body in motion will continue in motion until it be determined to a state of rest by another body, and that a body at rest will continue at rest until it be determined to a state of motion by another body. This indeed is self-evident. For if I suppose that a body, A, for example, is at rest, if I pay no regard to other bodies in motion, I can say nothing about the body A except that it is at rest. If it should afterwards happen that the body A should move, its motion could not certainly be a result of its former rest, for from its rest nothing could follow than that the body A should remain at rest. If, on the other hand, A be supposed to be in motion, so long as we regard A alone, the only thing we can affirm about it is that it moves. If it should afterwards happen that A should be at rest, the rest could not certainly be a result of the former motion, for from its motion nothing could follow but that A should move; the rest must therefore be a result of something which was not in A, that is to say, of an external cause by which it was determined to rest.

Axiom 1. All the modes by which one body is affected by another follow from the nature of the body affected, and at the same time from the nature of the affecting body, so that one and the same body may be moved in different ways according to the diversity of the nature of the moving bodies, and, on the other hand, different bodies may be moved in different ways by one and the same body.

Axiom 2. When a body in motion strikes against another which is at rest and immovable, it is reflected, in order that it may continue its motion, and the angle of the line of reflected motion with the plane of the body at rest against which it struck will be equal to the angle which the line of the motion of incidence makes with the same plane.

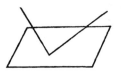

This much for simplest bodies which are distinguished from one another by motion and rest, speed and slowness alone; let us now advance to composite bodies.

Def. When a number of bodies of the same or of different magnitudes are pressed together by others, so that they lie one upon the other, or if they are in motion with the same or with different degrees of speed, so that they communicate their motion to one another in a certain fixed proportion — these bodies are said to be mutually united, and taken altogether they are said to compose one body or individual which is distinguished from other bodies by this union of bodies.

AXIOM 3. Whether it is easy or difficult to force the parts composing an individual to change their situation, and consequently whether it is easy or difficult for the individual to change its shape, depends upon whether the parts of the individual or of the compound body lie with less, or whether they lie with greater, surfaces upon one another. Hence bodies whose parts lie upon each other with greater surfaces I will call "hard"; those "soft" whose parts lie on one another with smaller surfaces; and those "fluid" whose parts move among each other.

LEMMA IV. *If a certain number of bodies be separated from the body or individual which is composed of a number of bodies, and if their place be supplied by the same number of other bodies of the same nature, the individual will retain the nature which it had before without any change of form.*

Demonstration. Bodies are not distinguished in respect of substance (Lem. 1); but that which makes the form of an individual is the union of bodies (by the preceding definition). This form, however (by hypothesis), is retained, although there may be a continuous change of the bodies. The individual, therefore, will retain its nature with regard both to substance and to mode, as before. — Q.E.D.

LEMMA V. *If the parts composing an individual become greater or less proportionately, so that they preserve towards one another the same kind of motion and rest, the individual will also retain the nature which it had before without any change of form.*

Demonstration. The demonstration is of the same kind as that immediately preceding.

LEMMA VI. *If any number of bodies composing an individual are compelled to divert into one direction the motion they previously had in another, but are nevertheless able to continue and reciprocally communicate their motions in the same manner as before, the individual will then retain its nature without any change of form.*

Demonstration. This is self-evident, for the individual is supposed to retain everything which, according to the definition, constitutes its form.

LEMMA VII. *The individual thus composed will, moreover, retain its nature whether it move as a whole or be at rest, or whether it move in this or that direction, provided that each part retain its own motion and communicate it as before to the rest.*

Demonstration. The proof is evident from the definition preceding Lemma 4.

Note. We thus see in what manner a composite individual can be affected in many ways and yet retain its nature. Up to this point we have conceived an individual to be composed merely of bodies which are distinguished from one another solely by motion and rest, speed and slowness, that is to say, to be composed of the most simple bodies. If we now consider an individual of another kind, composed of many individuals of diverse natures, we shall discover that it may be affected in many other ways, its nature nevertheless being preserved. For since each of its parts is composed of a number of bodies, each part (by the preceding Lemma), without any change of its nature, can move more slowly or more quickly, and consequently can communicate its motion more quickly or more slowly to the rest. If we now imagine a third kind of individual composed of these of the second kind, we shall discover that it can be affected in many other ways without any change of form. Thus, if we advance *ad infinitum*, we may easily conceive the whole of nature to be one individual whose parts, that is to say, all bodies, differ in infinite ways without any change of the whole individual. If it had been my object to consider specially the question of a body, I should have had to explain and demonstrate these things more fully. But, as I have already said, I have another end in view, and I have noticed them only because I can easily deduce from them those things which I have proposed to demonstrate.

Postulate 1. The human body is composed of a number of individual parts of diverse nature, each of which is composite to a high degree.

Postulate 2. Of the individual parts of which the human body is composed, some are fluid, some soft, and some hard.

Postulate 3. The individual parts composing the human body, and consequently the human body itself, are affected by external bodies in many ways.

Postulate 4. The human body needs for its preservation many other bodies by which it is, as it were, continually regenerated.

Postulate 5. When a fluid part of the human body is determined by an external body, so that it often strikes upon another which is soft, the fluid part changes the plane of the soft part and leaves upon it, as it were, some traces of the impelling external body.

Postulate 6. The human body can move and arrange external bodies in many ways.

PROPOSITION XIV. *The human mind is adapted to the perception of many things, and its aptitude increases in proportion to the number of ways in which its body can be disposed.*

Demonstration. The human body is affected (Post. 3 and 6) in many ways by external bodies, and is so disposed as to affect external bodies in many ways. But the human mind must perceive (Prop. 12, pt. 2) everything which happens in the human body. The human mind is therefore adapted, etc. — Q.E.D.

PROPOSITION XV. *The idea which constitutes the formal being of the human mind is not simple, but is composed of a number of ideas.*

Demonstration. The idea which constitutes the formal being of the human mind is the idea of a body (Prop. 13, pt. 2) which (Post. 1) is composed of a number of individuals composite to a high degree. But an idea of each individual composing the body must necessarily exist in God (Corol. Prop. 8, pt. 2); therefore (Prop. 7, pt. 2) the idea of the human body is composed of these several ideas of the component parts. — Q.E.D.

PROPOSITION XVI. *The idea of every way in which the human body is affected by external bodies must involve the nature of the human body, and at the same time the nature of the external body.*

Demonstration. All ways in which any body is affected follow at the same time from the nature of the affected body and from the nature of the affecting body (Ax. 1, following Corol. Lem. 3); therefore, the idea of these modifications (Ax. 4, pt. 1) necessarily involves the nature of each body, and therefore the idea of each way in which the human body is affected by an external body involves the nature of the human body and of the external body. — Q.E.D.

Corollary 1. Hence it follows, in the first place, that the human mind perceives the nature of many bodies together with that of its own body.

Corollary 2. It follows, secondly, that the ideas we have of external bodies indicate the constitution of our own body rather than the nature of external bodies. This I have explained in the Appendix of the First Part by many examples.

PROPOSITION XVII. *If the human body be affected in a way which involves the nature of any external body, the human mind will contemplate that external body as actually existing or as present, until the human body be affected by a modification which excludes the existence or presence of the external body.*

Demonstration. This is evident. For so long as the human body is thus affected, so long will the human mind (Prop. 12, pt. 2) contemplate this modification of the external body, that is to say (Prop. 16, pt. 2), it will have an idea of a mode actually existing which involves the nature of the external body, that is to say, an idea which does not exclude the existence or presence of the nature of the external body, but posits it; and therefore the mind (Corol. 1, Prop. 16, pt. 2) will contemplate the external body as actually existing, etc. — Q.E.D.

Corollary. The mind is able to contemplate external things by which the human body was once affected as if they were present, although they are not present and do not exist.

Demonstration. When external bodies so determine the fluid parts of the human body that they often strike upon the softer parts, the fluid parts change the plane of the soft parts (Post. 5); and thence it happens that the fluid parts are reflected from the new planes in a direction different from that in which they used to be reflected (Ax. 2, following Corol. Lem. 3), and that also afterwards, when they strike against these new planes by their own spontaneous motion, they are reflected in the same way as when they were impelled towards those planes by external bodies. Consequently, those fluid bodies produce a modification in the human body while they keep up this reflex motion similar to that produced by the presence of an external body. The mind, therefore (Prop. 12, pt. 2), will think as before, that is to say, it will again contemplate the external body as present (Prop. 17, pt. 2). This will happen as often as the fluid parts of the human body strike against those planes by their own spontaneous motion. Therefore, although the external bodies by which the human body was once affected do not exist, the mind will perceive them as if they were present so often as this action is repeated in the body. — Q.E.D.

Note. We see, therefore, how it is possible for us to contemplate things which do not exist as if they were actually present. This may indeed be produced by other causes, but I am satisfied with having here shown one cause through which I could explain it, just as if I had explained it through the true cause. I do not think, however, that I am far from the truth, since no postulate which I have assumed contains anything which is not confirmed by an experience that we cannot mistrust after we have proved the existence of the human body as we perceive it (Corol. following Prop. 13, pt. 2). Moreover (Corol. Prop. 17, pt. 2, and Corol. 2, Prop. 16, pt. 2), we clearly see what is the difference between the idea, for example, of Peter, which constitutes the essence of the mind itself of Peter, and the idea of Peter himself which is in another man; for example, in Paul. For the former directly manifests the essence of the body of Peter himself, nor does it involve existence unless so long as Peter exists; the latter, on the other hand, indicates rather the constitution of the body of Paul than the nature of Peter; and therefore so long as Paul's body exists with that constitution, so long will Paul's mind contemplate Peter as present, although he does not exist. But in order that we may retain the customary phraseology, we will give to those modifications of the human body, the ideas of which represent to us external bodies as if they were present, the name of *images of things*, although they do not actually reproduce the forms of the things. When the mind contemplates bodies in this way, we will say that it imagines. Here I wish it to be observed, in order that I may begin to show what *error* is, that these imaginations of the mind, regarded by themselves, contain no error, and that the mind is not in error because it imagines, but only in so far as it is considered as wanting in an idea which excludes the existence of those things which it imagines as present. For if the mind, when it imagines non-existent things to be present, could at the same time know that those things did not really exist, it would think its power of imagination to be a virtue of its nature and not a defect, especially if this faculty of imagining depended upon its own nature alone, that is to say (Def. 7, pt. 1), if this faculty of the mind were free.

PROPOSITION XVIII. *If the human body has at any time been simultaneously affected by two or more bodies, whenever the mind afterwards imagines one of them, it will also remember the others.*

Demonstration. The mind imagines a body (Corol. Prop. 17, pt. 2) because the human body is affected and disposed by the impressions of an external body, just as it was affected when certain of its parts received an impulse from the external body itself. But, by hypothesis, the body was at that time disposed in such a manner that the mind imagined two bodies at once; therefore it will imagine two at once now, and whenever it imagines one, it will immediately recollect the other. — Q.E.D.

Note. We clearly understand by this what memory is. It is nothing else than a certain concatenation of ideas, involving the nature of things which are outside the human body — a concatenation which corresponds in the mind to the order and concatenation of the modifications of the human body. I say, first, that it is a concatenation of those ideas only which involve the nature of things which are outside the human body, and not of those ideas which explain the nature of those things, for there are in truth (Prop. 16, pt. 2) ideas of the modifications of the human body which involve its nature as well as the nature of external bodies. I say, in the second place, that this concatenation takes place according to the order and concatenation of the modifications of the human body, that I may distinguish it from the concatenation of ideas which takes place according to the order of the intellect and enables the mind to perceive things through their first causes, and is the same in all men. Hence we can clearly understand how it is that the mind from the thought of one thing at once turns to the thought of another thing which is not in any way like the first. For example, from the thought of the word *pomum* a Roman immediately turned to the thought of the fruit which has no resemblance to the articulate sound *pomum*, nor anything in common with it except this that the body of that man was often affected by the thing and the sound; that is to say, he often heard the word *pomum* when he saw the fruit. In this manner each person will turn from one thought to another according to the manner in which the habit of each has arranged the images of things in the body. The soldier, for instance, if he sees the footsteps of a horse in the sand, will immediately turn from the thought of a horse to the thought of a horseman, and so to the thought of war. The countryman, on the other hand, from the thought of a horse will turn to the thought of his plough, his field, etc.; and thus each person will turn from one thought to this or that thought, according to the manner in which he has been accustomed to connect and bind together the images of things in his mind.

PROPOSITION XIX. *The human mind does not know the human body itself, nor does it know that the body exists except through ideas of modifications by which the body is affected.*

Demonstration. The human mind is the idea itself or the knowledge of the human body (Prop. 13, pt. 2). This knowledge (Prop. 9, pt. 2) is in God in so far as He is considered as affected by another idea of an individual thing. But because (Post. 4) the human body needs a number of bodies by which it is, as it were, continually regenerated, and because the order and connection of ideas is the same as the order and connection of causes (Prop. 7, pt. 2), this idea will be in God in so far as He is considered as affected by the ideas of a multitude of individual things.

God, therefore, has the idea of the human body or knows the human body in so far as He is affected by a multitude of other ideas, and not in so far as He forms the nature of the human mind; that is to say (Corol. 11, pt. 2), the human mind does not know the human body. But the ideas of the modifications of the body are in God in so far as He forms the nature of the human mind; that is to say (Prop. 12, pt. 2), the human mind perceives these modifications and, consequently (Prop. 16, pt. 2), the human body itself actually existing (Prop. 17, pt. 2). The human mind, therefore, perceives the human body, etc. — Q.E.D.

PROPOSITION XX. *There exists in God the idea or knowledge of the human mind, which follows in Him and is related to Him in the same way as the idea or knowledge of the human body.*

Demonstration. Thought is an attribute of God (Prop. 1, pt. 2), and therefore there must necessarily exist in God an idea of Himself (Prop. 3, pt. 2), together with an idea of all His modifications, and consequently (Prop. 11, pt. 2) an idea of the human mind. Moreover, this idea or knowledge of the mind does not exist in God in so far as He is infinite, but in so far as He is affected by another idea of an individual thing (Prop. 9, pt. 2). But the order and connection of ideas is the same as the order and connection of causes (Prop. 7, pt. 2). This idea or knowledge of the mind, therefore, follows in God, and is related to God in the same manner as the idea or knowledge of the body. — Q.E.D.

PROPOSITION XXI. *This idea of the mind is united to the mind in the same way as the mind itself is united to the body.*

Demonstration. We have shown that the mind is united to the body because the body is the object of the mind (Props. 12 and 13, pt. 2), therefore, by the same reasoning, the idea of the mind must be united with its object, the mind itself, in the same way as the mind itself is united to the body. — Q.E.D.

Note. This proposition is to be understood much more clearly from what has been said in the Note to Prop. 7, pt. 2, for we have there

shown that the idea of the body and the body, that is to say (Prop.
13, pt. 2), the mind and the body, are one and the same individual
which at one time is considered under the attribute of thought, and
at another under that of extension: the idea of the mind, therefore,
and the mind itself are one and the same thing, which is considered
under one and the same attribute, that of thought. It follows, I say,
that the idea of the mind and the mind itself exist in God from the
same necessity and from the same power of thought. For, indeed,
the idea of the mind, that is to say, the idea of the idea, is nothing but
the form of the idea in so far as this is considered as a mode of thought
and without relation to the object, just as a person who knows anything by that very fact knows that he knows, and knows that he
knows that he knows, and so on *ad infinitum*. But more on this
subject afterwards.

PROPOSITION XXII. *The human mind not only perceives the modifications of the body, but also the ideas of these modifications.*

Demonstration. The ideas of the ideas of modifications follow in
God and are related to God in the same way as the ideas themselves
of modifications. This is demonstrated like Prop. 20, pt. 2. But the
ideas of the modifications of the body are in the human mind (Prop.
12, pt. 2), that is to say, in God (Corol. Prop. 11, pt. 2), in so far as
He constitutes the essence of the human mind; therefore, the ideas of
these ideas will be in God in so far as He has the knowledge or idea
of the human mind; that is to say (Prop. 21, pt. 2), they will be in
the human mind itself, which, therefore, not only perceives the modifications of the body, but also the ideas of these modifications. —Q.E.D.

PROPOSITION XXIII. *The mind does not know itself except in so far as
it perceives the ideas of the modifications of the body.*

Demonstration. The idea or knowledge of the mind (Prop. 20, pt. 2)
follows in God and is related to God in the same way as the idea or
knowledge of the body. But since (Prop. 19, pt. 2) the human mind
does not know the human body itself, that is to say (Corol. Prop. 11,

pt. 2), since the knowledge of the human body is not related to God in so far as He constitutes the nature of the human mind, therefore the knowledge of the mind is not related to God in so far as He constitutes the essence of the human mind; and therefore (Corol. Prop. 11, pt. 2) the human mind so far does not know itself. Moreover, the ideas of the modifications by which the body is affected involve the nature of the human body itself (Prop. 16, pt. 2), that is to say (Prop. 13, pt. 2), they agree with the nature of the mind; therefore, a knowledge of these ideas will necessarily involve a knowledge of the mind. But (Prop. 22, pt. 2) the knowledge of these ideas is in the human mind itself, and therefore the human mind so far only has a knowledge of itself. — Q.E.D.

PROPOSITION XXIV. *The human mind does not involve an adequate knowledge of the parts composing the human body.*

Demonstration. The parts composing the human body pertain to the essence of the body itself only in so far as they communicate their motions to one another by some certain method (see Def. following Corol. Lem. 3), and not in so far as they can be considered as individual parts without relation to the human body. For the parts of the human body are individual (Post. 1), composite to a high degree, parts of which (Lem. 4) can be separated from the human body and communicate their motions (Ax. 1, following Lem. 3) to other bodies in another way, although the nature and form of the human body itself is closely preserved. Therefore (Prop. 3, pt. 2) the idea or knowledge of each part will be in God in so far as He is considered as affected (Prop. 9, pt. 2) by another idea of an individual thing, which individual thing is prior to the part itself in the order of Nature (Prop. 7, pt. 2). The same thing may be said of each part of the individual itself composing the human body, and therefore the knowledge of each part composing the human body exists in God in so far as He is affected by a number of ideas of things, and not in so far as He has the idea of the human body only, that is to say (Prop. 13, pt. 2), the idea which constitutes the nature of the human mind; and therefore (Corol. Prop. 11, pt. 2) the human mind does not involve an adequate knowledge of the parts composing the human body. — Q.E.D.

PROPOSITION XXV. *The idea of each modification of the human body does not involve an adequate knowledge of an external body.*

Demonstration. We have shown that the idea of a modification of the human body involves the nature of an external body so far as (Prop. 16, pt. 2) the external body determines the human body in some certain manner. But in so far as the external body is an individual which is not related to the human body, its idea or knowledge is in God (Prop. 9, pt. 2) in so far as He is considered as affected by the idea of another thing, which idea (Prop. 7, pt. 2) is by nature prior to the external body itself. Therefore the adequate knowledge of an external body is not in God in so far as He has the idea of the modification of the human body, or, in other words, the idea of the modification of the human body does not involve an adequate knowledge of an external body. — Q.E.D.

PROPOSITION XXVI. *The human mind perceives no external body as actually existing unless through the ideas of the modifications of its body.*

Demonstration. If the human body is in no way affected by any external body, then (Prop. 7, pt. 2) the idea of the human body, that is to say (Prop. 13, pt. 2), the human mind, is not affected in any way by the idea of the existence of that body, nor does it in any way perceive the existence of that external body. But in so far as the human body is affected in any way by any external body, so far (Prop. 16, pt. 2, with its Corol.) does it perceive the external body. — Q.E.D.

Corollary. In so far as the human mind imagines an external body, so far it has not an adequate knowledge of it.

Demonstration. When the human mind through the ideas of the modifications of its body contemplates external bodies, we say that it then imagines (Note, Prop. 17, pt. 2), nor can the mind (Prop. 26, pt. 2) in any other way imagine external bodies as actually existing. Therefore (Prop. 25, pt. 2) in so far as the mind imagines external bodies it does not possess an adequate knowledge of them. — Q.E.D.

PROPOSITION XXVII. *The idea of any modification of the human body does not involve an adequate knowledge of the human body itself.*

Demonstration. Every idea of any modification of the human body involves the nature of the human body in so far as the human body itself is considered as affected in a certain manner (Prop. 16, pt. 2). But in so far as the human body is an individual which can be affected in a multitude of other ways, its idea, etc. (See Demonst. Prop. 25, pt. 2.)

PROPOSITION XXVIII. *The ideas of the modifications of the human body, in so far as they are related only to the human mind, are not clear and distinct but confused.*

Demonstration. The ideas of the modifications of the human body involve the nature both of external bodies and of the human body itself (Prop. 16, pt. 2), and must involve the nature not only of the human body, but of its parts, for the modifications are ways (Post. 3) in which the parts of the human body, and consequently the whole body, is affected. But (Props. 24 and 25, pt. 2) an adequate knowledge of external bodies and of the parts composing the human body does not exist in God in so far as He is considered as affected by the human mind, but in so far as He is affected by other ideas. These ideas of modifications, therefore, in so far as they are related to the human mind alone, are like conclusions without premisses, that is to say, as is self-evident, they are confused ideas. — Q.E.D.

Note. The idea which forms the nature of the mind is demonstrated in the same way not to be clear and distinct when considered in itself. So also with the idea of the human mind, and the ideas of the ideas of the modifications of the human body, in so far as they are related to the mind alone, as every one may easily see.

PROPOSITION XXIX. *The idea of the idea of any modification of the human body does not involve an adequate knowledge of the human mind.*

Demonstration. The idea of a modification of the human body (Prop. 27, pt. 2) does not involve an adequate knowledge of the body itself, or, in other words, does not adequately express its nature, that is to say (Prop. 13, pt. 2), it does not correspond adequately with the nature of the human mind, and therefore (Ax. 6, pt. 1) the idea of this idea does not adequately express the nature of the human mind, nor involve an adequate knowledge of it. — Q.E.D.

Corollary. From this it is evident that the human mind, when it perceives things in the common order of Nature, has no adequate knowledge of itself nor of its own body, nor of external bodies, but only a confused and mutilated knowledge; for the mind does not know itself unless in so far as it perceives the ideas of the modifications of the body (Prop. 23, pt. 2). Moreover (Prop. 19, pt. 2), it does not perceive its body unless through those same ideas of the modifications by means of which alone (Prop. 26, pt. 2) it perceives external bodies. Therefore, in so far as it possesses these ideas it possesses an adequate knowledge neither of itself (Prop. 29, pt. 2), nor of its body (Prop. 27, pt. 2), nor of external bodies (Prop. 25, pt. 2), but merely (Prop. 28, pt. 2, together with the Note) a mutilated and confused knowledge. — Q.E.D.

Note. I say expressly that the mind has no adequate knowledge of itself, nor of its body, nor of external bodies, but has only a confused knowledge as often as it perceives things in the common order of Nature, that is to say, as often as it is determined to the contemplation of this or that *externally* — namely, by a chance coincidence, and not as often as it is determined *internally* — for the reason that it contem-plates[3] several things at once, and is determined to understand in what they differ, agree, or oppose one another; for whenever it is internally disposed in this or in any other way, it then contemplates things clearly and distinctly, as I shall show presently.

PROPOSITION XXX. *About the duration of our body we can have but a very inadequate knowledge.*

Demonstration. The duration of our body does not depend upon its essence (Ax. 1, pt. 2), nor upon the absolute nature of God (Prop.

³In this latter case. — TR.

21, pt. 1), but (Prop. 28, pt. 1) the body is determined to existence and action by causes which also are determined by others to existence and action in a certain and determinate manner, whilst these, again, are determined by others, and so on *ad infinitum*. The duration, therefore, of our body depends upon the common order of Nature and the constitution of things. But an adequate knowledge of the way in which things are constituted exists in God in so far as He possesses the ideas of all things, and not in so far as He possesses only the idea of the human body (Corol. Prop. 9, pt. 2). Therefore, the knowledge of the duration of our body is altogether inadequate in God in so far as He is only considered as constituting the nature of the human mind, that is to say (Corol. Prop. 11, pt. 2), this knowledge in our mind is altogether inadequate. — Q.E.D.

PROPOSITION XXXI. *About the duration of individual things which are outside us we can have but a very inadequate knowledge.*

Demonstration. Each individual thing, like the human body, must be determined to existence and action by another individual thing in a certain and determinate manner, and this again by another, and so on *ad infinitum* (Prop. 28, pt. 1). But we have demonstrated in the preceding proposition, from this common property of individual things, that we have but a very inadequate knowledge of the duration of our own body; therefore the same conclusion is to be drawn about the duration of individual things, that is to say, that we can have but a very inadequate knowledge of it. — Q.E.D.

Corollary. Hence it follows that all individual things are contingent and corruptible, for we can have no adequate knowledge concerning their duration (Prop. 31, pt. 2), and this is what is to be understood by us as their contingency and capability of corruption (Note 1, Prop. 33, pt. 1); for (Prop. 29, pt. 1) there is no other contingency but this. — Q.E.D.

PROPOSITION XXXII. *All ideas, in so far as they are related to God, are true.*

Demonstration. All the ideas which are in God always agree with those things of which they are the ideas (Corol. Prop. 7, pt. 2), and therefore (Ax. 6, pt. 1) they are all true. — Q.E.D.

PROPOSITION XXXIII. *In ideas there is nothing positive on account of which they are called false.*

Demonstration. If the contrary be. asserted, conceive, if it be possible, a positive mode of thought which shall constitute the form or error of falsity. This mode of thought cannot be in God (Prop. 32, pt. 2), but outside God it can neither be nor be conceived (Prop. 15, pt. 1), and therefore in ideas there is nothing positive on account of which they are called false. — Q.E.D.

PROPOSITION XXXIV. *Every idea which in us is absolute, that is to say, adequate and perfect, is true.*

Demonstration. When we say that an adequate and perfect idea is in us, we say nothing else than (Corol. Prop. 11, pt. 2) that an adequate and perfect idea exists in God in so far as He constitutes the essence of the human mind, and consequently (Prop. 32, pt. 2) we say nothing else than that this idea is true. — Q.E.D.

PROPOSITION XXXV. *Falsity consists in the privation of knowledge, which inadequate, that is to say, mutilated and confused ideas involve.*

Demonstration. There is nothing positive in ideas which can constitute a form of falsity (Prop. 33, pt. 2). But falsity cannot consist in absolute privation (for we say that minds and not bodies err and are mistaken); nor can it consist in absolute ignorance, for to be ignorant and to be in error are different. Falsehood, therefore, consists in the privation of knowledge which is involved by inadequate knowledge of things or by inadequate and confused ideas. — Q.E.D.

Note. In the note of Prop. 17, pt. 2, I have explained how error consists in the privation of knowledge; but for the sake of fuller explanation I will give an example. For instance, men are deceived because they think themselves free, and the sole reason for thinking so is that they are conscious of their own actions, and ignorant of the causes by which those actions are determined. Their idea of liberty therefore is this — that they know no cause for their own actions; for as to saying that their actions depend upon their will, these are words to which no idea is attached. What the will is, and in what manner it moves the body, everyone is ignorant, for those who pretend otherwise, and devise seats and dwelling-places of the soul, usually excite our laughter or disgust. Just in the same manner, when we look at the sun, we imagine his distance from us to be about 200 feet; the error not consisting solely in the imagination, but arising from our not knowing what the true distance is when we imagine, and what are the causes of our imagination. For although we may afterwards know that the sun is more than 600 diameters of the earth distant from us, we still imagine it near us, since we imagine it to be so near, not because we are ignorant of its true distance, but because a modification of our body involves the essence of the sun in so far as our body itself is affected by it.

PROPOSITION XXXVI. *Inadequate and confused ideas follow by the same necessity as adequate or clear and distinct ideas.*

Demonstration. All ideas are in God (Prop. 15, pt. 1), and in so far as they are related to God are true (Prop. 32, pt. 2) and (Corol. Prop. 7, pt. 2) adequate. No ideas, therefore, are inadequate or confused unless in so far as they are related to the individual mind of some person (see Props. 24 and 28, pt. 2). All ideas, therefore, both adequate and inadequate, follow by the same necessity (Corol. Prop. 6, pt. 2).—Q.E.D.

PROPOSITION XXXVII. *That which is common to everything (see Lemma 2), and which is equally in the part and in the whole, forms the essence of no individual thing.*

Demonstration. For if this be denied, let that which is common be conceived, if possible, to constitute the essence of some individual thing — the essence, for example, of B. Without B, therefore (Def. 2, pt. 2), that which is common can neither be nor be conceived. But this is contrary to the hypothesis. Therefore that which is common does not pertain to the essence of B, nor does it form the essence of any other individual thing. — Q.E.D.

PROPOSITION XXXVIII. *Those things which are common to everything, and which are equally in the part and in the whole, can only be adequately conceived.*

Demonstration. Let there be something, A, which is common to all bodies, and which is equally in the part of each body and in the whole. I say that A can only be adequately conceived. For the idea of A (Corol. Prop. 7, pt. 2) will necessarily be adequate in God, both in so far as He has the idea of the human body and in so far as He has the idea of its modifications, which (Props. 16, 25, and 27, pt. 2) involve the nature of the human body, and partly also the nature of external bodies; that is to say (Props. 12 and 13, pt. 2), this idea will necessarily be adequate in God in so far as He constitutes the human mind, or in so far as He has ideas which are in the human mind. The mind, therefore (Corol. Prop. 11, pt. 2), necessarily perceives A adequately, both in so far as it perceives itself or its own or any external body; nor can A be conceived in any other manner. — Q.E.D.

Corollary. Hence it follows that some ideas or notions exist which are common to all men, for (Lem. 2) all bodies agree in some things, which (Prop. 38, pt. 2) must be adequately, that is to say, clearly and distinctly, perceived by all.

PROPOSITION XXXIX. *There will exist in the human mind an adequate idea of that which is common and proper to the human body, and to any external bodies by which the human body is generally affected — of that which equally in the part of each of these external bodies and in the whole is common and proper.*

Demonstration. Let A be something which is common and proper to the human body and certain external bodies; let it exist equally in the human body and in those external bodies, and let it exist equally in the part of each external body and in the whole. An adequate idea of A itself will exist in God (Corol. Prop. 7, pt. 2), both in so far as He has the idea of the human body and in so far as He has the idea of the given external bodies. Let it be supposed that the human body is affected by an external body through that which it has in common with the external body, that is to say, by A. The idea of this modification will involve the property of A (Prop. 16, pt. 2), and therefore (Corol. Prop. 7, pt. 2) the idea of this modification in so far as it involves the property of A, will exist adequately in God in so far as He is affected by the idea of the human body, that is to say (Prop. 13, pt. 2), in so far as He constitutes the nature of the human mind. Therefore (Corol. Prop. 11, pt. 2), this idea is also adequate in the human mind. — Q.E.D.

Corollary. Hence it follows that the more things the body has in common with other bodies, the more things will the mind be adapted to perceive.

PROPOSITION XL. *Those ideas are also adequate which follow in the mind from ideas which are adequate in it.*

Demonstration. This is evident. For when we say that an idea follows in the human mind from ideas which are adequate in it, we do but say (Corol. Prop. 11, pt. 2) that in the divine intellect itself an idea exists of which God is the cause, not in so far as He is infinite, nor in so far as He is affected by the ideas of a multitude of individual things, but in so far only as He constitutes the essence of the human mind.

Note 1. I have thus explained the origin of those notions which are called common, and which are the foundations of our reasoning; but of some axioms or notions other causes exist which it would be advantageous to explain by our method, for we should thus be able to distinguish those notions which are more useful than others, and those which are scarcely of any use; those which are common; those which are clear and distinct only to those persons who do not suffer from prejudice; and, finally, those which are ill-founded. Moreover, it would be manifest whence these notions which are called *second*, and consequently the axioms founded upon them, have taken their origin; and other things, too, would be explained which I have thought about these matters at different times. Since, however, I have set apart this subject for another treatise, and because I do not wish to create disgust with excessive prolixity, I have determined to pass by this matter here. But not to omit anything which is necessary for us to know, I will briefly give the causes from which terms called *transcendental*, such as *being, thing, something*, have taken their origin. These terms have arisen because the human body, inasmuch as it is limited, can form distinctly in itself only a certain number of images at once. (For the explanation of the word *image* see Note, Prop. 17, pt. 2.) If this number be exceeded, the images will become confused; and if the number of images which the body is able to form distinctly be greatly exceeded, they will all run one into another. Since this is so, it is clear (Corol. Prop. 17, and Prop. 18, pt. 2) that in proportion to the number of images which can be formed at the same time in the body will be the number of bodies which the human mind can imagine at the same time. If the images in the body, therefore, are all confused, the mind will confusedly imagine all the bodies without distinguishing the one from the other, and will include them all, as it were, under one attribute — that of "being" or "thing." The same confusion may also be caused by lack of uniform force in the images and from other analogous causes, which there is no need to discuss here, the consideration of one cause being sufficient for the purpose we have in view. For it all comes to this, that these terms signify ideas in the highest degree confused. It is in this way that those notions have arisen which are called *universal*, such as, *man, horse, dog*, etc.; that is to say, so many images of men, for instance, are formed in the human body at once that they exceed the power of the imagination, not entirely, but to such a degree that the mind has no power to imagine the determinate number of men and the small differences of each, such as color and size, etc. It will therefore distinctly imagine that only in which all of them agree in so far as the body is affected by them, for by that the body was chiefly affected, that is to say, by each individual, and this it will express by the name *man*, covering thereby an infinite number of individuals; to imagine a determinate number of individuals being out of its power. But we must observe that these notions are not formed by all persons in the same way, but that they vary in each case according to the thing by which the body is more frequently affected, and which the mind more easily imagines or recollects. For example, those who have more frequently looked with admiration upon the stature of men, by the name *man* will understand an animal of erect stature, while those who have been in the habit of fixing their thoughts on something else will form another common image of men, describing man, for instance, as an animal capable of laughter, a biped without feathers, a rational animal, and so on — each person forming universal images of things according to the temperament of his own body. It is not, therefore, to be wondered at that so many controversies have arisen among those philosophers who have endeavored to explain natural objects by the images of things alone.

Note 2. From what has been already said, it clearly appears that we perceive many things and form universal ideas:

1. From individual things, represented by the senses to us in a mutilated and confused manner and without order to the intellect (Corol. Prop. 29, pt. 2). These perceptions I have therefore been in the habit of calling knowledge from vague experience.

2. From signs; as, for example, when we hear or read certain words, we recollect things and form certain ideas of them similar to them, through which ideas we imagine things (Note, Prop. 18, pt. 2). These two ways of looking at things I shall hereafter call knowledge of the first kind, opinion, or imagination.

3. From our possessing common notions and adequate ideas of the properties of things (Corol. Prop. 38, Prop. 39, with Corol. and Prop. 40, pt. 2). This I shall call reason and knowledge of the second kind.

Besides these two kinds of knowledge, there is a third, as I shall hereafter show, which we shall call intuitive science. This kind of knowing advances from an adequate idea of the formal essence of certain attributes of God to the adequate knowledge of the essence of things. All this I will explain by one example. Let there be three numbers given through which it is required to discover a fourth which shall be to the third as the second is to the first. A merchant does not hesitate to multiply the second and third together and divide the product by the first, either because he has not yet forgotten the things which he heard without any demonstration from his schoolmaster, or because he has seen the truth of the rule with the more simple numbers, or because from the 19th Prop. in the 7th book of Euclid he understands the common property of all proportionals.

But with the simplest numbers there is no need of all this. If the numbers 1, 2, 3, for instance, be given, everyone can see, much more clearly than by any demonstration that the fourth proportional is 6, because from the ratio in which we see by one intuition that the first stands to the second we conclude the fourth.

PROPOSITION XLI. *Knowledge of the first kind alone is the cause of falsity; knowledge of the second and third orders is necessarily true.*

Demonstration. To knowledge of the first kind we have said, in the preceding note, that all those ideas belong which are inadequate and confused, and, therefore (Prop. 35, pt. 2), this knowledge alone is the cause of falsity. Moreover, to knowledge of the second and third kind we have said that those ideas belong which are adequate, and, therefore, this knowledge (Prop. 34, pt. 2) is necessarily true. — Q.E.D.

PROPOSITION XLII. *It is the knowledge of the second and third, and not that of the first, kind which teaches us to distinguish the true from the false.*

Demonstration. This proposition is self-evident. For he who knows how to distinguish between the true and the false must have an adequate idea of the true and the false, that is to say (Note 2, Prop. 40, pt. 2), he must know the true and the false by the second or third kind of knowledge.

PROPOSITION XLIII. *He who has a true idea knows at the same time that he has a true idea, nor can he doubt the truth of the thing.*

Demonstration. A true idea in us is that which in God is adequate, in so far as He is manifested by the nature of the human mind (Corol.

Prop. 11, pt. 2). Let us suppose, therefore, that there exists in God, in so far as He is manifested by the nature of the human mind, an adequate idea, A. Of this idea there must necessarily exist in God an idea which is related to Him in the same way as the idea A (Prop. 20, pt. 2, the demonstration of which is universal). But the idea A is supposed to be related to God in so far as He is manifested by the nature of the human mind. The idea of the idea A must therefore be related to God in the same manner, that is to say (Corol. Prop. 11, pt. 2), this adequate idea of the idea A will exist in the mind itself which has the adequate idea A. He, therefore, who has an adequate idea, that is to say (Prop. 34, pt. 2), he who knows a thing truly, must at the same time have an adequate idea or a true knowledge of his knowledge, that is to say (as is self-evident), he must be certain. — Q.E.D.

Note. In the note to Prop. 21, pt. 2, I have explained what is the idea of an idea, but it is to be observed that the preceding proposition is evident by itself. For no one who has a true idea is ignorant that a true idea involves the highest certitude; to have a true idea signifying just this — to know a thing perfectly or as well as possible. No one, in fact, can doubt this unless he supposes an idea to be something dumb, like a picture on a tablet instead of being a mode of thought, that is to say, intelligence itself. Moreover, I ask who can know that he understands a thing unless he first of all understands that thing? That is to say, who can know that he is certain of anything unless he is first of all certain of that thing? Then, again, what can be clearer or more certain than a true idea as the standard of truth? Just as light reveals both itself and the darkness, so truth is the standard of itself and of the false. I consider what has been said to be a sufficient answer to the objection that if a true idea is distinguished from a false idea only in so far as it is said to agree with that of which it is the idea, the true idea therefore has no reality nor perfection above the false idea (since they are distinguished by an external sign alone), and consequently the man who has true ideas will have no greater reality or perfection than he who has false ideas only. I consider, too, that I have already replied to those who inquire why men have false ideas, and how a man can certainly know that he has ideas which agree with those things of which they are the ideas. For with regard to the difference between a true and a false idea, it is evident from

Prop. 35, pt. 2, that the former is related to the latter as being is to non-being. The causes of falsity, too, I have most clearly shown in Props. 19–35, including the note to the last. From what has there been said, the nature of the difference between a man who has true ideas and one who has only false ideas is clear. With regard to the last-mentioned point — how a man can know that he has an idea which agrees with that of which it is the idea — I have shown almost more times than enough that he knows it simply because he has an idea which agrees with that of which it is the idea, that is to say, because truth is its own standard. We must remember, besides, that our mind, in so far as it truly perceives things, is a part of the infinite intellect of God (Corol. Prop. 11, pt. 2), and therefore it must be that the clear and distinct ideas of the mind are as true as those of God.

PROPOSITION XLIV. *It is not of the nature of reason to consider things as contingent but as necessary.*

Demonstration. It is in the nature of reason to perceive things truly (Prop. 41, pt. 2), that is to say (Ax. 6, pt. 1), as they are in themselves, that is to say (Prop. 29, pt. 1), not as contingent but as necessary. — Q.E.D.

Corollary 1. Hence it follows that it is through the imagination alone that we look upon things as contingent both with reference to the past and the future.

Note. How this happens I will explain in a few words. We have shown above (Prop. 17, pt. 2, with Corol.) that, unless causes occur preventing the present existence of things, the mind always imagines them present before it, even if they do not exist. Again (Prop. 18, pt. 2), we have shown that, if the human body has once been simultaneously affected by two external bodies, whenever the mind afterwards imagines one it will immediately remember the other, that is to say, it will look upon both as present before it, unless causes occur which prevent the present existence of the things. No one doubts, too, that we imagine time because we imagine some bodies to move with a velocity less or greater than, or equal to, that of others. Let us therefore suppose a boy who yesterday, for the first time, in the morning saw Peter, at midday Paul, in the evening Simeon, and today in the morning again sees Peter. It is plain from Prop. 18, pt. 2, that as soon as he sees the morning light he will imagine the sun passing through the same part of the sky as on the day preceding, that is to say, he will imagine the whole day, and at the same time Peter will be connected in his imagination with the morning, Paul with midday, and Simeon with the evening. In the morning, therefore, the existence of Paul and Simeon will be imagined in relation to future time, while in the evening, if the boy should see Simeon, he will refer Peter and Paul to the past, since they will be connected with the past in his imagination. This process will be constant in proportion to the regularity with which he sees Peter, Paul, and Simeon in this order. If it should by some means happen that on some other evening, in the place of Simeon, he should see James, on the following morning he will connect in his imagination with the evening at one time Simeon and at another James, but not both together. For he is supposed to have seen one and then the other in the evening, but not both together. His imagination will therefore fluctuate, and he will connect with a future evening first one and then the other, that is to say, he will consider neither as certain, but both as a contingency in the future.

This fluctuation of the imagination will take place in the same way if the imagination is dealing with things which we contemplate in the same way with reference to past or present time, and consequently we imagine things related to time past, present, or future as contingent.

Corollary 2. It is of the nature of reason to perceive things under a certain form of eternity.

Demonstration. It is of the nature of reason to consider things as necessary and not as contingent (Prop. 44, pt. 2). This necessity of things it perceives truly (Prop. 41, pt. 2), that is to say (Ax. 6, pt. 1), as it is in itself. But (Prop. 16, pt. 1) this necessity of things is the necessity itself of the eternal nature of God. Therefore, it is of the nature of reason to consider things under this form of eternity. Moreover, the foundations of reason are notions which explain those things which are common to all (Prop. 38, pt. 2), and these things explain the essence of no individual thing (Prop. 37, pt. 2), and must therefore be conceived without any relation to time, but under a certain form of eternity. — Q.E.D.

PROPOSITION XLV. *Every idea of any body or actually existing individual thing necessarily involves the eternal and infinite essence of God.*

Demonstration. The idea of an individual thing actually existing necessarily involves both the essence and existence of the thing itself (Corol. Prop. 8, pt. 2). But individual things (Prop. 15, pt. 1) cannot be conceived without God, and since (Prop. 6, pt. 2) God is their cause in so far as He is considered under that attribute of which they are modes, their ideas (Ax. 4, pt. 1) must necessarily involve the conception of that attribute, or, in other words (Def. 6, pt. 1), must involve the eternal and infinite essence of God. — Q.E.D.

Note. By "existence" is to be understood here not duration, that is, existence considered in the abstract, as if it were a certain kind of quantity, but I speak of the nature itself of the existence which is assigned to individual things, because from the eternal necessity of the nature of God infinite numbers of things follow in infinite ways (Prop. 16, pt. 1). I repeat, that I speak of the existence itself of individual things in so far as they are in God. For although each individual thing is determined by another individual thing to existence in a certain way, the force, nevertheless, by which each thing perseveres in its existence follows from the eternal necessity of the nature of God (see Corol. Prop. 24, pt. 1).

PROPOSITION XLVI. *The knowledge of the eternal and infinite essence of God which each idea involves is adequate and perfect.*

Demonstration. The demonstration of the preceding proposition is universal, and whether a thing be considered as a part or as a whole, its idea, whether it be of a part or whole, will involve the eternal and infinite essence of God (Prop. 45, pt. 2). Therefore, that which gives a knowledge of the eternal and infinite essence of God is common to all, and is equally in the part and in the whole. This knowledge therefore (Prop. 38, pt. 2) will be adequate. — Q.E.D.

PROPOSITION XLVII. *The human mind possesses an adequate knowledge of the eternal and infinite essence of God.*

Demonstration. The human mind possesses ideas (Prop. 22, pt. 2) by which (Prop. 23, pt. 2) it perceives itself and its own body (Prop. 19, pt. 2), together with (Corol. 1, Prop. 16, and Prop. 17, pt. 2) external bodies, as actually existing. Therefore (Props. 45 and 46, pt. 2), it possesses an adequate knowledge of the eternal and infinite essence of God. — Q.E.D.

Note. Hence we see that the infinite essence and the eternity of God are known to all; and since all things are in God and are conceived through Him, it follows that we can deduce from this knowledge many things which we can know adequately, and that we can thus form that third sort of knowledge mentioned in Note 2, Prop. 40, pt. 2, of whose excellence and value the Fifth Part will be the place to speak. The reason why we do not possess a knowledge of God as distinct as that which we have of common notions is that we cannot imagine God as we can bodies; and because we have attached the name God to the images of things which we are in the habit of seeing, an error we can hardly avoid, inasmuch as we are continually affected by external bodies. Many errors of a truth consist merely in the application of the wrong names to things. For if a man says that the lines which are drawn from the center of the circle to the circumference are not equal, he understands by the circle, at all events for the time, something else than mathematicians understand by it. So when men make errors in calculation, the numbers which are in their minds are not those which are upon the paper. As far as their mind is concerned there is no error, although it seems as if there were because we think that the numbers in their minds are those which are upon the paper. If we did not think so, we should not believe them to be in error. For example, when I lately heard a man complaining that his court had flown into one of his neighbor's fowls, I understood what he meant, and therefore did not imagine him to be in error. This is the source from which so many controversies arise — that men either do not properly explain their own thoughts or do not properly interpret those of other people; for, in truth, when they most contradict one another, they either think the same things or something different, so that those things which they suppose to be errors and absurdities in another person are not so.

PROPOSITION XLVIII. *In the mind there is no absolute or free will, but the mind is determined to this or that volition by a cause which is also determined by another cause, and this again by another, and so on* ad infinitum.

Demonstration. The mind is a certain and determinate mode of thought (Prop. 11, pt. 2), and therefore (Corol. 2, Prop. 17, pt. 1) it cannot be the free cause of its own actions or have an absolute faculty of willing or not willing, but must be determined to this or that volition (Prop. 28, pt. 1) by a cause which is also determined by another cause, and this again by another, and so on *ad infinitum.* — Q.E.D.

Note. In the same manner it is demonstrated that in the mind there exists no absolute faculty of understanding, desiring, loving, etc. These and the like faculties, therefore, are either altogether fictitious or else are nothing but metaphysical or universal entities which we are in the habit of forming from individual cases. The intellect and will, therefore, are related to this or that idea or volition as rockiness is related to this or that rock, or as man is related to Peter or Paul. The reason why men imagine themselves to be free we have explained in the Appendix to the First Part. Before, however, I advance any further, I must observe that by the "will" I understand a faculty of affirming or denying, but not a desire — a faculty, I say, by which the mind affirms or denies that which is true or false, and not a desire by which the mind seeks a thing or turns away from it. But now that we have demonstrated that these faculties are universal notions which are not distinguishable from the individual notions from which they are formed, we must now inquire whether the volitions themselves are anything more than the ideas of things. We must inquire, I say, whether in the mind there exists any other affirmation or negation than that which the idea involves in so far as it is an idea. For this purpose see the following proposition, together with Def. 3, pt. 2, so that thought may not fall into pictures. For by "ideas" I do not understand the images which are formed at the back of the eye, or, if you please, in the middle of the brain, but rather the conceptions of thought.

PROPOSITION XLIX. *In the mind there is no volition or affirmation and negation except that which the idea, in so far as it is an idea, involves.*

Demonstration. In the mind there exists (Prop. 48, pt. 2) no absolute faculty of willing or not willing. Only individual volitions exist, that is to say, this and that affirmation and this and that negation. Let us conceive, therefore, any individual volition, that is, any mode of thought, by which the mind affirms that the three angles of a triangle are equal to two right angles. This affirmation involves the conception or idea of the triangle, that is to say, without it the affirmation cannot be conceived. For to say that A must involve the conception B is the same as saying that A cannot be conceived without B. Moreover, without the idea of the triangle this affirmation (Ax. 3, pt. 2) cannot be, and it can therefore neither be nor be conceived without that idea. But this idea of the triangle must involve this same affirmation that its three angles are equal to two right angles. Therefore also, *vice versa*, this idea of the triangle without this affirmation can neither be nor be conceived. Therefore (Def. 2, pt. 2) this affirmation pertains to the essence of the idea of the triangle, nor is it anything else besides this. Whatever, too, we have said of this volition (since it has been taken arbitrarily) applies to all other volitions, that is to say, they are nothing but ideas. — Q.E.D.

Corollary. The will and the intellect are one and the same.

Demonstration. The will and the intellect are nothing but the individual volitions and ideas themselves (Prop. 48, pt. 2, and its Note). But the individual volition and idea (Prop. 49, pt. 2) are one and the same. Therefore the will and the intellect are one and the same. — Q.E.D.

Note. I have thus removed what is commonly thought to be the cause of error. It has been proved above that falsity consists solely in the privation which mutilated and confused ideas involve. A false idea, therefore, in so far as it is false, does not involve certitude. Consequently, when we say that a man assents to what is false and does not doubt it, we do not say that he is certain, but merely that he does not doubt, that is to say, that he assents to what is false because there are no causes sufficient to make his imagination waver (Note, Prop. 44, pt. 2). Although, therefore, a man may be supposed to adhere to what is false, we shall never on that account say that he is certain. For by "certitude" we understand something positive (Prop. 43, pt. 2, with the Note), and not the privation of doubt; but by the privation of certitude we understand falsity. If the preceding proposition, however, is to be more clearly comprehended, a word or two must be added; it yet remains also that I should answer the objections which may be brought against our doctrine, and finally, in order to remove all scruples, I have thought it worth while to indicate some of its advantages. I say some, as the principal advantages will be better understood when we come to the Fifth Part. I begin, therefore, with the first, and I warn my readers carefully to distinguish between an idea or conception of the mind and the images of things formed by our imagination. Secondly, it is necessary that we should distinguish between ideas and the words by which things are signified. For it is because these three things, images, words, and ideas, are by many people either altogether confounded or not distinguished with sufficient accuracy and care that such ignorance exists about this doctrine of the will, so necessary to be known both for the purposes of speculation and for the wise government of life. Those who think that ideas consist of images which are formed in us by meeting with external bodies persuade themselves that those ideas of things of which we can form no similar image are not ideas, but mere fancies constructed by the free power of the will. They look upon ideas, therefore, as dumb pictures on a tablet and, being prepossessed with this prejudice, they do not see that an idea, in so far as it is an idea, involves affirmation or negation. Again, those who confound words with the idea or with the affirmation itself which the idea involves, think that they can will contrary to their perception because they affirm or deny something in words alone contrary to their perception. It will be easy for us, however, to divest ourselves of these prejudices if we attend to the nature of thought, which in no way involves the conception of extension, and by doing this we clearly see that an idea, since it is a mode of thought, is not an image of anything, nor does it consist of words. For the essence of words and images is formed of bodily motions alone, which involve in no way whatever the conception of thought.

Let this much suffice under this head. I pass on now to the objections to which I have already alluded.

The first is that it is supposed to be certain that the will extends itself more widely than the intellect, and is therefore different from it. The reason why men suppose that the will extends itself more widely than the intellect is because they say they have discovered that they do not need a larger faculty of assent — that is to say, of affirmation — and denial than that which they now have for the purpose of assenting to an infinite number of other things which we do not perceive, but that they do need a greater faculty for understanding them. The will, therefore, is distinguished from the intellect, the latter being finite, the former infinite. The second objection which can be made is that there is nothing which experience seems to teach more clearly than the possibility of suspending our judgment, so as not to assent to the things we perceive; and we are strengthened in this opinion because no one is said to be deceived in so far as he perceives a thing, but only in so far as he assents to it or dissents from it. For example, a man who imagines a winged horse does not therefore admit the existence of a winged horse, that is to say, he is not necessarily deceived unless he grants at the same time that a winged horse exists. Experience, therefore, seems to show nothing more plainly than that the will or faculty of assent is free and different from the faculty of the intellect.

Thirdly, it may be objected that one affirmation does not seem to contain more reality than another, that is to say, it does not appear that we need a greater power for affirming a thing to be true which is true than for affirming a thing to be true which is false. Nevertheless, we observe that one idea contains more reality or perfection than another, for as some objects are nobler than others, in the same proportion are their ideas more perfect. It appears indisputable, therefore, that there is a difference between the will and the intellect.

Fourthly, it may be objected that if a man does not act from freedom of the will, what would he do if he were in a state of equilibrium, like the ass of Buridan? Would he not perish from hunger and thirst? And if this be granted, do we not seem to conceive him as a statue of a man or as an ass? If I deny that he would thus perish, he will consequently determine himself and possess the power of going where he likes and doing what he likes.

There may be other objections besides these, but as I am not bound to discuss what every one may dream, I shall therefore make it my business to answer as briefly as possible those only which I have mentioned. In reply to the first objection, I grant that the will extends itself more widely than the intellect if by the intellect we understand only clear and distinct ideas, but I deny that the will extends itself more widely than the perceptions or the faculty of conception, nor, indeed, do I see why the faculty of will should be said to be infinite any more than the faculty of feeling; for as by the same faculty of will we can affirm an infinite number of things (one after the other, for we cannot affirm an infinite number of things at once), so also by the same faculty of feeling we can feel or perceive (one after another) an infinite number of bodies. If it be said that there are an infinite number of things which we cannot perceive, I reply that such things as these we can reach by no thought, and consequently by no faculty of will. But it is said that if God wished us to perceive those things, it would be necessary for Him to give us a larger faculty of perception, but not a larger faculty of will than He has already given us, which is the same thing as saying that if God wished us to understand an infinite number of other beings, it would be necessary for Him to give us a greater intellect, but not a more universal idea of being (in order to embrace that infinite number of beings) than He has given us. For we have shown that the will is a *universal* or the idea by which we explain all individual volitions, that is to say, that which is common to them all. It is not to be wondered at, therefore, that those who believe this common or universal idea of all the volitions to be a faculty should say that it extends itself infinitely beyond the limits of the intellect. For the universal is predicated of one or of many, or of an infinite number of individuals.

The second objection I answer by denying that we have free power of suspending judgment. For when we say that a person suspends judgment, we only say in other words that he sees that he does not perceive the thing adequately. The suspension of the judgment, therefore, is in truth a perception and not free will. In order that this may be clearly understood, let us take the case of a boy who imagines a horse and perceives nothing else. Since this imagination involves the existence of the horse (Corol. Prop. 17, pt. 2), and the boy does not perceive anything which negates its existence, he will necessarily contemplate it as present, nor will he be able to doubt its existence although he may not be certain of it. This is a thing which we daily experience in dreams, nor do I believe that there is any one who thinks that he has the free power during dreams of suspending his judgment upon those things which he dreams, and of causing himself not to dream those things which he dreams that he sees; and yet in dreams it nevertheless happens that we suspend our judgment, for we dream that we dream.

I grant, it is true, that no man is deceived in so far as he perceives, that is to say, I grant that mental images, considered in themselves, involve no error (Note, Prop. 17, pt. 2), but I deny that a man in so far as he perceives affirms nothing. For what else is it to perceive a winged horse than to affirm of the horse that it has wings? For if the mind perceived nothing else but this winged horse, it would regard it as present, nor would it have any reason for doubting its existence, nor any power of refusing assent to it, unless the image of the winged horse be joined to an idea which negates its existence, or the mind perceives that the idea of the winged horse which it has is inadequate. In either of the two latter cases it will necessarily deny or doubt the existence of the horse.

With regard to the third objection, what has been said will perhaps be a sufficient answer — namely, that the will is something universal, which is predicated of all ideas, and that it signifies that only which is common to them all, that is to say, affirmation. Its adequate essence, therefore, in so far as it is thus considered in the abstract, must be in every idea, and in this sense only must it be the same in all; but not in so far as it is considered as constituting the essence of an idea, for, so far, the individual affirmations differ just as the ideas differ. For example, the affirmation which the idea of a circle involves differs from that which the idea of a triangle involves, just as the idea of a circle differs from the idea of a triangle. Again, I absolutely deny that we need a power of thinking in order to affirm that to be true which is true, equal to that which we need in order to affirm that to be true which is false. For these two affirmations, if we look to the mind, are related to one another as being and non-being, for there is nothing positive in ideas which constitutes a form of falsity (Prop. 35, pt. 2, with its Note, and Note to Prop. 47, pt. 2).

Here, therefore, particularly is it to be observed how easily we are deceived when we confuse universals with individuals, and the entities of reason and abstractions with realities.

With regard to the fourth objection, I say that I entirely grant that if a man were placed in such a state of equilibrium he would perish of hunger and thirst, supposing he perceived nothing but hunger and thirst, and the food and drink which were equidistant from him.

If you ask me whether such a man would not be thought an ass rather than a man, I reply that I do not know; nor do I know what ought to be thought of a man who hangs himself, or of children, fools, and madmen.

It remains for me now to show what service to our own lives a knowledge of this doctrine is. This we shall easily understand from the remarks which follow. Notice —

1. It is of service in so far as it teaches us that we do everything by the will of God alone, and that we are partakers of the divine nature in proportion as our actions become more and more perfect and we more and more understand God. This doctrine, therefore, besides giving repose in every way to the soul, has also this advantage that it teaches us in what our highest happiness or blessedness consists, namely, in the knowledge of God alone, by which we are drawn to do those things only which love and piety persuade. Hence we clearly see how greatly those stray from the true estimation of virtue who expect to be distinguished by God with the highest rewards for virtue and the noblest actions as if for the completest servitude, just as if virtue itself and the service of God were not happiness itself and the highest liberty.

2. It is of service to us in so far as it teaches us how we ought to behave with regard to the things of fortune, or those which are not in our power, that is to say, which do not follow from our own nature; for it teaches us with equal mind to wait for and bear each form of fortune because we know that all things follow from the eternal decree of God, according to that same necessity by which it follows from the essence of a triangle that its three angles are equal to two right angles.

3. This doctrine contributes to the welfare of our social existence, since it teaches us to hate no one, to despise no one, to mock no one, to be angry with no one, and to envy no one. It teaches every one, moreover, to be content with his own, and to be helpful to his neighbor, not from any womanish pity, from partiality, or superstition, but by the guidance of reason alone, according to the demand of time and circumstance, as I shall show in the Third Part.

4. This doctrine contributes not a little to the advantage of common society, in so far as it teaches us by what means citizens are to be governed and led, not in order that they may be slaves, but that they may freely do those things which are best.

Thus I have discharged the obligation laid upon me in this Note, and with it I make an end of the Second Part, in which I think that I have explained the nature of the human mind and its properties at sufficient length, and, considering the difficulties of the subject, with sufficient clearness. I think, too, that certain truths have been established, from which much that is noble, most useful, and necessary to be known, can be deduced, as we shall partly see from what follows.

PART THREE

On the Origin and Nature of the Emotions

Most persons who have written about the emotions and man's conduct of life seem to discuss, not the natural things which follow the common laws of Nature, but things which are outside her. They seem indeed to consider man in Nature as a kingdom within a kingdom. For they believe that man disturbs rather than follows her order, that he has an absolute power over his own actions, and that he is altogether self-determined. They then proceed to attribute the cause of human weakness and changeableness, not to the common power of Nature, but to some vice of human nature which they therefore bewail, laugh at, mock, or, as is more generally the case, detest; whilst he who knows how to revile most eloquently or subtilly the weakness of the mind is looked upon as divine. It is true that very eminent men have not been wanting, to whose labor and industry we confess ourselves much indebted, who have written many excellent things about the right conduct of life, and who have given to mortals counsels full of prudence, but no one, so far as I know, has determined the nature and strength of the emotions, and what the mind is able to do toward controlling them. I remember, indeed, that the celebrated Descartes, although he believed that the mind is absolute master over its own actions, tried nevertheless to explain by their first causes human emotions, and at the same time to show the way by which the mind could obtain absolute power over them; but in my opinion he has shown nothing but the acuteness of his great intellect, as I shall make evident in the proper place, for I wish to return to those who prefer to detest and scoff at human emotions and actions than understand them. To such as these it will doubtless seem a marvelous thing for me to endeavor to treat by a geometrical method the vices and follies of men, and to desire by a sure method to demonstrate those things which these people cry out against as being opposed to reason, or as being vanities, absurdities, and monstrosities. The following is my reason for so doing. Nothing happens in Nature which can be attributed to any vice of Nature, for she is always the same and everywhere one. Her virtue is the same, and her power of acting, that is to say, her laws and rules, according to which all things are and are changed from form to form, are everywhere and always the same, so that there must also be one and the same method of understanding the nature of all things whatsoever, that is to say, by the universal laws and rules of Nature. The emotions, therefore, of hatred, anger, envy, considered in themselves, follow from the same necessity and virtue of Nature as other individual things; they have therefore certain causes through which they are to be understood, and certain properties which are just as worthy of being known as the properties of any other thing in the contemplation alone of which we delight. I shall, therefore, pursue the same method in considering the nature and strength of the emotions and the power of the mind over them which I pursued in our previous discussion of God and the mind, and I shall consider human actions and appetites just as if I were considering lines, planes, or bodies.

DEFINITIONS AND POSTULATES

DEF. I. I call that an *adequate* cause whose effect can be clearly and distinctly perceived by means of the cause. I call that an *inadequate* or partial cause whose effect cannot be understood by means of the cause alone.

DEF. II. I say that we act when anything is done, either within us or without us, of which we are the adequate cause, that is to say (by the preceding Def.), when from our nature anything follows, either within us or without us, which by that nature alone can be clearly and distinctly understood. On the other hand, I say that we suffer when anything is done within us, or when anything follows from our nature of which we are not the cause except partially.

DEF. III. By emotion I understand the modifications of the body by which the power of acting of the body itself is increased, diminished, helped, or hindered, together with the ideas of these modifications.

If, therefore, we can be the adequate cause of any of these modifications, I understand the emotion to be an action, otherwise it is a passive state.

Postulate I. The human body can be affected in many ways by which its power of acting is increased or diminished, and also in other ways which make its power of acting neither greater nor less.

This postulate or axiom is based upon Post. 1 and Lems. 5 and 7, following Prop. 13, pt. 2.

Postulate 2. The human body is capable of suffering many changes, and, nevertheless, can retain the impressions or traces of objects (Post 5, pt. 2), and consequently the same images of things. (For the definition of images see Note, Prop. 17, pt. 2.)

PROPOSITIONS

PROPOSITION I. *Our mind acts at times and at times suffers: in so far as it has adequate ideas, it necessarily acts; and in so far as it has inadequate ideas, it necessarily suffers.*

Demonstration. In every human mind some ideas are adequate, and others mutilated and confused (Note, Prop. 40, pt. 2). But the ideas which in any mind are adequate are adequate in God in so far as He forms the essence of that mind (Corol. Prop. 11, pt. 2), while those again which are inadequate in the mind are also adequate in God (by the same Corol.), not in so far as He contains the essence of that mind only, but in so far as He contains the ideas[1] of other things at the same time in Himself. Again, from any given idea some effect must necessarily follow (Prop. 36, pt. 1), of which God is the adequate cause (Def. 1, pt. 3), not in so far as He is infinite, but in so far as He is considered as affected with the given idea (Prop. 9, pt. 2). But of that effect of which God is the cause, in so far as He is affected by an idea which is adequate in any mind, that same mind is the adequate cause (Corol. Prop. 11, pt. 2). Our mind, therefore (Def. 2, pt. 3), in so far as it has adequate ideas, necessarily at times acts, which is the first thing we had to prove. Again, if there be anything which necessarily follows from an idea which is adequate in God, not in so far as He contains within Himself the mind of one man only, but also, together with this, the ideas[1] of other things, then the mind of that

[1] "Mentes," both in Paulus, Bruder, and Van Vloten and Land, but obviously a mistake for "ideas," as a reference to Corol. Prop. 11, pt. 2, will show. Kirchmann's translation omits "mentes" in the first passage marked, and renders, "insofern er andere Dinge in sich enthält." — TR.

man (Corol. Prop. 11, pt. 2) is not the adequate cause of that thing, but is only its partial cause, and therefore (Def. 2, pt. 3), in so far as the mind has inadequate ideas, it necessarily at times suffers. This was the second thing to be proved. Therefore our mind etc. — Q.E.D.

Corollary. Hence it follows that the mind is subject to passions in proportion to the number of inadequate ideas which it has, and that it acts in proportion to the number of adequate ideas which it has.

PROPOSITION II. *The body cannot determine the mind to thought, neither can the mind determine the body to motion nor rest, nor to anything else if there be anything else.*

Demonstration. All modes of thought have God for a cause in so far as He is a thinking thing, and not in so far as He is manifested by any other attribute (Prop. 6, pt. 2). That which determines the mind to thought, therefore, is a mode of thought and not of extension, that is to say (Def. 1, pt. 2), it is not the body. This is the first thing which was to be proved. Again, the motion and rest of the body must be derived from some other body, which has also been determined to motion or rest by another, and, absolutely, whatever arises in the body must arise from God, in so far as He is considered as affected by some mode of extension, and not in so far as He is considered as affected by any mode of thought (Prop. 6, pt. 2), that is to say, whatever arises in the body cannot arise from the mind, which is a mode of thought (Prop. 11, pt. 2). This is the second thing which was to be proved. Therefore, the body cannot determine, etc. — Q.E.D.

Note. This proposition will be better understood from what has been said in the Note of Prop. 7, pt. 2, that is to say, that the mind and the body are one and the same thing, conceived at one time under the attribute of thought, and at another under that of extension. For this reason, the order or concatenation of things is one, whether Nature be conceived under this or under that attribute, and consequently the order of the state of activity and passivity of our body is coincident in Nature with the order of the state of activity and passivity of the mind. This is also plain from the manner in which we have demonstrated Prop. 12, pt. 2.

Although these things are so, and no ground for doubting remains,

I scarcely believe, nevertheless, that, without a proof derived from
experience, men will be induced calmly to weigh what has been said,
so firmly are they persuaded that, solely at the bidding of the mind,
the body moves or rests, and does a number of things which depend
upon the will of the mind alone, and upon the power of thought.
For what the body can do no one has hitherto determined, that is to
say, experience has taught no one hitherto what the body, without
being determined by the mind, can do and what it cannot do from
the laws of Nature alone, in so far as nature is considered merely as
corporeal. For no one as yet has understood the structure of the body
so accurately as to be able to explain all its functions, not to mention
the fact that many things are observed in brutes which far surpass
human sagacity, and that sleepwalkers in their sleep do very many
things which they dare not do when awake — all this showing that
the body itself can do many things, from the laws of its own nature
alone, at which the mind belonging to that body is amazed. Again,
nobody knows by what means or by what method the mind moves
the body, nor how many degrees of motion it can communicate to
the body, nor with what speed it can move the body. So that it
follows that, when men say that this or that action of the body springs
from the mind which has command over the body, they do not know
what they say, and they do nothing but confess with pretentious
words that they know nothing about the cause of the action and see
nothing in it to wonder at. But they will say that, whether they know
or do not know by what means the mind moves the body, it is nevertheless in their experience that if the mind were not fit for thinking
the body would be inert. They say, again, it is in their experience
that the mind alone has power both to speak and be silent, and to do
many other things which they therefore think to be dependent on a
decree of the mind. But with regard to the first assertion, I ask them
if experience does not also teach that if the body be sluggish the mind
at the same time is not fit for thinking? When the body is asleep,
the mind slumbers with it and has not the power to think, as it has
when the body is awake. Again, I believe that all have discovered
that the mind is not always equally fitted for thinking about the same
subject, but in proportion to the fitness of the body for this or that
image to be excited in it will the mind be better fitted to contemplate
this or that object. But my opponents will say that from the laws of

Nature alone, in so far as it is considered to be corporeal merely, it cannot be that the causes of architecture, painting, and things of this sort, which are the results of human art alone, could be deduced, and that the human body, unless it were determined and guided by the mind, would not be able to build a temple. I have already shown, however, that they do not know what the body can do, nor what can be deduced from the consideration of its nature alone, and that they find that many things are done merely by the laws of Nature which they would never have believed to be possible without the direction of the mind, as, for example, those things which sleepwalkers do in their sleep, and at which they themselves are astonished when they wake. I adduce also here the structure itself of the human body, which so greatly surpasses in workmanship all those things which are constructed by human art, not to mention, what I have already proved, that an infinitude of things follows from Nature under whatever attribute it may be considered.

With regard to the second point, I should say that human affairs would be much more happily conducted if it were equally in the power of men to be silent and to speak; but experience shows over and over again that there is nothing which men have less power over than the tongue, and that there is nothing which they are less able to do than to govern their appetites, so that many persons believe that we do those things only with freedom which we seek indifferently, as the desire for such things can easily be lessened by the recollection of another thing which we frequently call to mind; it being impossible, on the other hand, to do those things with freedom which we seek with such ardor that the recollection of another thing is unable to mitigate it. But if, however, we had not found out that we do many things which we afterwards repent, and that when agitated by conflicting emotions we see that which is better and follow that which is worse, nothing would hinder us from believing that we do everything with freedom. Thus the infant believes that it is by free will that it seeks the breast; the angry boy believes that by free will he wishes vengeance; the timid man thinks it is with free will he seeks flight; the drunkard believes that by a free command of his mind he speaks the things which when sober he wishes he had left unsaid. Thus the madman, the chatterer, the boy, and others of the same kind, all believe that they speak by a free command of the mind, whilst, in truth, they have no power to restrain the impulse which they have to speak, so that experience itself, no less than reason, clearly teaches that men believe themselves to be free simply because they are conscious of their own actions, knowing nothing of the causes by which they are determined; it teaches, too, that the decrees of the mind are nothing but the appetites themselves, which differ, therefore, according to the different temper of the body. For every man determines all things from his emotion; those who are agitated by contrary emotions do not know what they want, whilst those who are agitated by no emotion are easily driven hither and thither. All this plainly shows that the decree of the mind, the appetite, and determination of the body are coincident in Nature, or rather that they are one and the same thing which, when it is considered under the attribute of thought and manifested by that, is called a "decree," and when it is considered under the attribute of extension and is deduced from the laws of motion and rest is called a "determination." This, however, will be better understood as we go on, for there is another thing which I wish to be observed here — that we cannot by a mental decree do a thing unless we recollect it. We cannot speak a word, for instance, unless we recollect it. But it is not in the free power of the mind either to recollect a thing or to forget it. It is believed, therefore, that the power of the mind extends only thus far — that from a mental decree we can speak or be silent about a thing only when we recollect it. But when we dream that we speak, we believe that we do so from a free decree of the mind, and yet we do not speak, or, if we do, it is the result of a spontaneous motion of the body. We dream, again, that we are concealing things, and that we do this by virtue of a decree of the mind like that by which, when awake, we are silent about things we know. We dream, again, that, from a decree of the mind, we do some things which we should not dare to do when awake. And I should like to know, therefore, whether there are two kinds of decrees in the mind — one belonging to dreams and the other free. If this be too great nonsense, we must necessarily grant that this decree of the mind which is believed to be free is not distinguishable from the imagination or memory, and is nothing but the affirmation which the idea necessarily involves in so far as it is an idea (Prop. 49, pt. 2). These decrees of the mind, therefore, arise in the mind by the same necessity as the ideas of things actually existing. Consequently, those who believe that they speak or are silent or do anything else from a free decree of the mind dream with their eyes open.

PROPOSITION III. *The actions of the mind arise from adequate ideas alone, but the passive states depend upon those alone which are inadequate.*

Demonstration. The first thing which constitutes the essence of the mind is nothing but the idea of an actually existing body (Props. 11 and 13, pt. 2). This idea is composed of a number of others (Prop. 15, pt. 2), some of which are adequate and others inadequate (Corol. Prop. 38, pt. 2, and Corol. Prop. 29, pt. 2). Everything, therefore, of which the mind is the proximate cause, and which follows from the nature of the mind, through which it must be understood, must necessarily follow from an adequate or from an inadequate idea. But in so far as the mind (Prop. 1, pt. 3) has inadequate ideas, so far it necessarily suffers; therefore the actions of the mind follow from adequate ideas alone, and the mind therefore suffers only because it has inadequate ideas. — Q.E.D.

Note. We see, therefore, that the passive states are not related to the mind, unless in so far as it possesses something which involves negation; in other words, unless in so far as it is considered as a part of Nature which by itself and without the other parts cannot be clearly and distinctly perceived. In the same way I could show that passive states are related to individual things, just as they are related to the mind, and that they cannot be perceived in any other way; but my purpose is to treat of the human mind alone.

PROPOSITION IV. *A thing cannot be destroyed except by an external cause.*

Demonstration. This proposition is self-evident, for the definition of any given thing affirms and does not deny the existence of the thing, that is to say, it posits the essence of the thing and does not negate it. So long, therefore, as we attend only to the thing itself, and not to external causes, we shall discover nothing in it which can destroy it. — Q.E.D.

PROPOSITION V. *In so far as one thing is able to destroy another are they of contrary natures, that is to say, they cannot exist in the same subject.*

Demonstration. If it were possible for them to come together or to coexist in the same subject, there would then be something in that subject able to destroy it, which (Prop. 4, pt. 3) is absurd. Therefore, in so far, etc. — Q.E.D.

PROPOSITION VI. *Each thing, in so far as it is in itself, endeavors to persevere in its being.*

Demonstration. Individual things are modes by which the attributes of God are expressed in a certain and determinate manner (Corol. Prop. 25, pt. 1), that is to say (Prop. 34, pt. 1), they are things which express in a certain and determinate manner the power of God by which He is and acts. A thing, too, has nothing in itself through which it can be destroyed, or which can negate its existence (Prop. 4, pt. 3), but, on the contrary, it is opposed to everything which could negate its existence (Prop. 5, pt. 3). Therefore, in so far as it can, and in so far as it is in itself, it endeavors to persevere in its own being. — Q.E.D.

PROPOSITION VII. *The effort by which each thing endeavors to persevere in its own being is nothing but the actual essence of the thing itself.*

Demonstration. From the given essence of anything certain things necessarily follow (Prop. 36, pt. 1), nor are things able to do anything else than what necessarily follows from their determinate nature (Prop. 29, pt. 1). Therefore, the power of a thing, or the effort by means of which it does or endeavors to do anything, either by itself or with others — that is to say (Prop. 6, pt. 3), the power or effort by which it endeavors to persevere in its being — is nothing but the given or actual essence of the thing itself. — Q.E.D.

PROPOSITION VIII. *The effort by which each thing endeavors to persevere in its own being does not involve finite but indefinite time.*

Demonstration. If it involved a limited time, which would determine the duration of the thing, then from that power alone by which the thing exists it would follow that, after that limited time, it could not exist but must be destroyed. But this (Prop. 4, pt. 3) is absurd. The effort, therefore, by which a thing exists does not involve definite time, but, on the contrary (Prop. 4, pt. 3), if the thing be destroyed by no external cause, by the same power by which it now exists it will always continue to exist, and this effort, therefore, by which it endeavors to persevere, etc. — Q.E.D.

PROPOSITION IX. — *The mind, both in so far as it has clear and distinct ideas and in so far as it has confused ideas, endeavors to persevere in its being for an indefinite time, and is conscious of this effort.*

Demonstration. The essence of the mind is composed of adequate and inadequate ideas (as we have shown in Prop. 3, pt. 3), and therefore (Prop. 7, pt. 3), both in so far as it has the former and in so far as it has the latter, it endeavors to persevere in its being, and endeavors to persevere in it for an indefinite time (Prop. 8, pt. 3). But since the mind (Prop. 23, pt. 2), through the ideas of the modifications of the body, is necessarily conscious of itself, it is therefore conscious (Prop. 7, pt. 3) of its effort. — Q.E.D.

Note. This effort, when it is related to the mind alone, is called "will," but when it is related at the same time both to the mind and the body is called "appetite," which is therefore nothing but the very essence of man, from the nature of which necessarily follow those things which promote his preservation, and thus he is determined to do those things. Hence there is no difference between appetite and desire, unless in this particular that desire is generally related to men in so far as they are conscious of their appetites, and it may therefore be defined as appetite of which we are conscious. From what has been said it is plain, therefore, that we neither strive for, wish, seek, nor desire anything because we think it to be good, but, on the contrary, we adjudge a thing to be good because we strive for, wish, seek, or desire it.

PROPOSITION X. *There can be no idea in the mind which excludes the existence of the body, for such an idea is contrary to the mind.*

Demonstration. There can be nothing in our body which is able to destroy it (Prop. 5, pt. 3), and there cannot be, therefore, in God an idea of any such thing in so far as He has the idea of the body (Corol. Prop. 9, pt. 2); that is to say (Props. 11 and 13, pt. 2), no idea of any such thing can exist in our mind, but, on the contrary, since (Props. 11 and 13, pt. 2) the first thing which constitutes the essence of the mind is the idea of a body actually existing, the first and chief thing belonging to our mind is the effort (Prop. 7, pt. 3) to affirm the existence of our body, and therefore the idea which denies the existence of our body is contrary to our mind. — Q.E.D.

PROPOSITION XI. *If anything increases, diminishes, helps, or limits our body's power of action, the idea of that thing increases, diminishes, helps, or limits our mind's power of thought.*

Demonstration. This proposition is evident from Prop. 7, pt. 2, and also from Prop. 14, pt. 2.

Note. We thus see that the mind can suffer great changes, and can pass now to a greater and now to a lesser perfection; these passive states explaining to us the emotions of joy and sorrow. By "joy," therefore, in what follows, I shall understand the passive states through which the mind passes to a greater perfection; by "sorrow," on the other hand, the passive states through which it passes to a less perfection. The emotion of joy, related at the same time both to the mind and the body, I call "pleasurable excitement" (*titillatio*) or "cheerfulness"; that of sorrow I call "pain" or "melancholy." It is, however, to be observed that pleasurable excitement and pain are related to a man when one of his parts is affected more than the others; cheerfulness and melancholy, on the other hand, when all parts are equally affected. What the nature of desire is I have explained in the note of Prop. 9, pt. 3; and besides these three — joy, sorrow, and desire — I know of no other primary emotion; the others springing from these, as I shall show in what follows. But before I advance any further, I should like to explain more fully Prop. 10, pt. 3, so that we may more clearly understand in what manner one idea is contrary to another.

In the note of Prop. 17, pt. 2, we have shown that the idea which forms the essence of the mind involves the existence of the body so long as the body exists. Again, from Corol. Prop. 8, pt. 2, and its note, it follows that the present existence of our mind depends solely upon this — that the mind involves the actual existence of the body. Finally, we have shown that the power of the mind by which it imagines and remembers things also depends upon this — that it involves the actual existence of the body (Props. 17 and 18, pt. 2, with the note). From these things it follows that the present existence of the mind and its power of imagination are negated as soon as the mind ceases to affirm the present existence of the body. But the cause by which the mind ceases to affirm this existence of the body cannot be the mind itself (Prop. 4, pt. 2), nor can it be the body's ceasing to be; for (Prop. 6, pt. 2) the mind does not affirm the existence of the body because the body began to exist, and therefore, by the same reasoning, it does not cease to affirm the existence of the body because the body ceases to be, but (Prop. 17, pt. 2) because of another idea excluding the present existence of our body, and consequently of our mind, and contrary, therefore, to the idea which forms the essence of our mind.

PROPOSITION XII. *The mind endeavors as much as possible to imagine those things which increase or assist the body's power of acting.*

Demonstration. The human mind will contemplate any external body as present so long as the human body is affected in a way which involves the nature of that external body (Prop. 17, pt. 2), and consequently (Prop. 7, pt. 2) as long as the human mind contemplates any external body as present, that is to say (Note, Prop. 17, pt. 2), imagines it, so long is the human body affected in a way which involves the nature of that external body. Consequently, as long as the mind imagines those things which increase or assist our body's power of action, so long is the body affected in a way which increases or assists that power (Post. 1, pt. 3), and consequently (Prop. 11, pt. 3) so long the mind's power of thought is increased or assisted; therefore (Props. 6 and 9, pt. 3) the mind endeavors as much as possible to imagine those things. — Q.E.D.

PROPOSITION XIII. *Whenever the mind imagines those things which lessen or limit the body's power of action, it endeavors as much as possible to recollect what excludes the existence of these things.*

Demonstration. So long as the mind imagines anything of this sort, the power of the body and of the mind is lessened or limited (as we have shown in the preceding proposition). Nevertheless, the mind will continue to imagine these things until it imagines some other thing which will exclude their present existence (Prop. 17, pt. 2); that is to say, as we have just shown, the power of the mind and of the body is diminished or limited until the mind imagines something which excludes the existence of these things. This, therefore (Prop. 9, pt. 3), the mind will endeavor to imagine or recollect as much as possible. — Q.E.D.

Corollary. Hence it follows that the mind is averse to imagine those things which lessen or hinder its power and that of the body.

Note. From what has been said we can clearly see what love is and what hatred is. *Love* is nothing but joy accompanied with the idea of an external cause, and *hatred* is nothing but sorrow with the accompanying idea of an external cause. We see, too, that he who loves a thing necessarily endeavors to keep it before him and to preserve it, and, on the other hand, he who hates a thing necessarily endeavors to remove and destroy it. But we shall speak at greater length upon these points in what follows.

PROPOSITION XIV. *If the mind at any time has been simultaneously affected by two emotions, whenever it is afterwards affected by one of them, it will also be affected by the other.*

Demonstration. If the human body has at any time been simultaneously affected by two bodies, whenever the mind afterwards imagines one of them, it will immediately remember the other (Prop. 18, pt. 2). But the imaginations of the mind indicate rather the emotions of our body than the nature of external bodies (Corol. 2, Prop. 16, pt. 2), and therefore if the body, and consequently the mind (Def. 3, pt. 3), has been at any time, etc. — Q.E.D.

PROPOSITION XV. *Anything may be accidentally the cause of joy, sorrow, or desire.*

Demonstration. Let the mind be supposed to be affected at the same time by two emotions, its power of action not being increased or diminished by one, while it is increased or diminished by the other (Post. 1, pt. 3). From the preceding proposition it is plain that when the mind is afterwards affected by the first emotion through its true cause which (by hypothesis) of itself neither increases nor diminishes the mind's power of thinking, it will at the same time be affected by the other emotion which does increase or diminish that power, that is to say (Note, Prop. 11, pt. 3), it will be affected with joy or sorrow; and thus the thing itself will be the cause of joy or of sorrow, not of itself, but accidentally. In the same way it can easily be shown that the same thing may accidentally be the cause of desire. — Q.E.D.

Corollary. The fact that we have contemplated a thing with an emotion of joy or sorrow, of which it is not the efficient cause, is a sufficient reason for being able to love or hate it.

Demonstration. For this fact alone is a sufficient reason (Prop. 14, pt. 3) for its coming to pass that the mind in imagining the thing afterwards is affected with the emotion of joy or sorrow, that is to say (Prop. 11, pt. 3), that the power of the mind and of the body is increased or diminished, etc., and, consequently (Prop. 12, pt. 3), that the mind desires to imagine the thing or (Corol. Prop. 13, pt. 3) is averse to doing so, that is to say (Note, Prop. 13, pt. 3), that the mind loves the thing or hates it. — Q.E.D.

Note. We now understand why we love or hate certain things from no cause which is known to us, but merely from sympathy or antipathy, as they say. To this class, too, as we shall show in the following propositions, are to be referred those objects which affect us with joy or sorrow solely because they are somewhat like objects which usually affect us with those emotions. I know indeed that the writers who first introduced the words "sympathy" and "antipathy" desired thereby to signify certain hidden qualities of things, but, nevertheless, I believe that we shall be permitted to understand by those names qualities which are plain and well known.

PROPOSITION XVI. *If we imagine a certain thing to possess something which resembles an object which usually affects the mind with joy or sorrow, although the quality in which the thing resembles the object is not the efficient cause of these emotions, we shall nevertheless, by virtue of the resemblance alone, love or hate the thing.*

Demonstration. The quality in which the thing resembles the object we have contemplated in the object itself (by hypothesis) with the emotion of joy or sorrow, and since (Prop. 14, pt. 3), whenever the mind is affected by the image of this quality, it is also affected by the former or latter emotion, the thing which is perceived by us to possess this quality will be (Prop. 15, pt. 3) accidentally the cause of joy or sorrow. Therefore (by the preceding Corol.), although the quality in which the thing resembles the object is not the efficient cause of these emotions, we shall nevertheless love the thing or hate it. — Q.E.D.

PROPOSITION XVII. *If we imagine that a thing that usually affects us with the emotion of sorrow has any resemblance to an object which usually affects us equally with a great emotion of joy, we shall at the same time hate the thing and love it.*

Demonstration. This thing (by hypothesis) is of itself the cause of sorrow, and (Note, Prop. 13, pt. 3) in so far as we imagine it with this emotion we hate it; but in so far as we imagine it to resemble an object which usually affects us equally with a great emotion of joy do we love it with an equally great effort of joy (Prop. 16, pt. 3), and so we shall both hate it and love it at the same time. — Q.E.D.

Note. This state of mind which arises from two contrary emotions is called "vacillation of the mind." It is related to emotion as doubt is related to the imagination (Note, Prop. 44, pt. 2). Nor do vacillation and doubt differ from one another except as greater and less. It is to be observed that in the preceding proposition I have deduced these vacillations of the mind from causes which occasion the one emotion directly and the other contingently. This I have done because the emotions could thus be more easily deduced from what preceded, and not because I deny that these vacillations often originate from the object itself which is the efficient cause of both emotions. For the human body (Post. 1, pt. 2) is composed of a number of individual parts of different natures, and therefore (Ax. 1, after Lem. 3, following Prop. 13, pt. 2) it can be affected by one and the same body in very many and in different ways. On the other hand, the same object can be affected in a number of different ways, and consequently can affect the same part of the body in different ways. It is easy, therefore, to see how one and the same object may be the cause of many and contrary emotions.

PROPOSITION XVIII. *A man is affected by the image of a past or future thing with the same emotion of joy or sorrow as that with which he is affected by the image of a present thing.*

Demonstration. As long as a man is affected by the image of anything, he will contemplate the thing as present although it does not exist (Prop. 17, pt. 2, with Corol.), nor does he imagine it as past or future unless in so far as its image is connected with that of past or future time (Note, Prop. 44, pt. 2). Therefore the image of the thing considered in itself alone is the same whether it be related to future, past, or present time, that is to say (Corol. 2, Prop. 16, pt. 2), the state of the body or the emotion is the same whether the image be that of a past, present, or future thing. The emotion, therefore, of joy and sorrow is the same whether the image be that of a past, present, or future thing. — Q.E.D.

Note 1. I call a thing here past or future in so far as we have been or shall be affected by it, for example, in so far as we have seen a thing or are about to see it, in so far as it has strengthened us or will strengthen us, has injured or will injure us. For in so far as we thus imagine it do we affirm its existence, that is to say, the body is affected by no emotion which excludes the existence of the thing, and therefore

(Prop. 17, pt. 2) the body is affected by the image of the thing in the same way as if the thing itself were present. But because it generally happens that those who possess much experience hesitate when they think of a thing as past or future, and doubt greatly concerning its issue (Note, Prop. 44, pt. 2), therefore the emotions which spring from such images of things are not so constant, but are generally disturbed by the images of other things, until men become more sure of the issue.

Note 2. From what has now been said we understand the nature of Hope, Fear, Confidence, Despair, Gladness, Remorse. *Hope* is nothing but unsteady joy, arising from the image of a future or past thing about whose issue we are in doubt. *Fear*, on the other hand, is an unsteady sorrow, arising from the image of a doubtful thing. If the doubt be removed from these emotions, then hope and fear become *confidence* and *despair*, that is to say, joy or sorrow, arising from the image of a thing for which we have hoped or which we have feared. *Gladness*, again, is joy arising from the image of a past thing whose issues we have doubted. *Remorse* is the sorrow which is opposed to gladness.

PROPOSITION XIX. *He who imagines that what he loves is destroyed will sorrow, but if he imagines that it is preserved he will rejoice.*

Demonstration. The mind endeavors as much as it can to imagine those things which increase or assist the body's power of action (Prop. 12, pt. 3), that is to say (Note, Prop. 13, pt. 3), to imagine those things which it loves. But the imagination is assisted by those things which posit the existence of the object and is restrained by those which exclude its existence (Prop. 17, pt. 2). Therefore, the images of things which posit the existence of the beloved object assist the mind's effort to imagine it, that is to say (Note, Prop. 11, pt. 3), they affect the mind with joy; whilst those, on the other hand, which exclude the existence of the beloved object restrain that same effort of the mind, that is to say (Note, Prop. 11, pt. 3), they affect the mind with sorrow. He, therefore, who imagines that what he loves is destroyed, etc. — Q.E.D.

PROPOSITION XX. *He who imagines that what he hates is destroyed will rejoice.*

Demonstration. The mind (Prop. 13, pt. 3) endeavors to imagine those things which exclude the existence of whatever lessens or limits the body's power of action, that is to say (Note, Prop. 13, pt. 3), it endeavors to imagine those things which exclude the existence of what it hates, and therefore the image of the thing which excludes the existence of what the mind hates assists this endeavor of the mind, that is to say (Note, Prop. 11, pt. 3), affects the mind with joy. He, therefore, who imagines that what he hates is destroyed will rejoice. — Q.E.D.

PROPOSITION XXI. *He who imagines that what he loves is affected with joy or sorrow will also be affected with joy or sorrow, and these emotions will be greater or less in the lover as they are greater or less in the thing loved.*

Demonstration. The images of things (Prop. 19, pt. 3) which posit the existence of the beloved object assist the effort of the mind to imagine it; but joy posits the existence of the thing which rejoices, and the greater the joy, the more is existence posited, for (Note, Prop. 11, pt. 3) joy is the transition to a greater perfection. The image, therefore, in the lover of the joy of the beloved object assists the effort of his mind to imagine the object, that is to say (Note, Prop. 11, pt. 3), affects the lover with joy proportionate to the joy of the object he loves. This was the first thing to be proved. Again, in so far as anything is affected with sorrow, so far is it destroyed, and the destruction is greater as the sorrow with which it is affected is greater (Note, Prop. 11, pt. 3). Therefore (Prop. 19, pt. 3), he who imagines that what he loves is affected with sorrow will also be affected with sorrow, and it will be greater as this emotion shall have been greater in the object beloved. — Q.E.D.

PROPOSITION XXII. *If we imagine that a person affects with joy a thing which we love, we shall be affected with love toward him. If, on the contrary, we imagine that he affects it with sorrow, we shall also be affected with hatred toward him.*

Demonstration. He who affects with joy or sorrow the thing we love affects us also with joy or sorrow whenever we imagine the beloved object so affected (Prop. 21, pt. 3). But this joy or sorrow is supposed to exist in us accompanied with the idea of an external cause; therefore (Note, Prop. 13, pt. 3), if we imagine that a person affects with joy or sorrow a thing which we love, we shall be affected with love or hatred toward him. — Q.E.D.

Note. Prop. 21 explains to us what "commiseration" is, which we may define as sorrow which springs from another's loss. By what name the joy is to be called which springs from another's good I do not know. Love toward the person who has done good to another we shall call "favor," whilst hatred toward him who has done evil to another we shall call "indignation" (*indignatio*). It is to be observed, too, that we not only feel pity for the object which we have loved, as we showed in Prop. 21, but also for that to which we have been attached by no emotion, provided only we adjudge it to be like ourselves (as I shall show hereafter), and so we shall regard with favor him who has done any good to the object which is like us, and, on the contrary, be indignant with him who has done it any harm.

PROPOSITION XXIII. *He who imagines that what he hates is affected with sorrow will rejoice; if, on the other hand, he imagines it to be affected with joy he will be sad; and these emotions will be greater or less in him in proportion as their contraries are greater or less in the object he hates.*

Demonstration. In so far as the hated thing is affected with sorrow is it destroyed, and the destruction is greater as the sorrow is greater (Note, Prop. 11, pt. 3). He, therefore (Prop. 20, pt. 3), who imagines that the thing which he hates is affected with sorrow will on the contrary be affected with joy, and the joy will be the greater in proportion as he imagines the hated thing to be affected with a greater sorrow. This was the first thing to be proved. Again, joy posits the existence of the thing which rejoices (Note, Prop. 11, pt. 3), and it does so the more in proportion as the joy is conceived to be greater. If a person, therefore, imagines that he whom he hates is affected with joy, this idea (Prop. 13, pt. 3) will restrain the effort of the mind of him who hates, that is to say (Note, Prop. 11, pt. 3), he will be affected with sorrow. — Q.E.D.

Note. This joy can hardly be solid and free from any mental conflict. For, as I shall show directly in Prop. 27, in so far as we imagine that what is like ourselves is affected with sorrow, we must be sad; and, on the contrary, if we imagine it to be affected with joy, we rejoice. Here, however, we are considering merely hatred.

PROPOSITION XXIV. *If we imagine that a person affects with joy a thing which we hate, we are therefore affected with hatred toward him. On the other hand, if we imagine that he affects it with sorrow, we are therefore affected with love toward him.*

Demonstration. This proposition is proved in the same manner as Prop. 22, pt. 3, which see.

Note. These and the like emotions of hatred are related to *envy*, which is therefore nothing but hatred in so far as it is considered to dispose a man so that he rejoices over the evil and is saddened by the good which befalls another.

PROPOSITION XXV. *We endeavor to affirm everything, both concerning ourselves and concerning the beloved object which we imagine will affect us or the object with joy, and, on the contrary, we endeavor to deny everything that will affect either it or ourselves with sorrow.*

Demonstration. Everything which we imagine as affecting the beloved object with joy or sorrow affects us also with joy or sorrow (Prop. 21, pt. 3). But the mind (Prop. 12, pt. 3) endeavors as much as it can to imagine those things which affect us with joy, that is to say (Prop. 17, pt. 2 and its Corol.), it endeavors to consider them as present. On the contrary (Prop. 13, pt. 3), it endeavors to exclude the existence of what affects us with sorrow; therefore we endeavor to affirm everything both concerning ourselves and concerning the beloved object which we imagine will affect us or it with joy, etc. — Q.E.D.

PROPOSITION XXVI. *If we hate a thing, we endeavor to affirm concerning it everything which we imagine will affect it with sorrow, and, on the other hand, to deny everything concerning it which we imagine will affect it with joy.*

Demonstration. This proposition follows from Prop. 23, as the preceding proposition follows from Prop. 21.

Note. We see from this how easily it may happen that a man should think too much of himself or of the beloved object, and, on the contrary, should think too little of what he hates. When a man thinks too much of himself, this imagination is called "pride," and is a kind of delirium because he dreams with his eyes open that he is able to do all those things to which he attains in imagination alone, regarding them therefore as realities, and rejoicing in them so long as he cannot imagine anything to exclude their existence and limit his power of action. Pride, therefore, is that joy which arises from a man's thinking too much of himself. The joy which arises from thinking too much of another is called "over-estimation," and that which arises from thinking too little of another is called "contempt."

PROPOSITION XXVII. *Although we may not have been moved toward a thing by any emotion, yet if it is like ourselves, whenever we imagine it to be affected by any emotion, we are affected by the same.*

Demonstration. The images of things are modifications of the human body, and the ideas of these modifications represent to us external bodies as if they were present (Note, Prop. 17, pt. 2), that is to say (Prop. 16, pt. 2), these ideas involve both the nature of our own body and at the same time the present nature of the external body. If, therefore, the nature of the external body be like that of our body, then the idea of the external body which we imagine will involve a modification of our body like that of the external body. Therefore, if we imagine any one who is like ourselves to be affected with any emotion, this imagination will express a modification of our body like that emotion, and therefore we shall be affected with a similar emotion ourselves because we imagine something like us to be affected with the same. If, on the other hand, we hate a thing which is like ourselves, we shall so far (Prop. 23, pt. 3) be affected with an emotion contrary and not similar to that with which it is affected. — Q.E.D.

Note. This imitation of emotions, when it is connected with sorrow, is called "commiseration" (see Note, Prop. 22, pt. 3), and where it is connected with desire is called "emulation," which is nothing else than the desire which is engendered in us for anything because we imagine that other persons, who are like ourselves, possess the same desire.

Corollary 1. If we imagine that a person to whom we have been moved by no emotion affects with joy a thing which is like us, we shall therefore be affected with love toward him. If, on the other hand, we imagine that he affects it with sorrow, we shall be affected with hatred toward him.

Demonstration. This corollary follows from the preceding proposition, just as Prop. 22, pt. 3, follows from Prop. 21, pt. 3.

Corollary 2. If we pity a thing, the fact that its misery affects us with sorrow will not make us hate it.

Demonstration. If we could hate the thing for this reason, we should then (Prop. 23, pt. 3) rejoice over its sorrow, which is contrary to the hypothesis.

Corollary 3. If we pity a thing, we shall endeavor as much as possible to free it from its misery.

Demonstration. That which affects with sorrow the thing that we pity, affects us likewise with the same sorrow (Prop. 27, pt. 3), and we shall, therefore, endeavor to devise every means by which we may take away or destroy the existence of the cause of the sorrow (Prop. 13, pt. 3), that is to say (Note, Prop. 9, pt. 3), we shall seek to destroy it or shall be determined thereto, and therefore we shall endeavor to free from its misery the thing we pity.

Note. This will or desire of doing good, arising from our pity for the object which we want to benefit, is called "benevolence," which is, therefore, simply the desire which arises from commiseration. With regard to the love or hatred toward the person who has done good or evil to the thing we imagine to be like ourselves, see Note, Prop. 22, pt. 3.

PROPOSITION XXVIII. *We endeavor to bring into existence everything which we imagine conduces to joy, and to remove or destroy everything opposed to it, or which we imagine conduces to sorrow.*

Demonstration. We endeavor to imagine as much as possible all those things which we think conduce to joy (Prop. 12, pt. 3), that is to say (Prop. 17, pt. 2), we strive as much as possible to perceive them as present or actually existing. But the mind's effort or power in thinking is equal to and correspondent with the body's effort or power in acting, as clearly follows from Corol. Prop. 7, pt. 2, and Corol. Prop. 11, pt. 2, and therefore absolutely whatever conduces to joy we endeavor to make exist, that is to say (Note, Prop. 9, pt. 3), we seek after it and aim at it. This is the first thing which was to be proved. Again, if we imagine that a thing which we believe causes us sorrow, that is to say (Note, Prop. 13, pt. 3), which we hate, is destroyed, we shall rejoice (Prop. 20, pt. 3), and therefore (by the first part of this demonstration) we shall endeavor to destroy it, or (Prop. 13, pt. 3) to remove it from us, so that we may not perceive it as present. This is the second thing which was to be proved. We endeavor, therefore, to bring into existence, etc. — Q.E.D.

PROPOSITION XXIX. *We shall endeavor to do everything which we imagine men will look upon with joy, and, on the contrary, we shall be averse to doing anything to which we imagine men[2] are averse.*

Demonstration. If we imagine men to love or hate a thing, we shall therefore love or hate it (Prop. 27, pt. 3), that is to say (Note, Prop. 13, pt. 3), we shall therefore rejoice or be sad at the presence of the thing, and therefore (Prop. 28, pt. 3) everything which we imagine that men love or look upon with joy, we shall endeavor to do, etc. — Q.E.D.

[2] Both here and in what follows I understand by the word "men," men to whom we are moved by no emotion.

Note. This effort to do some things and omit doing others, solely because we wish to please men, is called "ambition," especially if our desire to please the common people is so strong that our actions or omissions to act are accompanied with injury to ourselves or to others. Otherwise this endeavor is usually called "humanity." Again, the joy with which we imagine another person's action, the purpose of which is to delight us, I call "praise," and the sorrow with which we turn away from an action of a contrary kind I call "blame."

PROPOSITION XXX. *If a person has done anything which he imagines will affect others with joy, he also will be affected with joy, accompanied with an idea of himself as its cause, that is to say, he will look upon himself with joy. If, on the other hand, he has done anything which he imagines will affect others with sorrow, he will look upon himself with sorrow.*

Demonstration. He who imagines that he affects others with joy or sorrow will necessarily be affected with joy or sorrow (Prop. 27, pt. 3). But since man is conscious of himself (Props. 19 and 23, pt. 2) by means of the modifications by which he is determined to act, therefore he who has done anything which he imagines will affect others with joy will be affected with joy accompanied with a consciousness of himself as its cause, that is to say, he will look upon himself with joy, and, on the other hand, etc. — Q.E.D.

Note. Since love (Note, Prop. 13, pt. 3) is joy attended with the idea of an external cause, and hatred is sorrow attended with the idea of an external cause, the joy and sorrow spoken of in this proposition will be a kind of love and hatred. But because love and hatred are related to external objects, we will therefore give a different name to the emotions which are the subject of this proposition, and we will call this kind of joy which is attended with the idea of an external cause "self-exaltation," and the sorrow opposed to it we will call "shame." The reader is to understand that this is the case in which joy or sorrow arises because the man believes that he is praised or blamed, otherwise I shall call this joy accompanied with the idea of an external cause "contentment with one's-self," and the sorrow opposed to it "repentance." Again, since (Corol. Prop. 17, pt. 2) it may happen that the joy with which a person imagines that he affects other people is only imaginary, and since (Prop. 25, pt. 3) every one endeavors to imagine concerning himself what he supposes will affect himself with joy, it may easily happen that the self-exalted man becomes proud, and imagines that he is pleasing everybody when he is offensive to everybody.

PROPOSITION XXXI. *If we imagine that a person loves, desires, or hates a thing which we ourselves love, desire, or hate, we shall on that account love, desire, or hate the thing more steadily. If, on the other hand, we imagine that he is averse to the thing we love or loves the thing to which we are averse, we shall then suffer vacillation of mind.*

Demonstration. If we imagine that another person loves a thing, on that very account we shall love it (Prop. 27, pt. 3). But we are supposed to love it independently of this, and a new cause for our love is therefore added, by which it is strengthened, and consequently the object we love will be loved by us on this account the more steadily. Again, if we imagine that a person is averse to a thing, on that very account we shall be averse to it (Prop. 27, pt. 3); but if we suppose that we at the same time love it, we shall both love the thing and be averse to it, that is to say (Note, Prop. 17, pt. 3), we shall suffer vacillation of mind.— Q.E.D.

Corollary. It follows from this proposition and from Prop. 28, pt. 3 that every one endeavors as much as possible to make others love what he loves, and to hate what he hates. Hence the poet says —

> Speremus pariter, pariter metuamus amantes;
> Ferreus est, si quis, quod sinit alter, amat.[3]

This effort to make every one approve what we love or hate is in truth ambition (Note, Prop. 29, pt. 3), and so we see that each person by nature desires that other persons should live according to his way of thinking; but if everyone does this, then all are a hindrance to one

[3]Ovid, *Amores*, Bk. II, Elegy 19, lines 5 and 4 (Spinoza has transposed the lines):
    As lovers let us hope and fear alike:
    Of iron is he who loves what the other leaves. — ED.

another, and if everyone wishes to be praised or beloved by the rest, then they all hate one another.

PROPOSITION XXXII. *If we imagine that a person enjoys a thing which only one can possess, we do all we can to prevent his possessing it.*

Demonstration. If we imagine that a person enjoys a thing, that will be a sufficient reason (Prop. 27, pt. 3, with Corol. 1) for making us love the thing and desiring to enjoy it. But (by hypothesis) we imagine that his enjoyment of the thing is an obstacle to our joy, and therefore (Prop. 28, pt. 3) we endeavor to prevent his possessing it. — Q.E.D.

Note. We see, therefore, that the nature of man is generally constituted so as to pity those who are in adversity and envy those who are in prosperity, and (Prop. 32, pt. 3) he envies with a hatred which is the greater in proportion as he loves what he imagines another possesses. We see also that from the same property of human nature from which it follows that men pity one another it also follows that they are envious and ambitious. If we will consult experience, we shall find that she teaches the same doctrine, especially if we consider the first years of our life. For we find that children, because their body is, as it were, continually in equilibrium, laugh and cry merely because they see others do the same; whatever else they see others do they immediately wish to imitate; everything which they think is pleasing to other people they want. And the reason is, as we have said, that the images of things are the modifications themselves of the human body, or the ways in which it is affected by external causes and disposed to this or that action.

PROPOSITION XXXIII. *If we love a thing which is like ourselves, we endeavor as much as possible to make it love us in return.*

Demonstration. We endeavor as much as possible to imagine before everything else the thing we love (Prop. 12, pt. 3). If, therefore, it be like ourselves, we shall endeavor to affect it with joy before everything else (Prop. 29, pt. 3), that is to say, we shall endeavor as much as possible to cause the beloved object to be affected with joy attended with the idea of ourselves, or, in other words (Note, Prop. 13, pt. 3), we try to make it love us in return. — Q.E.D.

PROPOSITION XXXIV. *The greater the emotion with which we imagine that a beloved object is affected toward us, the greater will be our self-exaltation.*

Demonstration. We endeavor as much as possible to make a beloved object love us in return (Prop. 33, pt. 3), that is to say (Note, Prop. 13, pt. 3), to cause it to be affected with joy attended with the idea of ourselves. In proportion, therefore, as we imagine the beloved object to be affected with a joy of which we are the cause, will our endeavor be assisted, that is to say (Prop. 11, pt. 3 with Note), will be the greatness of the joy with which we are affected. But since we rejoice because we have affected with joy another person like ourselves, we shall look upon ourselves with joy (Prop. 30, pt. 3); and therefore the greater the emotion with which we imagine that the beloved object is affected toward us, the greater will be the joy with which we shall look upon ourselves, that is to say (Note, Prop. 30, pt. 3), the greater will be our self-exaltation. — Q.E.D.

PROPOSITION XXXV. *If I imagine that an object beloved by me is united to another person by the same or by a closer bond of friendship than that by which I myself alone held the object, I shall be affected with hatred toward the beloved object itself, and shall envy that other person.*

Demonstration. The greater the love with which a person imagines a beloved object to be affected toward him, the greater will be his self-exaltation (Prop. 34, pt. 3), that is to say (Note, Prop. 30, pt. 3), the more will he rejoice. Therefore (Prop. 28, pt. 3), he will endeavor as much as he can to imagine the beloved object united to him as closely as possible, and this effort or desire is strengthened if he imagines that another person desires for himself the same object (Prop. 31, pt. 3). But this effort or desire is supposed to be checked by the image of the beloved object itself attended by the image of the person whom it connects with itself. Therefore (Note, Prop. 11, pt. 3) the lover on this account will be affected with sorrow attended with the idea of the beloved object as its cause together with the image of another person, that is to say (Note, Prop. 13, pt. 3), he will be affected with hatred toward the beloved object and at the same time toward this other person (Corol. Prop. 15, pt. 3), whom he will envy (Prop. 23, pt. 3) as being delighted with it. — Q.E.D.

Note. This hatred toward a beloved object when joined with envy is called "jealousy," which is therefore nothing but a vacillation of the mind springing from the love and hatred both felt together, and attended with the idea of another person whom we envy. Moreover, this hatred toward the beloved object will be greater in proportion to the joy with which the jealous man has been usually affected from the mutual affection between him and his beloved, and also in proportion to the emotion with which he had been affected toward the person who is imagined to unite to himself the beloved object. For if he has hated him, he will for that very reason hate the beloved object (Prop. 24, pt. 3) because he imagines it to affect with joy that which he hates, and also (Corol. Prop. 15, pt. 3) because he is compelled to connect the image of the beloved object with the image of him whom he hates. This feeling is generally excited when the love is love toward a woman. The man who imagines that the woman he loves prostitutes herself to another is not merely troubled because his appetite is restrained, but he turns away from her because he is obliged to connect the image of a beloved object with the privy parts and with what is excremental in another man; and in addition to this, the jealous person is not received with the same favor which the beloved object formerly bestowed on him — a new cause of sorrow to the lover, as I shall show.

PROPOSITION XXXVI. *He who recollects a thing with which he has once been delighted desires to possess it with every condition which existed when he was first delighted with it.*

Demonstration. Whatever a man has seen together with an object which has delighted him will be (Prop. 15, pt. 3) contingently a cause of joy, and therefore (Prop. 28, pt. 3) he will desire to possess it all, together with the object which has delighted him, that is to say, he will desire to possess the object with every condition which existed when he was first delighted with it. — Q.E.D.

Corollary. If, therefore, the lover discovers that one of these conditions be wanting, he will be sad.

Demonstration. For in so far as he discovers that any one condition is wanting does he imagine something which excludes the existence of the object. But since (Prop. 36, pt. 3) he desires the object or condition from love, he will therefore be sad (Prop. 19, pt. 3) in so far as he imagines that condition to be wanting. — Q.E.D.

Note. This sorrow, in so far as it is related to the absence of what we love, is called "longing."

PROPOSITION XXXVII. *The desire which springs from sorrow or joy, from hatred or love, is greater in proportion as the emotion is greater.*

Demonstration. Sorrow lessens or limits a man's power of action (Note, Prop. 11, pt. 3), that is to say (Prop. 7, pt. 3), it lessens or limits the effort by which a man endeavors to persevere in his own being, and therefore (Prop. 5, pt. 3) it is opposed to this effort; consequently, if a man be affected with sorrow, the first thing he attempts is to remove that sorrow; but (by the definition of sorrow) the greater it is, the greater is the human power of action to which it must be opposed, and so much the greater, therefore, will be the power of action with which the man will endeavor to remove it, that is to say (Note, Prop. 9, pt. 3), with the greater eagerness or desire will he struggle to remove it. Again, since joy (Note, Prop. 11, pt. 3) increases or assists a man's power of action, it is easily demonstrated, by the same method, that there is nothing which a man who is affected with joy desires more than to preserve it, and his desire is in proportion to his joy. Again, since hatred and love are themselves emotions either of joy or sorrow, it follows in the same manner that the effort, desire, or eagerness which arises from hatred or love will be greater in proportion to the hatred or love. — Q.E.D.

PROPOSITION XXXVIII. *If a man has begun to hate a beloved thing, so that his love of it is altogether destroyed, he will for this very reason hate it more than he would have done if he had never loved it, and his hatred will be in greater proportion to his previous love.*

Demonstration. If a man begins to hate a thing which he loves, a constraint is put upon more appetites than if he had never loved it. For love is joy (Note, Prop. 13, pt. 3), which a man endeavors to preserve as much as possible (Prop. 28, pt. 3), both by looking on the beloved object as present (Note, Prop. 13, pt. 3) and by affecting it with joy as much as possible (Prop. 21, pt. 3); this effort (Prop. 37, pt. 3) to preserve the joy of love being the greater in proportion as his love is greater, and so also is the effort to bring the beloved object to love him in return (Prop. 33, pt. 3). But these efforts are restrained by the hatred toward the beloved object (Corol. Prop. 13, and Prop. 23, pt. 3); therefore the lover (Note, Prop. 11, pt. 3), for this reason, also will be affected with sorrow, and that the more as the love had been greater, that is to say, in addition to the sorrow which was the cause of the hatred there is another produced by his having loved the object, and consequently he will contemplate with a greater emotion of sorrow the beloved object, that is to say (Note, Prop. 13, pt. 3), he will hate it more than he would have done if he had not loved it, and his hatred will be in proportion to his previous love. — Q.E.D.

PROPOSITION XXXIX. *If a man hates another he will endeavor to do him evil unless he fears a greater evil will therefore arise to himself; and, on the other hand, he who loves another will endeavor to do him good by the same rule.*

Demonstration. To hate a person (Note, Prop. 13, pt. 3) is to imagine him as a cause of sorrow, and therefore (Prop. 28, pt. 3) he who hates another will endeavor to remove or destroy him. But if he fears lest a greater grief or, which is the same thing, a greater evil should fall upon himself, and one which he thinks he can avoid by refraining from inflicting the evil he meditated, he will desire not to do it (Prop. 28, pt. 3); and this desire will be stronger than the former with which he was possessed of inflicting the evil, and will prevail over it (Prop. 37, pt. 3). This is the first part of the proposition. The second is demonstrated in the same way. Therefore if a man hates another, etc. — Q.E.D.

Note. By "good" I understand here every kind of joy and everything that conduces to it, chiefly, however, anything that satisfies longing, whatever that thing may be. By "evil" I understand every kind of sorrow, and chiefly whatever thwarts longing. For we have shown above (Note, Prop. 9, pt. 3) that we do not desire a thing because we adjudge it to be good, but, on the contrary, we call it good because we desire it, and, consequently, everything to which we are averse we call evil. Each person, therefore, according to his emotion judges or estimates what is good and what is evil, what is better and what is worse, and what is the best and what is the worst. Thus the covetous man thinks plenty of money to be the best thing and poverty the worst. The ambitious man desires nothing like glory, and on the other hand dreads nothing like shame. To the envious person, again, nothing is more pleasant than the misfortune of another, and nothing more disagreeable than the prosperity of another. And so each person according to his emotion judges a thing to be good or evil, useful or useless. We notice, moreover, that this emotion by which a man is so disposed as not to will the thing he wills, and to will that which he does not will, is called "fear," which may therefore be defined as that "apprehension" which leads a man to avoid an evil in the future by incurring a lesser evil (Prop. 28, pt. 3). If the evil feared is shame, then the fear is called "modesty." If the desire of avoiding the future is restrained by the fear of another evil, so that the man does not know what he most wishes, then this apprehension is called "consternation," especially if both the evils feared are very great.

PROPOSITION XL. *If we imagine that we are hated by another without having given him any cause for it, we shall hate him in return.*

Demonstration. If we imagine that another person is affected with hatred, on that account we shall also be affected with it (Prop. 27, pt. 3), that is to say, we shall be affected with sorrow (Note, Prop. 13, pt. 3), accompanied with the idea of an external cause. But (by hypothesis) we imagine no cause for this sorrow except the person himself who hates us, and therefore, because we imagine ourselves hated by another, we shall be affected with sorrow accompanied with the idea of him who hates us, that is to say (Note, Prop. 13, pt. 3), we shall hate him. — Q.E.D.

Note. If we imagine that we have given just cause for the hatred, we shall then (Prop. 30, pt. 3, with its Note) be affected with shame. This, however (Prop. 25, pt. 3), rarely happens.

This reciprocity of hatred may also arise from the fact that hatred is followed by an attempt to bring evil upon him who is hated (Prop. 39, pt. 3). If, therefore, we imagine that we are hated by any one else, we shall imagine him as the cause of some evil or sorrow, and thus we shall be affected with sorrow or apprehension accompanied with the idea of the person who hates us as a cause, that is to say, we shall hate him in return, as we have said above.

Corollary 1. If we imagine that the person we love is affected with hatred toward us, we shall be agitated at the same time both with love and hatred. For in so far as we imagine that we are hated are we determined (Prop. 40, pt. 3) to hate him in return. But (by hypothesis) we love him, notwithstanding, and therefore we shall be agitated both by love and hatred.

Corollary 2. If we imagine that an evil has been brought upon us through the hatred of some person toward whom we have hitherto been moved by no emotion, we shall immediately endeavor to return that evil upon him.

Demonstration. If we imagine that another person is affected with hatred toward us, we shall hate him in return (Prop. 40, pt. 3), and (Prop. 26, pt. 3) we shall endeavor to devise and (Prop. 39, pt. 3) bring upon him everything which can affect him with sorrow. But (by hypothesis) the first thing of this kind we imagine is the evil brought upon ourselves, and therefore we shall immediately endeavor to bring that upon him. — Q.E.D.

Note. The attempt to bring evil on those we hate is called "anger," and the attempt to return the evil inflicted on ourselves is called "vengeance."

PROPOSITION XLI. *If we imagine that we are beloved by a person without having given any cause for the love (which may be the case by Corol. Prop. 15, pt. 3, and by Prop. 16, pt. 3), we shall love him in return.*

Demonstration. This proposition is demonstrated in the same way as the preceding, to the note of which the reader is also referred.

Note. If we imagine that we have given just cause for love, we shall pride ourselves upon it (Prop. 30, pt. 3, with its Note). This frequently occurs (Prop. 25, pt. 3), and we have said that the contrary takes place when we believe that we are hated by another person (Note, Prop. 40, pt. 3). This reciprocal love, and consequently (Prop. 39, pt. 3) this attempt to do good to the person who loves us, and who (by the same Prop. 39, pt. 3) endeavors to do good to us, is called "thankfulness" or "gratitude," and from this we can see how much readier men are to revenge themselves than to return a benefit.

Corollary. If we imagine that we are loved by a person we hate, we shall at the same time be agitated both by love and hatred. This is demonstrated in the same way as the preceding proposition.

Note. If the hatred prevail, we shall endeavor to bring evil upon the person by whom we are loved. This emotion is called "cruelty," especially if it is believed that the person who loves has not given any ordinary reason for hatred.

PROPOSITION XLII. *If, moved by love or hope of self-exaltation, we have conferred a favor upon another person, we shall be sad if we see that the favor is received with ingratitude.*

Demonstration. If we love a thing which is of the same nature as ourselves, we endeavor as much as possible to cause it to love us in return (Prop. 33, pt. 3). If we confer a favor, therefore, upon any one because of our love toward him, we do it with a desire by which we are possessed that we may be loved in return, that is to say (Prop. 34, pt. 3), from the hope of self-exaltation or (Note, Prop. 30, pt. 3) of joy, and we shall consequently (Prop. 12, pt. 3) endeavor as much as possible to imagine this cause of self-exaltation or to contemplate it as actually existing. But (by hypothesis) we imagine something else which excludes the existence of that cause, and, therefore (Prop. 19, pt. 3), this will make us sad. — Q.E.D.

PROPOSITION XLIII. *Hatred is increased through return of hatred, but may be destroyed by love.*

Demonstration. If we imagine that the person we hate is affected with hatred toward us, a new hatred is thereby produced (Prop. 40, pt. 3), the old hatred still remaining (by hypothesis). If, on the other hand, we imagine him to be affected with love toward us, in so far as we imagine it (Prop. 30, pt. 3) shall we look upon ourselves with joy and endeavor (Prop. 29, pt. 3) to please him, that is to say (Prop. 41, pt. 3), in so far shall we endeavor not to hate him nor to affect him with sorrow. This effort (Prop. 37, pt. 3) will be greater or less as the emotion from which it arises is greater or less, and, therefore, should it be greater than that which springs from hatred, and by which (Prop. 26, pt. 3) we endeavor to affect with sorrow the object we hate, then it will prevail and banish hatred from the mind. — Q.E.D.

PROPOSITION XLIV. *Hatred which is altogether overcome by love passes into love, and the love is therefore greater than if hatred had not preceded it.*

Demonstration. The demonstration is of the same kind as that of Prop. 38, pt. 3. For if we begin to love a thing which we hated, or upon which we were in the habit of looking with sorrow, we shall rejoice for the very reason that we love; and to this joy which love involves (see its definition in the note of Prop. 13, pt. 3) a new joy is added which springs from the fact that the effort to remove the sorrow which hatred involves (Prop. 37, pt. 3) is so much assisted, there being also present before us, as the cause of our joy, the idea of the person whom we hated.

Note. Notwithstanding the truth of this proposition, no one will try to hate a thing or will wish to be affected with sorrow in order that he may rejoice the more, that is to say, no one will desire to inflict loss on himself in the hope of recovering the loss, or to become ill in the hope of getting well, inasmuch as every one will always try to preserve his being and to remove sorrow from himself as much as possible. Moreover, if it can be imagined that it is possible for us to desire to hate a person in order that we may love him afterwards the more, we must always desire to continue the hatred. For the love will be the greater as the hatred has been greater, and therefore we shall always desire the hatred to be more and more increased. Upon the same principle we shall desire that our sickness may continue and increase in order that we may afterwards enjoy the greater pleasure when we get well, and therefore we shall always desire sickness, which (Prop. 6, pt. 3) is absurd.

PROPOSITION XLV. *If we imagine that any one like ourselves is affected with hatred toward an object like ourselves which we love, we shall hate him.*

Demonstration. The beloved object hates him who hates it (Prop. 40, pt. 3), and therefore we who love it, who imagine that any one hates it, imagine also that it is affected with hatred, that is to say, with sorrow (Note, Prop. 13, pt. 3), and consequently (Prop. 21, pt. 3) we are sad, our sadness being accompanied with the idea of the person, as the cause thereof, who hates the beloved object, that is to say (Note, Prop. 13, pt. 3), we shall hate him. — Q.E.D.

PROPOSITION XLVI. *If we have been affected with joy or sorrow by any one who belongs to a class or nation different from our own, and if our joy or sorrow is accompanied with the idea of this person as its cause, under the common name of his class or nation, we shall not love or hate him merely, but the whole of the class or nation to which he belongs.*

Demonstration. This proposition is demonstrated in the same way as Prop. 16, pt. 3.

PROPOSITION XLVII. *The joy which arises from our imagining that what we hate has been destroyed or has been injured is not unaccompanied with some sorrow.*

Demonstration. This is evident from Prop. 27, pt. 3, for in so far as we imagine an object like ourselves affected with sorrow shall we be sad.

Note. This proposition may also be demonstrated from Corol.,

Prop. 17, pt. 2. For as often as we recollect the object, although it does not actually exist, we contemplate it as present, and the body is affected in the same way as if it were present. Therefore, so long as the memory of the object remains, we are so determined as to contemplate it with sorrow, and this determination, while the image of the object abides, is restrained by the recollection of those things which exclude the existence of the object, but is not altogether removed. Therefore we rejoice only so far as the determination is restrained, and hence it happens that the joy which springs from the misfortune of the object we hate is renewed as often as we recollect the object. For, as we have already shown, whenever its image is excited, inasmuch as this involves the existence of the object, we are so determined as to contemplate it with the same sorrow with which we were accustomed to contemplate it when it really existed. But because we have connected with this image other images which exclude its existence, the determination to sorrow is immediately restrained, and we rejoice anew; and this happens as often as this repetition takes place. This is the reason why we rejoice as often as we call to mind any evil that is past, and why we like to tell tales about the dangers we have escaped, since, whenever we imagine any danger, we contemplate it as if it were about to be, and are so determined as to fear it — a determination which is again restrained by the idea of freedom, which we connected with the idea of the danger when we were freed from it, and this idea of freedom again makes us fearless, so that we again rejoice.

PROPOSITION XLVIII. *Love and hatred toward any object, for example, toward Peter, are destroyed if the joy and the sorrow which they respectively involve be joined to the idea of another cause; and they are respectively diminished in proportion as we imagine that Peter has not been their sole cause.*

Demonstration. This is plain from the very definition of love and hatred (see Note, Prop. 13, pt. 3), joy being called love to Peter and sorrow being called hatred to him, solely because he is considered to be the cause of this or that emotion. Whenever, therefore, we can no longer consider him either partially or entirely its cause, the emotion toward him ceases or is diminished. — Q.E.D.

PROPOSITION XLIX. *For the same reason, love or hatred toward an object we imagine to be free must be greater than toward an object which is under necessity.*

Demonstration. An object which we imagine to be free must (Def. 7, pt. 1) be perceived through itself and without others. If, therefore, we imagine it to be the cause of joy or sorrow, we shall for that reason alone love or hate it (Note, Prop. 13, pt. 3), and that, too, with the greatest love or the greatest hatred which can spring from the given emotion (Prop. 48, pt. 3). But if we imagine that the object which is the cause of that emotion is necessary, then (by the same Def. 7, pt. 1) we shall imagine it as the cause of that emotion, not alone, but together with other causes, and so (Prop. 48, pt. 3) our love or hatred toward it will be less. — Q.E.D.

Note. Hence it follows that our hatred or love toward one another is greater than toward other things because we think we are free. We must take into account also the imitation of emotions which we have discussed in Props. 27, 34, 40, and 43, pt. 3.

PROPOSITION L. *Anything may be accidentally the cause either of hope or fear.*

Demonstration. This proposition is demonstrated in the same way as Prop. 15, pt. 3, which see, together with Note 2, Prop. 18, pt. 3.

Note. Things which are accidentally the causes either of hope or fear are called good or evil omens. In so far as the omens are the cause of hope and fear (by the Def. of hope and fear in Note 2, Prop. 18, pt. 3) are they the cause of joy or of sorrow, and consequently (Corol. Prop. 15, pt. 3) so far do we love them or hate them, and (Prop. 28, pt. 3) endeavor to use them as means to obtain those things for which we hope, or to remove them as obstacles or causes of fear. It follows, too, from Prop. 25, pt. 3, that our natural constitution is such that we easily believe the things we hope for, and believe with difficulty those we fear, and that we think too much of the former and too little of the latter. Thus have superstitions arisen, by which men are everywhere disquieted. I do not consider it worth while to go any further and to explain here all those vacillations of mind which arise from hope and fear, since it follows from the definition alone of these emotions that hope cannot exist without fear, nor fear without hope (as we shall explain more at length in the proper place). Besides, in so far as we hope for a thing or fear it, we love it or hate it, and therefore everything which has been said about hatred and love can easily be applied to hope and fear.

PROPOSITION LI. *Different men may be affected by one and the same object in different ways, and the same man may be affected by one and the same object in different ways at different times.*

Demonstration. The human body (Post. 3, pt. 2) is affected by external bodies in a number of ways. Two men, therefore, may be affected in different ways at the same time, and, therefore (Ax. 1, after Lemma 3, following Prop. 13, pt. 2), they can be affected by one and the same object in different ways. Again (Post. 3, pt. 2), the human body may be affected now in this and now in that way, and, consequently (by the axiom just quoted), it may be affected by one and the same object in different ways at different times. — Q.E.D.

Note. We thus see that it is possible for one man to love a thing and for another man to hate it, for this man to fear what this man does not fear, and for the same man to love what before he hated, and to dare to do what before he feared. Again, since each judges according to his own emotion what is good and what is evil, what is better and what is worse (Note, Prop. 39, pt. 3), it follows that men may change in their judgment as they do in their emotions,[4] and hence it comes to pass that when we compare men we distinguish them solely by the difference in their emotions, calling some "brave," others "timid," and others by other names. For example, I shall call a man brave who despises an evil which I usually fear, and if, besides this, I consider the fact that his desire of doing evil to a person whom

---

[4] That this may be the case, although the human mind is part of the divine intellect, we have shown in Corol., Prop. 12, pt. 2.

he hates or doing good to one whom he loves is not restrained by that fear of evil by which I am usually restrained, I call him "audacious." On the other hand, the man who fears an evil which I usually despise will appear "timid," and if, besides this, I consider that his desire is restrained by the fear of an evil which has no power to restrain me, I call him "pusillanimous"; and in this way everybody will pass judgment. Finally, from this nature of man and the inconstancy of his judgment, in consequence of which he often judges things from mere emotion, and the things which he believes contribute to his joy or his sorrow, and which, therefore, he endeavors to bring to pass or remove (Prop. 28, pt. 3), are often only imaginary — to say nothing about what we have demonstrated in the Second Part of this book about the uncertainty of things — it is easy to see that a man may often be himself the cause of his sorrow or his joy, or of being affected with sorrow or joy accompanied with the idea of himself as its cause, so that we can easily understand what repentance and what self-approval are. Repentance is sorrow accompanied with the idea of one's self as the cause, and self-approval is joy accompanied with the idea of one's self as the cause; and these emotions are very intense because men believe themselves free (Prop. 49, pt. 3).

PROPOSITION LII. *An object which we have seen before together with other objects, or which we imagine possesses nothing which is not common to it with many other objects, we shall not contemplate so long as that which we imagine possesses something peculiar.*

Demonstration. Whenever we imagine an object which we have seen with others, we immediately call these to mind (Prop. 18, pt. 2, with Note), and thus from the contemplation of one object we immediately fall to contemplating another. This also is our way with an object which we imagine to possess nothing except what is common to a number of other objects. For this is the same thing as supposing that we contemplate nothing in it which we have not seen before with other objects. On the other hand, if we suppose ourselves to imagine in an object something peculiar which we have never seen before, it is the same as saying that the mind, while it contemplates that object, holds nothing else in itself to the contemplation of which it can pass, turning away from the contemplation of the object, and therefore it is determined to the contemplation solely of the object. Therefore an object, etc. — Q.E.D.

Note. This mental modification or imagination of a particular thing, in so far as it alone occupies the mind, is called "astonishment," and if it is excited by an object we dread, we call it "consternation," because astonishment at the evil so fixes us in the contemplation of itself that we cannot think of anything else by which we might avoid the evil. On the other hand, if the objects at which we are astonished are human wisdom, industry, or anything of this kind, inasmuch as we consider that their possessor is by so much superior to ourselves, the astonishment goes by the name of "veneration"; whilst, if the objects are human anger, envy, or anything of this sort, it goes by the name of "horror." Again, if we are astonished at the wisdom or industry of a man we love, then our love on that account (Prop. 12, pt. 3) will be greater, and this love, united to astonishment or veneration, we call "devotion." In the same manner it is possible to conceive of hatred, hope, confidence, and other emotions being joined to astonishment, so that more emotions may be deduced than are indicated by the words in common use. From this we see that names have been invented for emotions from common usage rather than from accurate knowledge of them.

To astonishment is opposed contempt, which is usually caused, nevertheless, by our being determined to astonishment, love, or fear toward an object either because we see that another person is astonished at, loves or fears this same object, or because at first sight it appears like other objects at which we are astonished or which we love or fear (Prop. 15, with Corol. pt. 3, and Prop. 27, pt. 3). But if the presence of the object or a more careful contemplation of it should compel us to deny that there exists in it any cause for astonishment, love, fear, etc., then, from its presence itself, the mind remains determined to think rather of those things which are not in it than of those which are in it, although from the presence of an object the mind is accustomed to think chiefly about what is in the object. We may also observe that as devotion springs from astonishment at a thing we love, so "derision" springs from the contempt of a thing we hate or fear, whilst "scorn" arises from the contempt of folly, as veneration arises from astonishment at wisdom. We may also conceive of love, hope, glory, and other emotions being joined to contempt, and thus deduce other emotions which also we are not in the habit of distinguishing by separate words.

PROPOSITION LIII. *When the mind contemplates itself and its own power of acting, it rejoices, and it rejoices in proportion to the distinctness with which it imagines itself and its power of action.*

Demonstration. Man has no knowledge of himself except through the modifications of his own body and their ideas (Props. 19 and 23, pt. 2); whenever, therefore, it happens that the mind is able to contemplate itself it is thereby supposed to pass to a greater perfection, that is to say (Note, Prop. 11, pt. 3), it is supposed to be affected with joy, and the joy is greater in proportion to the distinctness with which it imagines itself and its power of action. — Q.E.D.

Corollary. The more a man imagines that he is praised by other men, the more is this joy strengthened; for the more a man imagines that he is praised by others, the more does he imagine that he affects others with joy accompanied by the idea of himself as a cause (Note, Prop. 29, pt. 3), and therefore (Prop. 27, pt. 3) he is affected with greater joy accompanied with the idea of himself. — Q.E.D.

PROPOSITION LIV. *The mind endeavors to imagine those things only which posit its power of acting.*

Demonstration. The effort or power of the mind is the essence of the mind itself (Prop. 7, pt. 3), but the essence of the mind, as is self-evident, affirms only that which the mind is and is able to do, and does not affirm that which the mind is not and cannot do, and therefore the mind endeavors to imagine those things only which affirm or posit its power of acting. — Q.E.D.

PROPOSITION LV. *When the mind imagines its own weakness it necessarily sorrows.*

Demonstration. The essence of the mind affirms only that which the mind is and is able to do, or, in other words, it is the nature of the mind to imagine those things only which posit its power of acting (Prop. 54, pt. 3). If we say, therefore, that the mind, while it contemplates itself, imagines its own weakness, we are merely saying in other words that the effort of the mind to imagine something which posits its power of acting is restrained, that is to say (Note, Prop. 11, pt. 3), the mind is sad. — Q.E.D.

Corollary. This sorrow is strengthened in proportion as the mind imagines that it is blamed by others. This is demonstrated in the same way as Corol. Prop. 53, pt. 3.

Note. This sorrow, accompanied with the idea of our own weakness, is called "humility," and the joy which arises from contemplating ourselves is called "self-love" or "self-approval." Inasmuch as this joy recurs as often as a man contemplates his own virtues or his own power of acting, it comes to pass that everyone loves to tell of his own deeds and to display the powers both of his body and mind, and that for this reason men become an annoyance to one another. It also follows that men are naturally envious (Note, Prop. 24, and Note, Prop. 32, pt. 3), that is to say, they rejoice over the weaknesses of their equals and sorrow over their strength. For whenever a person imagines his own actions he is affected with joy (Prop. 53, pt. 3), and his joy is the greater in proportion as he imagines that his actions express more perfection, and he imagines them more distinctly, that is to say (by what has been said in Note 1, Prop. 40, pt. 2), in proportion as he is able to distinguish them from others and to contemplate them as individual objects. A man's joy in contemplating himself will therefore be greatest when he contemplates something in himself which he denies of other people. For if he refers that which he affirms of himself to the universal idea of man or of animal nature, he will not so much rejoice; on the other hand, he will be sad if he imagines that his own actions, when compared with those of other people, are weaker than theirs, and this sorrow he will endeavor to remove (Prop. 28, pt. 3), either by misinterpreting the actions of his equals or giving as great a lustre as possible to his own. It appears, therefore, that men are by nature inclined to hatred and envy, and we must add that their education assists them in this propensity, for parents are accustomed to excite their children to follow virtue by the stimulus of honor and envy alone. But an objection perhaps may be raised that we not infrequently venerate men and admire their virtues. In order to remove this objection I will add the following corollary.

Corollary. No one envies the virtue of a person who is not his equal.

Demonstration. Envy is nothing but hatred (Note, Prop. 24, pt. 3), that is to say (Note, Prop. 13, pt. 3), sorrow, or, in other words (Note, Prop. 11, pt. 3), a modification by which the effort of a man or his power of action is restrained. But (Note, Prop. 9, pt. 3) a man neither endeavors to do nor desires anything except what can follow from his given nature, therefore a man will not desire to affirm of himself any power of action or, which is the same thing, any virtue which is peculiar to another nature and foreign to his own. His desire, therefore, cannot be restrained, that is to say (Note, Prop. 11, pt. 3), he cannot feel any sorrow because he contemplates a virtue in another person altogether unlike himself, and, consequently, he cannot envy that person, but will only envy one who is his own equal, and who is supposed to possess the same nature. — Q.E.D.

Note. Since, therefore, we have said in Note, Prop. 52, pt. 3, that we venerate a man because we are astonished at his wisdom and bravery, etc., this happens because (as is evident from the proposition itself) we imagine that he specially possesses these virtues, and that they are not common to our nature. We therefore envy them no more than we envy trees their height or lions their bravery.

PROPOSITION LVI. *Of joy, sorrow, and desire, and consequently of every emotion which either, like vacillation of mind, is compounded of these or, like love, hatred, hope, and fear, is derived from them, there are just as many kinds as there are kinds of objects by which we are affected.*

Demonstration. Joy and sorrow, and consequently the emotions which are compounded of these or derived from them, are passive states (Note, Prop. 11, pt. 3). But (Prop. 1, pt. 3) we necessarily suffer in so far as we have inadequate ideas, and (Prop. 3, pt. 3) only in so far as we have them; that is to say (see Note, Prop. 40, pt. 2), we necessarily suffer only in so far as we imagine, or (see Prop. 17, pt. 2, with its Note) in so far as we are affected with an emotion which involves the nature of our body and that of an external body. The nature, therefore, of each passive state must necessarily be explained in such a manner that the nature of the object by which we are affected is expressed. The joy, for example, which springs from an object A involves the nature of that object A, and the joy which springs from B involves the nature of that object B and therefore these two emotions of joy are of a different nature because they arise from causes of a different nature. In like manner the emotion of sorrow which arises from one object is of a different kind from that which arises from another cause, and the same thing is to be understood of love, hatred, hope, fear, vacillation of mind, etc., so that there are necessarily just as many kinds of joy, sorrow, love, hatred, etc., as there are kinds of objects by which we are affected. But desire is the essence itself or nature of a person in so far as this nature is conceived from its given constitution as determined toward any action (Note, Prop. 9, pt. 3), and, therefore, as a person is affected by external causes with this or that kind of joy, sorrow, love, hatred, etc., that is to say, as his nature is constituted in this or that way, so must his desire vary and the nature of one desire differ from that of another, just as the emotions from which each desire arises differ. There are as many kinds of desires, therefore, as there are kinds of joy, sorrow, love, etc., and, consequently (as we have just shown), as there are kinds of objects by which we are affected. — Q.E.D.

Note. Amongst the different kinds of emotions, which (by the preceding Prop.) must be very great in number, the most remarkable are *voluptuousness, drunkenness, lust, avarice,* and *ambition,* which are nothing but notions of love or desire, which explain the nature of this or that emotion through the objects to which they are related. For by "voluptuousness," "drunkenness," "lust," "avarice," and "ambition" we understand nothing but an immoderate love or desire for good living, for drinking, for women, for riches, and for glory. It is to be observed that these emotions, in so far as we distinguish them by the object alone to which they are related, have no contraries. For "temperance," "sobriety," and "chastity," which we are in the habit of opposing to voluptuousness, drunkenness, and lust, are not emotions nor passions, but merely indicate the power of the mind which restrains these emotions.

The remaining kinds of emotions I cannot explain here (for they are as numerous as are the varieties of objects), nor, if I could explain them, is it necessary to do so. For it is sufficient for the purpose we have in view, the determination, namely, of the strength of the emotions and the mind's power over them, to have a general definition of each kind of emotion. It is sufficient for us, I say, to understand the common properties of the mind and the emotions so that we may determine what and how great is the power of the mind to govern and constrain the emotions. Therefore, although there is a great difference between this or that emotion of love, of hatred, or of desire — for example, between the love toward children and the love toward a wife — it is not worth while for us to take cognizance of these differences, or to investigate the nature and origin of the emotions any further.

PROPOSITION LVII. *The emotion of one person differs from the corresponding emotion of another as much as the essence of the one person differs from that of the other.*

Demonstration. This proposition is evident from Ax. 1, following Lem. 3, after Note, Prop. 13, pt. 2. Nevertheless, we will demonstrate it from the definitions of the three primitive emotions. All emotions are related to desire, joy, or sorrow, as the definitions show which we have given of those emotions. But desire is the very nature or essence of a person (Note, Prop. 9, pt. 3), and therefore the desire of one person differs from the desire of another as much as the nature or essence of the one differs from that of the other. Again, joy and sorrow are emotions by which the power of a person or his effort to persevere in his own being is increased or diminished, helped, or limited (Prop. 11, pt. 3, with its Note). But by the effort to persevere in his own being, in so far as it is related at the same time to the mind and the body, we understand appetite and desire (Note, Prop. 9, pt. 3), and therefore joy and sorrow are desire or appetite in so far as the latter is increased, diminished, helped, or limited by external causes, that is to say (Note, Prop. 9, pt. 3), they are the nature itself of each person.

The joy or sorrow of one person therefore differs from the joy or sorrow of another as much as the nature or essence of one person differs from that of the other, and consequently the emotion of one person differs from the corresponding emotion of another, etc. — Q.E.D.

Note. Hence it follows that the feelings of animals which are called irrational (for after we have learned the origin of the mind we can in no way doubt that brutes feel) differ from human emotions as much as the nature of a brute differs from that of a man. Both the man and the horse, for example, are swayed by the lust to propagate, but the horse is swayed by equine lust and the man by that which is human. The lusts and appetites of insects, fishes, and birds must vary in the same way; and so, although each individual lives contented with its own nature and delights in it, nevertheless the life with which it is contented and its joy are nothing but the idea or soul of that individual, and so the joy of one differs in character from the joy of the other as much as the essence of the one differs from the essence of the other. Finally, it follows from the preceding proposition that the joy by which the drunkard is enslaved is altogether different from the joy which is the portion of the philosopher — a thing I wished just to hint in passing. So much, therefore, for the emotions which are related to man in so far as he is passive. It remains that I should say a few words about those things which are related to him in so far as he acts.

PROPOSITION LVIII. *Besides the joys and sorrows which are passive, there are other emotions of joy and sorrow which are related to us in so far as we act.*

Demonstration. When the mind conceives itself and its own power of acting, it is rejoiced (Prop. 53, pt. 3). But the mind necessarily contemplates itself whenever it conceives a true or adequate idea (Prop. 43, pt. 2); and as (Note 2, Prop. 40, pt. 2) it does conceive some adequate ideas, it is rejoiced in so far as it conceives them or, in other words (Prop. 1, pt. 3), in so far as it acts. Again, the mind, both in so far as it has clear and distinct ideas and in so far as it has confused ideas, endeavors to persevere in its own being (Prop. 9, pt. 3). But by this effort we understand desire (Note, Prop. 9, pt. 3), and therefore desire also is related to us in so far as we think, that is to say (Prop. 1, pt. 3), in so far as we act. — Q.E.D.

PROPOSITION LIX. *Amongst all the emotions which are related to the mind in so far as it acts, there are none which are not related to joy or desire.*

Demonstration. All the emotions are related to desire, joy, or sorrow, as the definitions we have given of them show. By sorrow, however, we understand that the mind's power of acting is lessened or limited (Prop. 11, pt. 3, and its Note), and, therefore, in so far as the mind suffers sorrow, is its power of thinking, that is to say (Prop. 1, pt. 3), its power of acting, lessened or limited. Therefore no emotions of sorrow can be related to the mind in so far as it acts, but only emotions of joy and desire, which (by the preceding Prop.) are also so far related to the mind. — Q.E.D.

Note. All the actions which follow from the emotions which are related to the mind in so far as it thinks I ascribe to *fortitude*, which I divide into *strength of mind* (*animositas*) and *generosity*. By "strength of mind" I mean the desire by which each person endeavors from the dictates of reason alone to preserve his own being. By "generosity" I mean the desire by which, from the dictates of reason alone, each person endeavors to help other people and to join them to him in friendship. Those actions, therefore, which have for their aim the advantage only of the doer I ascribe to strength of mind, whilst those which aim at the advantage of others I ascribe to generosity. Temperance, therefore, sobriety, and presence of mind in danger are a species of strength of mind, while moderation and mercy are a species of generosity.

I have now, I think, explained the principal emotions and vacillations of the mind which are compounded of the three primary emotions — desire, joy, and sorrow — and have set them forth through their first causes. From what has been said it is plain that we are disturbed by external causes in a number of ways, and that, like the waves of the sea agitated by contrary winds, we fluctuate in our ignorance of our future and destiny. I have said, however, that I have only explained the principal mental complications, and not all which may exist. For by the same method which we have pursued above it would be easy to show that love unites itself to repentance, scorn, shame, etc.; but I think it has already been made clear to all that the emotions can be combined in so many ways, and that so many variations can arise, that no limits can be assigned to their number. It is sufficient for my purpose to have enumerated only those which are of consequence; the rest, of which I have taken no notice, being more curious than important. There is one constantly recurring characteristic of love which I have yet to note: that while we are enjoying the thing which we desired the body acquires from that fruition a new disposition by which it is otherwise determined, and the images of other things are excited in it, and the mind begins to imagine and to desire other things. For example, when we imagine anything which usually delights our taste, we desire to enjoy it by eating it. But whilst we enjoy it the stomach becomes full, and the constitution of the body becomes altered. If, therefore, the body being now otherwise disposed, the image of the food, in consequence of its being present, and therefore also the effort or desire to eat it, become more intense, then this new disposition of the body will oppose this effort or desire, and consequently the presence of the food which we desired will become hateful to us, and this hatefulness is what we call "loathing" or "disgust." As for the external modifications of the body which are observed in the emotions, such as trembling, paleness, sobbing, laughter, and the like, I have neglected to notice them because they belong to the body alone without any relationship to the mind. A few things remain to be said about the definitions of the emotions, and I will therefore here repeat the definitions in order, appending to them what is necessary to be observed in each.

DEFINITIONS OF THE EMOTIONS

I. *Desire* is the essence itself of man in so far as it is conceived as determined to any action by any one of his modifications.

Explanation. We have said above, in the Note of Prop. 9, pt. 3, that desire is appetite which is self-conscious, and that appetite is the essence itself of man in so far as it is determined to such acts as contribute to his preservation. But in the same note I have taken care to remark that in truth I cannot recognize any difference between human appetite and desire. For whether a man be conscious of his appetite or not, it remains one and the same appetite, and so, lest I might appear to be guilty of tautology, I have not explained desire by appetite, but have tried to give such a definition of desire as would include all the efforts of human nature to which we give the name of appetite, desire, will, or impulse. For I might have said that desire is the essence itself of man in so far as it is considered as determined to any action; but from this definition it would not follow (Prop. 23, pt. 2) that the mind could be conscious of its desire or appetite, and therefore, in order that I might include the cause of this consciousness, it was necessary (by the same proposition) to add the words, *in so far as it is conceived as determined to any action by any one of his modifications*. For by a modification of the human essence we understand any constitution of that essence, whether it be innate, whether it be conceived through the attribute of thought alone or of extension alone, or whether it be related to both. By the word "desire," therefore, I understand all the efforts, impulses, appetites, and volitions of a man, which vary according to his changing disposition, and not infrequently are so opposed to one another that he is drawn hither and thither, and knows not whither he ought to turn.

II. *Joy* is man's passage from a less to a greater perfection.

III. *Sorrow* is man's passage from a greater to a less perfection.

Explanation. I say passage, for joy is not perfection itself. If a man were born with the perfection to which he passes, he would possess it without the emotion of joy — a truth which will appear the more clearly from the emotion of sorrow, which is the opposite to joy. For that sorrow consists in the passage to a less perfection, but not in the less perfection itself, no one can deny, since in so far as a man shares any perfection he cannot be sad. Nor can we say that sorrow consists in the privation of a greater perfection, for privation is nothing. But the emotion of sorrow is a reality, and it therefore must be the reality of the passage to a lesser perfection, or the reality by which man's power of acting is diminished or limited (Note, Prop. 11, pt. 3). As for the definitions of cheerfulness, pleasurable excitement, melancholy, and grief, I pass these by because they are related rather to the body than to the mind, and are merely different kinds of joy or of sorrow.

IV. *Astonishment* is the imagination of an object in which the mind remains fixed because this particular imagination has no connection with others.

Explanation. In the Note of Prop. 18, pt. 2, we have shown that that which causes the mind from the contemplation of one thing

immediately to pass to the thought of another is that the images of
these things are connected one with the other, and are so arranged
that the one follows the other — a process which cannot be conceived
when the image of the thing is new, for the mind will be held in the
contemplation of the same object until other causes determine it to
think of other things. The imagination, therefore, considered in itself,
of a new object is of the same character as other imaginations; and
for this reason I do not class astonishment among the emotions nor
do I see any reason why I should do it, since this abstraction of the
mind arises from no positive cause by which it is abstracted from other
things, but merely from the absence of any cause by which from the
contemplation of one thing the mind is determined to think other
things. I acknowledge, therefore (as I have shown in Note, Prop. 11,
pt. 3), only three primitive or primary emotions — those of joy,
sorrow, and desire; and the only reason which has induced me to
speak of astonishment is that it has been the custom to give other
names to certain emotions derived from the three primitives whenever these emotions are related to objects at which we are astonished.
This same reason also induces me to add the definition of contempt.

V. *Contempt* is the imagination of an object which so little touches
the mind that the mind is moved by the presence of the object to
imagine those qualities which are not in it rather than those which
are in it. (See Note, Prop. 52, pt. 3.)

The definitions of veneration and scorn I pass by here because they
give a name, so far as I know, to none of the emotions.

VI. *Love* is joy with the accompanying idea of an external cause.

Explanation. This definition explains with sufficient clearness the
essence of love; that which is given by some authors who define love
to be the will of the lover to unite himself to the beloved object,
expressing not the essence of love but one of its properties, and in as
much as these authors have not seen with sufficient clearness what is
the essence of love, they could not have a distinct conception of its
properties, and consequently their definition has by everybody been
thought very obscure. I must observe, however, when I say that it
is a property in a lover to will a union with the beloved object, that
I do not understand by will a consent or deliberation or a free decree
of the mind (for that this is a fiction we have demonstrated in Prop.
48, pt. 2), nor even a desire of the lover to unite himself with the

beloved object when it is absent, nor a desire to continue in its presence when it is present, for love can be conceived without either one or the other of these desires; but by will I understand the satisfaction that the beloved object produces in the lover by its presence by virtue of which the joy of the lover is strengthened or at any rate supported.

VII. *Hatred* is sorrow with the accompanying idea of an external cause.

Explanation. What is to be observed here will easily be seen from what has been said in the explanation of the preceding definition. (See, moreover, Note, Prop. 13, pt. 3.)

VIII. *Inclination* (*propensio*) is joy with the accompanying idea of some object as being accidentally the cause of the joy.

IX. *Aversion* is sorrow with the accompanying idea of some object which is accidentally the cause of the sorrow. (See Note, Prop. 15, pt. 3.)

X. *Devotion* is love toward an object which astonishes us.

Explanation. That astonishment arises from the novelty of the object we have shown in Prop. 52, pt. 3. If, therefore, it should happen that we often imagine the object at which we are astonished, we shall cease to be astonished at it, and hence we see that the emotion of devotion easily degenerates into simple love.

XI. *Derision* is joy arising from the imagination that something we despise is present in an object we hate.

Explanation. In so far as we despise a thing we hate do we deny its existence (Note, Prop. 52, pt. 3), and so far (Prop. 20, pt. 3) do we rejoice. But inasmuch as we suppose that a man hates what he ridicules, it follows that this joy is not solid. (See Note, Prop. 47, pt. 3.)

XII. *Hope* is a joy not constant, arising from the idea of something future or past, about the issue of which we sometimes doubt.

XIII. *Fear* is a sorrow not constant, arising from the idea of something future or past, about the issue of which we sometimes doubt. (See Note 2, Prop. 18, pt. 3.)

Explanation. From these definitions it follows that there is no hope without fear nor fear without hope, for the person who wavers in hope and doubts concerning the issue of anything is supposed to imagine something which may exclude its existence, and so far, therefore, to be sad (Prop. 19, pt. 3), and consequently, while he wavers in hope, to fear lest his wishes should not be accomplished. So also the person who fears, that is to say, who doubts whether what he hates will not come to pass, imagines something which excludes the existence of what he hates, and therefore (Prop. 20, pt. 3) is rejoiced, and consequently so far hopes that it will not happen.

XIV. *Confidence* is joy arising from the idea of a past or future object from which cause for doubting is removed.

XV. *Despair* is sorrow arising from the idea of a past or future object from which cause for doubting is removed.

Explanation. Confidence, therefore, springs from hope and despair from fear, whenever the reason for doubting the issue is taken away — a case which occurs either because we imagine a thing past or future to be present and contemplate it as present, or because we imagine other things which exclude the existence of those which made us to doubt.

For although we can never be sure about the issue of individual objects (Corol. Prop. 31, pt. 2), it may nevertheless happen that we do not doubt it. For elsewhere we have shown (Note, Prop. 49, pt. 2) that it is one thing not to doubt and another to possess certitude, and so it may happen that from the image of an object either past or future we are affected with the same emotion of joy or sorrow as that by which we should be affected from the image of an object present, as we have demonstrated in Prop. 18, pt. 3, to which, together with the note, the reader is referred.

XVI. *Gladness* (*gaudium*) is joy with the accompanying idea of something past which, unhoped for, has happened.

XVII. *Remorse* is sorrow with the accompanying idea of something past which, unhoped for, has happened.

XVIII. *Commiseration* is sorrow with the accompanying idea of evil which has happened to some one whom we imagine like ourselves (Note, Prop. 22, and Note, Prop. 27, pt. 3).

Explanation. Between commiseration and compassion there seems to be no difference, except perhaps that commiseration refers rather to an individual emotion and compassion to it as a habit.

XIX. *Favor* is love toward those who have benefited others.

XX. *Indignation* is hatred toward those who have injured others.

Explanation. I am aware that these names in common bear a different meaning. But my object is not to explain the meaning of words but the nature of things, and to indicate them by words whose customary meaning shall not be altogether opposed to the meaning which I desire to bestow upon them. I consider it sufficient to have said this once for all. As far as the cause of these emotions is concerned, see Corol. 1, Prop. 27, pt. 3, and Note, Prop. 22, pt. 3.

XXI. *Overestimation* consists in thinking too highly of another person in consequence of our love for him.

XXII. *Contempt* consists in thinking too little of another person in consequence of our hatred for him.

Explanation. Over-estimation and contempt are therefore respectively effects or properties of love or hatred, and so overestimation may be defined as love in so far as it affects a man so that he thinks too much of the beloved object; and, on the contrary, contempt may be defined as hatred in so far as it affects a man so that he thinks too little of the object he hates. (See Note, Prop. 26, pt. 3.)

XXIII. *Envy* is hatred in so far as it affects a man so that he is sad at the good fortune of another person and is glad when any evil happens to him.

Explanation. To envy is generally opposed compassion (*misericordia*), which may therefore be defined as follows, notwithstanding the usual signification of the word:

XXIV. *Compassion* is love in so far as it affects a man so that he is glad at the prosperity of another person and is sad when any evil happens to him.

Explanation. With regard to the other properties of envy, see Note, Prop. 24, and Note, Prop. 32, pt. 3. These are emotions of joy and sorrow which are attended by the idea of an external object as their cause, either of itself or accidentally. I pass now to consider other emotions which are attended by the idea of something within us as the cause.

XXV. *Self-satisfaction* is the joy which is produced by contemplating ourselves and our own power of action.

XXVI. *Humility* is the sorrow which is produced by contemplating our impotence or helplessness.

Self-satisfaction is opposed to humility in so far as we understand by the former the joy which arises from contemplating our power of action, but in so far as we understand by it joy attended with the idea of something done, which we believe has been done by a free decree of our mind, it is opposed to repentance, which we may thus define:

XXVII. *Repentance* is sorrow accompanied with the idea of something done which we believe has been done by a free decree of our mind.

Explanation. We have shown what are the causes of these emotions in Note, Prop. 51, pt. 3; Props. 53 and 54, pt. 3; and Prop. 55, pt. 3, together with its Note. With regard to a free decree of the mind, see Note, Prop. 35, pt. 2. Here, however, I must observe that it is not to be wondered at that sorrow should always follow all those actions which are from custom called wicked, and that joy should follow those which are called good. But that this is chiefly the effect of education will be evident from what we have before said. Parents, by reprobating what are called bad actions, and frequently blaming their children whenever they commit them, while they persuade them to what are called good actions, and praise their children when they perform them, have caused the emotions of sorrow to connect themselves with the former, and those of joy with the latter. Experience proves this, for custom and religion are not the same everywhere; but, on the contrary, things which are sacred to some are profane to others, and what are honorable with some are disgraceful with others. Education alone, therefore, will determine whether a man will repent of any deed or boast of it.

XXVIII. *Pride* is thinking too much of ourselves, through self-love.

Explanation. Pride differs, therefore, from overestimation, inasmuch as the latter is related to an external object, but pride to the man himself who thinks of himself too highly. As overestimation, therefore, is an effect or property of love, so pride is an effect or property of self-love, and it may therefore be defined as love of ourselves or self-satisfaction, in so far as it affects us so that we think too highly of ourselves. (See Note, Prop. 26, pt. 3.)

To this emotion a contrary does not exist, for no one, through hatred of himself, thinks too little of himself; indeed, we may say that no one thinks too little of himself, in so far as he imagines himself unable to do this or that thing. For whatever he imagines that he cannot do, that thing he necessarily imagines, and by his imagination is so disposed that he is actually incapable of doing what he imagines he cannot do. So long, therefore, as he imagines himself unable to do this or that thing, so long is he not determined to do it, and, consequently, so long it is impossible for him to do it. If, however, we pay attention to what depends upon opinion alone, we shall be able to conceive it possible for a man to think too little of himself, for it may happen that while he sorrowfully contemplates his own weakness he will imagine himself despised by everybody, although nothing could be further from their thoughts than to despise him. A man may also think too little of himself if in the present he denies something of himself in relation to a future time of which he is not sure; for example, when he denies that he can conceive of nothing with certitude, and that he can desire and do nothing which is not wicked and base. We may also say that a man thinks too little of himself when we see that, from an excess of fear or shame, he does not dare to do what others who are his equals dare to do. This emotion, to which I will give the name of "despondency," may therefore be opposed to pride; for as self-satisfaction springs from pride, so despondency springs from humility, and it may therefore be defined thus:

XXIX. *Despondency* is thinking too little of ourselves through sorrow.

Explanation. We are, nevertheless, often in the habit of opposing humility to pride, but only when we attend to their emotions rather than to their nature. For we are accustomed to call a man proud who boasts too much (Note, Prop. 30, pt. 3), who talks about nothing but his own virtues and other people's vices, who wishes to be preferred to everybody else, and who marches along with that stateliness and pomp which belong to others whose position is far above his. On the other hand, we call a man humble who often blushes, who confesses his own faults and talks about the virtues of others, who yields to every one, who walks with bended head, and who neglects to adorn himself. These emotions — humility and despondency — are very rare, for human nature, considered in itself, struggles against them as much as it can (Props. 13 and 54, pt. 3), and hence those who have the most credit for being abject and humble are generally the most ambitious and envious.

XXX. *Self-exaltation* is joy with the accompanying idea of some action we have done which we imagine people praise.

XXXI. *Shame* is sorrow with the accompanying idea of some action which we imagine people blame.

Explanation. With regard to these emotions see Note, Prop. 30, pt. 3. A difference, however, is here to be observed between shame and modesty. Shame is sorrow which follows a deed of which we are ashamed. Modesty is the dread or fear of shame which keeps a man from committing any disgraceful act. To modesty is usually opposed impudence, which indeed is not an emotion, as I shall show in the proper place; but the names of emotions, as I have already said, are matters rather of custom than indications of the nature of the emotions. I have thus discharged the task which I set myself of explaining the emotions of joy and sorrow. I will advance now to those which I ascribe to desire.

XXXII. *Regret* is the desire or longing to possess something, the emotion being strengthened by the memory of the object itself, and at the same time being restrained by the memory of other things which exclude the existence of the desired object.

Explanation. Whenever we recollect a thing, as we have often said, we are thereby necessarily disposed to contemplate it with the same emotion as if it were present before us. But this disposition or effort, while we are awake, is generally restrained by the images of things which exclude the existence of the thing which we recollect. Whenever, therefore, we recollect a thing which affects us with any kind of joy, we thereby endeavor to contemplate it with the same emotion of joy as if it were present — an attempt which is, however, immediately restrained by the memory of that which excludes the existence of the thing. Regret, therefore, is really a sorrow which is opposed to the joy which arises from the absence of what we hate. (See Note, Prop. 47, pt. 3.) But because the name "regret" seems to connect this emotion with desire, I therefore ascribe it to desire.

XXXIII. *Emulation* is the desire which is begotten in us of a thing because we imagine that other persons have the same desire.

Explanation. He who seeks flight because others seek it, he who fears because he sees others fear, or even he who withdraws his hand and moves his body as if his hand were burning because he sees that another person has burned his hand, such as these, I say, although they may indeed imitate the emotion of another, are not said to emulate it; not because we have recognized one cause for emulation and another for imitation, but because it has been the custom to call that man only emulous who imitates what we think noble, useful, or pleasant. With regard to the cause of emulation, see also Prop. 27, pt. 3, with the Note. For the reason why envy is generally connected with this emotion, see Prop. 32, pt. 3, with its Note.

XXXIV. *Thankfulness* or *gratitude* is the desire or endeavor of love with which we strive to do good to others who, from a similar emotion of love, have done good to us (Prop. 39, with Note, Prop. 41, pt. 3).

XXXV. *Benevolence* is the desire to do good to those whom we pity (Note, Prop. 27, pt. 3).

XXXVI. *Anger* is the desire by which we are impelled, through hatred, to injure those whom we hate (Prop. 39, pt. 3).

XXXVII. *Vengeance* is the desire which, springing from mutual hatred, urges us to injure those who, from a similar emotion, have injured us (Corol. 2, Prop. 40, pt. 3, with Note).

XXXVIII. *Cruelty* or *ferocity* is the desire by which a man is impelled to injure any one whom we love or pity.

Explanation. To cruelty is opposed mercy, which is not a passive state, but a power of the mind by which a man restrains anger and vengeance.

XXXIX. *Fear* is the desire of avoiding the greater of two dreaded evils by the less (Note, Prop. 39, pt. 3).

XL. *Audacity* is the desire by which we are impelled to do something which is accompanied with a danger which our equals fear to meet.

XLI. A person is said to be *pusillanimous* whose desire is restrained by the fear of a danger which his equals dare to meet.

Explanation. Pusillanimity, therefore, is nothing but the dread of some evil which most persons do not usually fear, and therefore I do not ascribe it to the emotions resulting from desire. I wished; notwithstanding, to explain it here because, in so far as we attend to desire, pusillanimity is the true opposite of the emotion of audacity.

XLII. *Consternation* is affirmed of the man whose desire of avoiding evil is restrained by astonishment at the evil which he fears.

Explanation. Consternation is therefore a kind of pusillanimity. But because consternation springs from a double fear, it may be more aptly defined as that dread which holds a man stupefied or vacillating, so that he cannot remove an evil. I say "stupefied," in so far as we understand his desire of removing the evil to be restrained by his astonishment. I say also "vacillating," in so far as we conceive the same desire to be restrained by the fear of another evil which equally tortures him, so that he does not know which of the two evils to avoid. See Note, Prop. 39, and Note, Prop. 52, pt. 3. With regard to pusillanimity and audacity, see Note, Prop. 51, pt. 3.

XLIII. *Courtesy* or *moderation* is the desire of doing those things which please men and omitting those which displease them.

XLIV. *Ambition* is the immoderate desire of glory.

Explanation. Ambition is a desire which increases and strengthens all the emotions (Props. 27 and 31, pt. 3), and that is the reason why it can hardly be kept under control. For so long as a man is possessed by any desire, he is necessarily at the same time possessed by this. "Every noble man," says Cicero, "is led by glory, and even the philosophers who write books about despising glory place their names on the title page."

XLV. *Luxuriousness* is the immoderate desire or love of good living.

XLVI. *Drunkenness* is the immoderate desire and love of drinking.

XLVII. *Avarice* is the immoderate desire and love of riches.

XLVIII. *Lust* is the immoderate desire and love of sexual intercourse.

Explanation. This desire of sexual intercourse is usually called lust, whether it be held within bounds or not. I may add that the five last-mentioned emotions (as we have shown in Note, Prop. 56, pt. 3) have no contraries, for moderation is a kind of ambition (see Note, Prop. 29, pt. 3), and I have already observed that temperance, sobriety, and chastity show a power and not a passion of the mind. Even supposing that an avaricious, ambitious, or timid man refrains from an excess of eating, drinking, or sexual intercourse, avarice, ambition, and fear are not therefore the opposites of voluptuousness, drunkenness, or lust. For the avaricious man generally desires to swallow as much meat and drink as he can, provided only it belong to another person. The ambitious man, too, if he hopes he can keep it a secret, will restrain himself in nothing and, if he lives amongst drunkards and libertines, will be more inclined to their vices just because he is ambitious. The timid man, too, does what he does not will; and although, in order to avoid death, he may throw his riches into the sea, he remains avaricious; nor does the lascivious man cease to be lascivious because he is sorry that he cannot gratify his desire. Absolutely, therefore, these emotions have reference not so much to the acts themselves of eating and drinking as to the appetite and love itself. Consequently, nothing can be opposed to these emotions but nobility of soul and strength of mind, as we shall see afterwards.

The definitions of jealousy and the other vacillations of the mind I pass over in silence, both because they are compounded of the emotions which we have already defined, and also because many of them have no names — a fact which shows that, for the purposes of life, it is sufficient to know these combinations generally. Moreover, it follows from the definitions of the emotions which we have explained that they all arise from desire, joy, or sorrow, or rather that there are none but these three, which pass under names varying as their relations and external signs vary. If, therefore, we attend to these primitive emotions and to what has been said above about the nature of the mind, we shall be able here to define the emotions in so far as they are related to the mind alone.

General definition of the emotions. Emotion which is called *animi pathema* is a confused idea by which the mind affirms of its body, or any part of it, a greater or less power of existence than before; and this increase of power being given, the mind itself is determined to one particular thought rather than to another.

Explanation. I say, in the first place, that an emotion or passion of the mind *is a confused idea.* For we have shown (Prop. 3, pt. 3) that the mind suffers only in so far as it has inadequate or confused ideas. I say again, *by which the mind affirms of its body, or any part of it, a greater or less power of existence than before.* For all ideas which we possess of bodies indicate the actual constitution of our body rather than the nature of the external body (Corol. 2, Prop. 16, pt. 2); but this idea which constitutes the reality of an emotion must indicate or express the constitution of the body or of some part of it; which constitution the body or any part of it possesses from the fact that its power of action or force of existence is increased or diminished, helped or limited. But it is to be observed that when I say "a greater or less power of existence than before," I do not mean that the mind compares the present with the past constitution of the body, but that the idea which constitutes the reality of an emotion affirms something of the body which actually involves more or less reality than before. Moreover, since the essence of the mind (Props. 11 and 13, pt. 2) consists in its affirmation of the actual existence of its body, and since we understand by perfection the essence itself of the thing, it follows that the mind passes to a greater or less perfection when it is able to affirm of its body, or some part of it, something which involves a greater or less reality than before. When, therefore, I have said that the mind's power of thought is increased or diminished, I have wished to be understood as meaning nothing else than that the mind has formed an idea of its body, or some part of its body, which expresses more or less reality than it had hitherto affirmed of the body. For the value of ideas and the actual power of thought are measured by the value of the object. Finally, I added, "which being given, the mind itself is determined to one particular thought rather than to another," that I might also express the nature of desire in addition to that of joy and sorrow, which is explained by the first part of the definition.

PART FOUR

Of Human Bondage; or of the Strength of the Emotions

PREFACE

The impotence of man to govern or restrain the emotions I call "bondage," for a man who is under their control is not his own master, but is mastered by fortune, in whose power he is, so that he is often forced to follow the worse, although he sees the better before him. I propose in this part to demonstrate why this is, and also to show what of good and evil the emotions possess. But before I begin I should like to say a few words about perfection and imperfection, and about good and evil. If a man has proposed to do a thing and has accomplished it, he calls it perfect, and not only he, but every one else who has really known or has believed that he has known the mind and intention of the author of that work will call it perfect too. For example, having seen some work (which I suppose to be as yet not finished), if we know that the intention of the author of that work is to build a house, we shall call the house imperfect; while, on the other hand, we shall call it perfect as soon as we see the work has been brought to the end which the author had determined for it. But if we see any work such as we have never seen before, and if we do not know the mind of the workman, we shall then not be able to say whether the work is perfect or imperfect.[1] This seems to have been the first signification of these words; but afterwards men began to form universal ideas — to think out for themselves types of houses, buildings, castles, and to prefer some types of things to others; and so it happened that each person called a thing perfect which seemed to agree with the universal idea which he had formed of that thing, and, on the

[1] A translation cannot show the etymology of the word *perfect* as it is shown in the original Latin, so that this passage may perhaps seem rather obscure. It is only necessary, however, to bear in mind that "perfect" and "accomplished," are expressible by the same word in Latin, and that "accomplish" is the primary meaning of *perficere* [complete]. — TR.

187

other hand, he called a thing imperfect which seemed to agree less
with his typal conception, although, according to the intention of the
workman, it had been entirely completed. This appears to be the only
reason why the words "perfect" and "imperfect" are commonly
applied to natural objects which are not made with human hands;
for men are in the habit of forming, both of natural as well as of arti-
ficial objects, universal ideas which they regard as types of things,
and which they think Nature has in view, setting them before herself
as types, too; it being the common opinion that she does nothing
except for the sake of some end. When, therefore, men see something
done by Nature which does not altogether answer to that typal conception which they have of the thing, they think that Nature herself
has failed or committed an error, and that she has left the thing imperfect. Thus we see that the custom of applying the words "perfect"
and "imperfect" to natural objects has arisen rather from prejudice
than from true knowledge of them. For we have shown in the Appendix
to the First Part of this work that Nature does nothing for the sake
of an end, for that eternal and infinite Being whom we call God or
Nature acts by the same necessity by which He exists; for we have
shown that He acts by the same necessity of Nature as that by which
He exists (Prop. 16, pt. 1). The reason or cause, therefore, why God
or Nature acts and the reason why He exists are one and the same.
Since, therefore, He exists for no end, He acts for no end; and since
He has no principle or end of existence, He has no principle or end of
action. A final cause, as it is called, is nothing, therefore, but human
desire, in so far as this is considered as the principle or primary cause
of anything. For example, when we say that the having a house to
live in was the final cause of this or that house, we merely mean that
a man, because he imagined the advantages of a domestic life, desired
to build a house. Therefore, having a house to live in, in so far as it
is considered as a final cause, is merely this particular desire, which is
really an efficient cause, and is considered as primary because men
are usually ignorant of the causes of their desires; for, as I have often
said, we are conscious of our actions and desires, but ignorant of the
causes by which we are determined to desire anything. As for the
vulgar opinion that Nature sometimes fails or commits an error, or
produces imperfect things, I class it amongst those fictions mentioned
in the Appendix to the First Part.

Perfection, therefore, and imperfection are really only modes of thought, that is to say, notions which we are in the habit of forming from the comparison with one another of individuals of the same species or genus, and this is the reason why I have said, in Def. 6, pt. 2, that by reality and perfection I understand the same thing; for we are in the habit of referring all individuals in Nature to one genus which is called the most general, that is to say, to the notion of being, which embraces absolutely all the individual objects in Nature. In so far, therefore, as we refer the individual objects in Nature to this genus and compare them one with another, and discover that some possess more being or reality than others, in so far do we call some more perfect than others; and in so far as we assign to the latter anything which, like limitation, termination, impotence, etc., involves negation, shall we call them imperfect because they do not affect our minds so strongly as those we call perfect, but not because anything which really belongs to them is wanting, or because Nature has committed an error. For nothing belongs to the nature of anything except that which follows from the necessity of the nature of the efficient cause, and whatever follows from the necessity of the nature of the efficient cause necessarily happens.

With regard to good and evil, these terms indicate nothing positive in things, considered in themselves, nor are they anything else than modes of thought, or notions which we form from the comparison of one thing with another. For one and the same thing may at the same time be both good and evil or indifferent. Music, for example, is good to a melancholy person, bad to one mourning, while to a deaf man it is neither good nor bad. But although things are so, we must retain these words. For since we desire to form for ourselves an idea of man upon which we may look as a model of human nature, it will be of service to us to retain these expressions in the sense I have mentioned. By "good," therefore, I understand in the following pages everything which we are certain is a means by which we may approach nearer and nearer to the model of human nature we set before us. By "evil," on the contrary, I understand everything which we are certain hinders us from reaching that model. Again, I shall call men more or less perfect or imperfect in so far as they approach more or less nearly to this same model. For it is to be carefully observed that when I say that an individual passes from a less to a greater perfection and *vice versa*, I do not understand that from one essence or form he is changed into another (for a horse, for instance, would be as much destroyed if it were changed into a man as if it were changed into an insect), but rather we conceive that his power of action, in so far as it is understood by his own nature, is increased or diminished. Finally, by "perfection" generally, I understand as I have said, reality, that is to say, the essence of any object in so far as it exists and acts in a certain manner, no regard being paid to its duration. For no individual thing can be said to be more perfect because for a longer time it has persevered in existence; inasmuch as the duration of things cannot be determined by their essence, the essence of things involving no fixed or determined period of existence; any object, whether it be more or less perfect, always being able to persevere in existence with the same force as that with which it commenced existence. All things, therefore, are equal in this respect.

DEFINITIONS

I. By good, I understand that which we certainly know is useful to us.

II. By evil, on the contrary, I understand that which we certainly know hinders us from possessing anything that is good.

With regard to these two definitions, see the close of the preceding preface.

III. I call individual things contingent in so far as we discover nothing whilst we attend to their essence alone, which necessarily posits their existence or which necessarily excludes it.

IV. I call these individual things possible, in so far as we are ignorant, whilst we attend to the causes from which they must be produced, whether these causes are determined to the production of these things. In Note 1, Prop. 33, pt. 1, I made no difference between possible and contingent because there was no occasion there to distinguish them accurately.

V. By contrary emotions I understand in the following pages those which, although they may be of the same kind, draw a man in different directions; such as voluptuousness and avarice, which are both a species of love, and are not contrary to one another by nature, but only by accident.

VI. What I understand by emotion felt toward a thing future, present, and past, I have explained in Notes 1 and 2, Prop. 18, pt. 3, to which the reader is referred.

Here, however, it is to be observed that it is the same with time as it is with place; for as beyond a certain limit we can form no distinct imagination of distance, that is to say, as we usually imagine all objects to be equally distant from us, and as if they were on the same plane, if their distance from us exceeds 200 feet, or if their distance from the position we occupy is greater than we can distinctly imagine — so we imagine all objects to be equally distant from the present time, and refer them as if to one moment, if the period to which their existence belongs is separated from the present by a longer interval than we can usually imagine distinctly.

VII. By end for the sake of which we do anything, I understand appetite.

VIII. By virtue and power I understand the same thing, that is to say (Prop. 7, pt. 3), virtue, in so far as it is related to man, is the essence itself or nature of the man in so far as it has the power of effecting certain things which can be understood through the laws of its nature alone.

AXIOM

There is no individual thing in Nature which is not surpassed in strength and power by some other thing, but any individual thing being given, another and a stronger is also given by which the former can be destroyed.

PROPOSITIONS

PROPOSITION I. *Nothing positive contained in a false idea is removed by the presence of the true in so far as it is true.*

Demonstration. Falsity consists in nothing but the privation of knowledge which inadequate ideas involve (Prop. 35, pt. 2), nor do they possess anything positive on account of which they are called false (Prop. 33, pt. 2); on the contrary, in so far as they are related to God, they are true (Prop. 32, pt. 2). If, therefore, anything positive contained in a false idea were removed by the presence of the true in so far as it is true, a true idea would be removed by itself, which (Prop. 4, pt. 3) is absurd. Nothing positive, therefore, etc. — Q.E.D.

Note. This proposition can be understood more clearly from Corol. 2, Prop. 16, pt. 2. For an imagination is an idea which indicates the present constitution of the human body rather than the nature of an external body, not indeed distinctly but confusedly, so that the mind is said to err. For example, when we look at the sun, we imagine his distance from us to be about 200 feet, and in this we are deceived so long as we remain in ignorance of the true distance. When this is known, the error is removed, but not the imagination, that is to say, the idea of the sun which manifests his nature in so far only as the body is affected by him; so that, although we know his true distance, we nevertheless imagine him close to us. For, as we have shown in Note, Prop. 35, pt. 2, it is not because we are ignorant of the sun's true distance that we imagine him to be so close to us, but because the mind conceives the magnitude of the sun just in so far as the body is affected by him. So when the rays of the sun falling upon a surface of water are reflected to our eyes, we imagine him to be in the water, although his true place is known to us. So with the other imaginations by which the mind is deceived; whether they indicate the natural constitution of the body or an increase or diminution in its power of action, they are not opposed to the truth, nor do they disappear with the presence of the truth. We know that, when we groundlessly fear any evil, the fear vanishes when we hear correct intelligence; but we also know, on the other hand, that, when we fear an evil which will actually come upon us, the fear vanishes when we hear false intelligence, so that the imaginations do not disappear with the presence of the truth, in so far as it is true, but because other imaginations arise which are stronger and which exclude the present existence of the objects we imagine, as we have shown in Prop. 17, pt. 2.

PROPOSITION II. *We suffer in so far as we are a part of Nature, which part cannot be conceived by itself nor without the other parts.*

Demonstration. We are said to suffer when anything occurs in us of which we are only the partial cause (Def. 2, pt. 3), that is to say (Def. 1, pt. 3), anything which cannot be deduced from the laws of our own nature alone; we suffer, therefore, in so far as we are a part of Nature, which part cannot be conceived by itself nor without the other parts. — Q.E.D.

PROPOSITION III. *The force by which man perseveres in existence is limited, and infinitely surpassed by the power of external causes.*

Demonstration. This is evident from the Axiom, pt. 4. For any man being given, there is given something else — for example, A — more powerful than he is, and A being given, there is again given something, B, more powerful than A, and so on *ad infinitum.* Hence the power of man is limited by the power of some other object, and is infinitely surpassed by the power of external causes. — Q.E.D.

PROPOSITION IV. *It is impossible that a man should not be a part of Nature, and that he should suffer no changes but those which can be understood through his own nature alone, and of which he is the adequate cause.*

Demonstration. The power by which individual things and consequently man preserve their being is the actual power of God or Nature (Corol. Prop. 24, pt. 1), not in so far as it is infinite, but in so far as it can be manifested by the actual essence of man (Prop. 7, pt. 3). The power therefore of man, in so far as it is manifested by his actual essence, is part of the infinite power of God or Nature, that is to say (Prop. 34, pt. 1), part of His essence. This was the first thing to be proved. Again, if it were possible that man could suffer no changes but those which can be understood through his nature alone, it would follow (Props. 4 and 6, pt. 3) that he could not perish, but that he would exist for ever necessarily; and this necessary existence must result from a cause whose power is either finite or infinite, that is to say, either from the power of man alone, which would be able to place at a distance from himself all other changes which could take their origin from external causes, or it must result from the infinite power of Nature by which all individual things would be so directed that man could suffer no changes but those tending to his preservation.

But the first case (by the preceding proposition whose demonstration is universal and capable of application to all individual objects) is absurd; therefore if it were possible for a man to suffer no changes but those which could be understood through his own nature alone, and consequently (as we have shown) that he should always necessarily exist, this must follow from the infinite power of God; and, therefore, (Prop. 16, pt. 1) from the necessity of the divine nature, in so far as it is considered as affected by the idea of any one man, the whole order of Nature, in so far as it is conceived under the attributes of thought and extension, would have to be deduced. From this it would follow (Prop. 21, pt. 1) that man would be infinite, which (by the first part of this demonstration) is an absurdity. It is impossible, therefore, that a man can suffer no changes but those of which he is the adequate cause. — Q.E.D.

Corollary. Hence it follows that a man is necessarily always subject to passions, and that he follows and obeys the common order of Nature, accommodating himself to it as far as the nature of things requires.

PROPOSITION V. *The force and increase of any passion and its perseverance in existence are not limited by the power by which we endeavor to persevere in existence, but by the power of an external cause compared with our own power.*

Demonstration. The essence of a passion cannot be explained by our essence alone (Defs. 1 and 2, pt. 3), that is to say (Prop. 7, pt. 3), the power of a passion cannot be limited by the power by which we endeavor to persevere in our being, but (as has been shown in Prop. 16, pt. 2) must necessarily be limited by the power of an external cause compared with our own power. — Q.E.D.

PROPOSITION VI. *The other actions or power of a man may be so far surpassed by force of some passion or emotion that the emotion may obstinately cling to him.*

Demonstration. The force and increase of any passion and its perseverance in existence are limited by the power of an external cause compared with our own power (Prop. 5, pt. 4), and therefore (Prop. 3, pt. 4) may surpass the power of man. — Q.E.D.

PROPOSITION VII. *An emotion cannot be restrained nor removed unless by an opposed and stronger emotion.*

Demonstration. An emotion, in so far as it is related to the mind, is an idea by which the mind affirms a greater or less power of existence for its body than the body possessed before (by the general definition of emotions at the end of Third Part). Whenever, therefore, the mind is agitated by any emotion, the body is at the same time affected with a modification by which its power of action is increased or diminished. Again, this modification of the body (Prop. 5, pt. 4) receives from its own cause a power to persevere in its own being, a power, therefore, which cannot be restrained nor removed unless by a bodily cause (Prop. 6, pt. 2) affecting the body with a modification contrary to the first (Prop. 5, pt. 3), and stronger than it (Ax., pt. 4). Thus the mind (Prop. 12, pt. 2) is affected by the idea of a modification stronger than the former and contrary to it, that is to say (by the general definition of the emotions), it will be affected with an emotion stronger than the former and contrary to it, and this stronger emotion will exclude the existence of the other or remove it. Thus an emotion cannot be restrained nor removed unless by an opposed and stronger emotion. — Q.E.D.

Corollary. An emotion, in so far as it is related to the mind, cannot be restrained nor removed unless by the idea of a bodily modification opposed to that which we suffer and stronger than it. For the emotion which we suffer cannot be restrained nor removed unless by an opposed and stronger emotion (Prop. 7, pt. 4); that is to say (by the geneal definition of the emotions), it cannot be removed unless by the idea of a bodily modification stronger than that which affects us, and opposed to it.

PROPOSITION VIII. *Knowledge of good or evil is nothing but an emotion of joy or sorrow in so far as we are conscious of it.*

Demonstration. We call a thing good which contributes to the preservation of our being, and we call a thing evil if it is an obstacle to the preservation of our being (Defs. 1 and 2, pt. 4), that is to say (Prop. 7, pt. 3), a thing is called by us good or evil as it increases or diminishes, helps or restrains, our power of action. In so far, therefore (Defs. of *joy* and *sorrow* in Note, Prop. 11, pt. 3), as we perceive that any object affects, us with joy or sorrow do we call it good or evil, and therefore the knowledge of good or evil is nothing but an idea of joy or sorrow which necessarily follows from the emotion itself of joy or sorrow (Prop. 22, pt. 2). But this idea is united to the emotion in the same way as the mind is united to the body (Prop. 21, pt. 2), or, in other words (as we have shown in the Note, Prop. 21, pt. 2), this idea is not actually distinguished from the emotion itself, that is to say (by the general definition of the emotions), it is not actually distinguished from the idea of the modification of the body unless in conception alone. This knowledge, therefore, of good and evil is nothing but the emotion itself of joy and sorrow in so far as we are conscious of it. — Q.E.D.

PROPOSITION IX. *If we imagine the cause of an emotion to be actually present with us, that emotion will be stronger than if we imagined the cause not to be present.*

Demonstration. The imagination is an idea by which the mind contemplates an object as present (see the definition of the imagination in Note, Prop. 17, pt. 2), an idea which nevertheless indicates the constitution of the human body rather than the nature of the external object (Corol. 2, Prop. 16, pt. 2). Imagination, therefore (by the general definition of the emotions), is an emotion in so far as it indicates the constitution of the body. But the imagination (Prop. 17, pt. 2) increases in intensity in proportion as we imagine nothing which excludes the present existence of the external object. If, therefore, we imagine the cause of an emotion to be actually present with us, that emotion will be intenser or stronger than if we imagined the cause not to be present. — Q.E.D.

Note. When I said (in Prop. 18, pt. 3) that we are affected by the image of an object in the future or the past with the same emotion with which we should be affected if the object we imagined were actually present, I was careful to warn the reader that this was true in so far only as we attend to the image alone of the object itself, for the image is of the same nature, whether we have imagined the object or not; but I have not denied that the image becomes weaker when we contemplate as present other objects which exclude the present existence of the future object. This exception I neglected to make, because I had determined to treat in this part of my work of the strength of the emotions.

Corollary. The image of a past or future object, that is to say, of an object which we contemplate in relation to the past or future to the exclusion of the present, other things being equal, is weaker than the image of a present object, and consequently the emotion toward a future or past object, other things being equal, is weaker then than the emotion toward a present object.

PROPOSITION X. *We are affected with regard to a future object which we imagine will soon be present more powerfully than if we imagine that the time at which it will exist is further removed from the present, and the memory of an object which we imagine has but just passed away also affects us more powerfully than if we imagine the object to have passed away some time ago.*

Demonstration. In so far as we imagine that an object will quickly be present or has not long since passed away, do we imagine something which excludes the presence of the object less than if we imagine that the time of its existence is at a great distance from the present, either in the future or the past (as is self-evident), and, therefore (Prop. 9, pt. 4), so far shall we be affected more strongly with regard to it. — Q.E.D.

Note. From the observations which we made upon Def. 6, pt. 4, it follows that all objects which are separated from the present time by a longer interval than our imagination has any power to determine affect us equally slightly, although we know them to be separated from one another by a large space of time.

PROPOSITION XI. *The emotion toward an object which we imagine as necessary, other things being equal, is stronger than that toward an object that is possible, contingent, or not necessary.*

Demonstration. In so far as we imagine any object to be necessary do we affirm its existence, and, on the other hand, we deny its existence in so far as we imagine it to be not necessary (Note 1, Prop. 33, pt. 1), and therefore (Prop. 9, pt. 4) the emotion toward a necessary object, other things being equal, is stronger than that which we feel toward one that is not necessary. — Q.E.D.

PROPOSITION XII. *The emotion toward an object which we know does not exist in the present, and which we imagine as possible, other things being equal, is stronger than the emotion toward a contingent object.*

Demonstration. In so far as we imagine an object as contingent, we are not affected by the image of any other object which posits the existence of the first (Def. 3, pt. 4), but, on the contrary (by hypothesis), we imagine some things which exclude its present existence. But in so far as we imagine any object in the future to be possible do we imagine some things which posit its existence (Def. 4, pt. 4), that is to say (Note 2, Prop. 18, pt. 3), things which foster hope or fear, and therefore the emotion toward a possible object is stronger, etc. — Q.E.D.

Corollary. The emotion toward an object which we know does not exist in the present, and which we imagine as contingent, is much weaker than if we imagined that the object were present to us.

Demonstration. The emotion toward an object which we imagine to exist in the present is stronger than if we imagined it as future (Corol. Prop. 9, pt. 4), and is much stronger if we imagine the future to be at a great[1] distance from the present time (Prop. 10, pt. 4). The emotion, therefore, toward an object which we imagine will not exist for a long time is so much feebler than if we imagined it as present, and nevertheless (Prop. 12, pt. 4) is stronger than if we imagined it as contingent;

---

[1] *Non multum distare*, Ed. Pr. Corrected from Dutch version. — TR.

and therefore the emotion toward a contingent object is much feebler than if we imagined the object to be present to us. — Q.E.D.

PROPOSITION XIII. *The emotion toward a contingent object which we know does not exist in the present, other things being equal, is much weaker than the emotion toward a past object.*

Demonstration. In so far as we imagine an object as contingent, we are affected with no image of any other object which posits the existence of the first (Def. 3, pt. 4). On the contrary, we imagine (by hypothesis) certain things which exclude its present existence. But in so far as we imagine it in relationship to past time are we supposed to imagine something which brings it back to the memory or which excites its image (Prop. 18, pt. 2, with the Note), and therefore so far causes us to contemplate it as present (Corol. Prop. 17, pt. 2). Therefore (Prop. 9, pt. 4), the emotion toward a contingent object which we know does not exist in the present, other things being equal, will be weaker than the emotion toward a past object. — Q.F.D.

PROPOSITION XIV. *No emotion can be restrained by the true knowledge of good and evil in so far as it is true, but only in so far as it is considered as an emotion.*

Demonstration. An emotion is an idea by which the mind affirms a greater or less power of existence for the body than it possessed before (by the general definition of the emotions); and, therefore (Prop. 1, pt. 4), this idea has nothing positive which can be removed by the presence of the truth, and, consequently, the true knowledge of good and evil, in so far as it is true, can restrain no emotion. But in so far as it is an emotion (see Prop. 8, pt. 4) will it restrain any other emotion, provided that the latter be the weaker of the two (Prop. 7, pt. 4). — Q.E.D.

PROPOSITION XV. *Desire which arises from a true knowledge of good and evil can be extinguished or restrained by many other desires which take their origin from the emotions by which we are agitated.*

Demonstration. From the true knowledge of good and evil, in so far as this (Prop. 8, pt. 4) is an emotion, necessarily arises desire (Def. 1 of the emotions, pt. 3), which is greater in proportion as the emotion from which it springs is greater (Prop. 37, pt. 3). But this desire (by hypothesis), because it springs from our understanding something truly, follows therefore in us in so far as we act (Prop. 1, pt. 3), and therefore must be understood through our essence alone (Def. 2, pt. 3), and consequently its strength and increase must be limited by human power alone (Prop. 7, pt. 3). But the desires which spring from the emotions by which we are agitated are greater as the emotions themselves are greater, and therefore their strength and increase (Prop. 5, pt. 4) must be limited by the power of external causes — a power which, if it be compared with our own, infinitely surpasses it (Prop. 3, pt. 4). The desires, therefore, which take their origin from such emotions as these may be much stronger than that which takes its origin from a true knowledge of good and evil, and the former (Prop. 7, pt. 4) may be able to restrain and extinguish the latter. — Q.E.D.

PROPOSITION XVI. *The desire which springs from a knowledge of good and evil can be easily extinguished or restrained, in so far as this knowledge is connected with the future, by the desire of things which in the present are sweet.*

Demonstration. The emotion toward an object which we imagine as future is weaker than toward that which we imagine as present (Corol. Prop. 9, pt. 4). But the desire which springs from a true knowledge of good and evil, even although the knowledge be of objects which are good at the present time, may be extinguished or restrained by any casual desire (Prop. 15, pt. 4, the demonstration of this proposition being universal), and therefore the desire which springs from a knowledge of good and evil, in so far as this knowledge is connected with the future, can be easily restrained or extinguished. — Q.E.D.

PROPOSITION XVII. *The desire which springs from a true knowledge of good and evil can be still more easily restrained, in so far as this*

knowledge is connected with objects which are contingent, by the
desire of objects which are present.

Demonstration. This proposition is demonstrated in the same way
as the preceding proposition from Corol. Prop. 12, pt. 4.

Note. In these propositions I consider that I have explained why
men are more strongly influenced by an opinion than by true reason,
and why the true knowledge of good and evil causes disturbance in
the mind, and often gives way to every kind of lust, whence the saying
of the poet, *"Video meliora proboque, deteriora sequor."*[2] The same
thought appears to have been in the mind of the Preacher when he
said, "He that increaseth knowledge increaseth sorrow."[3] I say these
things not because I would be understood to conclude, therefore, that
it is better to be ignorant than to be wise, or that the wise man in
governing his passions is nothing better than the fool, but I say them
because it is necessary for us to know both the strength and weakness
of our nature, so that we may determine what reason can do and
what it cannot do in governing our emotions. This, moreover, let it
be remembered, is the Part in which I meant to treat of human weakness alone, all consideration of the power of reason over the passions
being reserved for a future portion of the book.

PROPOSITION XVIII. *The desire which springs from joy, other things*
being equal, is stronger than that which springs from sorrow.

Demonstration. Desire is the very essence of man (Def. 1 of the
emotions, pt. 3), that is to say (Prop. 7, pt. 3), the effort by which a
man strives to persevere in his being. The desire, therefore, which
springs from joy, by that very emotion of joy (by the definition of
joy in Note, Prop. 11, pt. 3) is assisted or increased, while that which
springs from sorrow, by that very emotion of sorrow (by the same
Note) is lessened or restrained, and so the force of the desire which
springs from joy must be limited by human power, together with the

[2] Ovid, *Metamorphoses*, Bk. viii (*Jason and Medea*), 1. 20:

> I see a better course, and I approve;
> Yet follow I the worse. — ED.

[3] Ecclesiastes 1: 18. — ED.

power of an external cause, while that which springs from sorrow must be limited by human power alone. The latter is, therefore, weaker than the former. — Q.E.D.

Note. I have thus briefly explained the causes of human impotence and want of stability, and why men do not obey the dictates of reason. It remains for me now to show what it is which reason prescribes to us, which emotions agree with the rules of human reason, and which, on the contrary, are opposed to these rules. Before, however, I begin to demonstrate these things by our full geometrical method, I should like briefly to set forth here these dictates of reason in order that what I have in my mind about them may be easily comprehended by all. Since reason demands nothing which is opposed to nature, it demands, therefore, that every person should love himself, should seek his own profit — what is truly profitable to him — should desire everything that really leads man to greater perfection, and absolutely that every one should endeavor, as far as in him lies, to preserve his own being. This is all true as necessarily as that the whole is greater than its part (Prop. 6, pt. 3). Again, since virtue (Def. 8, pt. 4) means nothing but acting according to the laws of our own nature, and since no one endeavors to preserve his being (Prop. 7, pt. 3) except in accordance with the laws of his own nature, it follows: *First*, that the foundation of virtue is that endeavor itself to preserve our own being, and that happiness consists in this — that a man can preserve his own being. *Secondly*, it follows that virtue is to be desired for its own sake, nor is there anything more excellent or more useful to us than virtue, for the sake of which virtue ought to be desired. *Thirdly*, it follows that all persons who kill themselves are impotent in mind, and have been thoroughly overcome by external causes opposed to their nature. Again, from Post. 4, pt. 2, it follows that we can never free ourselves from the need of something outside us for the preservation of our being, and that we can never live in such a manner as to have no intercourse with objects which are outside us. Indeed, so far as the mind is concerned, our intellect would be less perfect if the mind were alone and understood nothing but itself. There are many things, therefore, outside us which are useful to us, and which, therefore, are to be sought. Of all these, none more excellent can be discovered than those which exactly agree with our nature. If, for example, two individuals of exactly the same nature are joined together, they make up a single individual, doubly stronger than each alone. Nothing, therefore, is more useful to man than man. Men can desire, I say, nothing more excellent for the preservation of their being than that all should so agree at every point that the minds and bodies of all should form, as it were, one mind and one body; that all should together endeavor as much as possible to preserve their being, and that all should together seek the common good of all. From this it follows that men who are governed by reason, that is to say, men who, under the guidance of reason, seek their own profit, desire nothing for themselves which they do not desire for other men, and that, therefore, they are just, faithful, and honorable.

These are those dictates of reason which I purposed briefly to set forth before commencing their demonstration by a fuller method, in order that, if possible, I might win the attention of those who believe that this principle — that every one is bound to seek his own profit — is the foundation of impiety, and not of virtue and piety. Having now briefly shown that this belief of theirs is the contrary of the truth, I proceed, by the same method as that which we have hitherto pursued, to demonstrate what I have said.

PROPOSITION XIX. *According to the laws of his own nature each person necessarily desires that which he considers to be good, and avoids that which he considers to be evil.*

Demonstration. The knowledge of good and evil (Prop. 8, pt. 4) is the emotion itself of joy or sorrow, in so far as we are conscious of it, and, therefore (Prop. 28, pt. 3), each person necessarily desires that which he considers to be good, and avoids that which he considers to be evil. But this desire is nothing but the essence itself or nature of man (Def. of appetite in Note, Prop. 9, pt. 3, and Def. 1 of the emotions, pt. 3). Therefore, according to the laws of his own nature alone, he necessarily desires or avoids, etc. — Q.E.D.

PROPOSITION XX. *The more each person strives and is able to seek his own profit, that is to say, to preserve his being, the more virtue does he possess; on the other hand, in so far as each person neglects his own profit, that is to say, neglects to preserve his own being, is he impotent.*

Demonstration. Virtue is human power itself, which is limited by the essence alone of man (Def. 8, pt. 4), that is to say (Prop. 7, pt. 3), which is limited by the effort alone by which man endeavors to per-severe in his being. The more, therefore, each person strives and is able to preserve his being, the more virtue does he possess, and, con-sequently (Props. 4 and 6, pt. 3), in proportion as he neglects to preserve his being is he impotent. — Q.E.D.

Note. No one, therefore, unless defeated by external causes and those which are contrary to his nature, neglects to seek his own profit or preserve his being. No one, I say, refuses food or kills himself from a necessity of his nature, but only when forced by external causes. The compulsion may be exercised in many ways. A man kills himself under compulsion by another when that other turns the right hand, with which the man had by chance laid hold of a sword and compels him to direct the sword against his own heart; or the command of a tyrant may compel a man, as it did Seneca, to open his own veins, that is to say, he may desire to avoid a greater evil by a less. External and hidden causes also may so dispose his imagination and may so affect his body as to cause it to put on another nature contrary to that which it had at first, and one whose idea cannot exist in the mind (Prop. 10, pt. 3); but a very little reflection will show that it is as impossible that a man, from the necessity of his nature, should endeavor not to exist, or to be changed into some other form, as it is that some-thing should be begotten from nothing.

PROPOSITION XXI. *No one can desire to be happy, to act well and live well, who does not at the same time desire to be, to act, and to live, that is to say, actually to exist.*

Demonstration. The demonstration of this proposition, or rather the proposition itself. is self-evident, and is also evident from the definition of desire. For desire (Def. 1 of the emotions, pt. 3), whether it be desire of living or acting happily or well, is the very essence of man, that is to say (Prop. 7, pt. 3), the endeavor by which every one

strives to preserve his own being. No one, therefore, can desire, etc.
— Q.E.D.

PROPOSITION XXII. *No virtue can be conceived prior to this (the endeavor, namely, after self-preservation).*

Demonstration. The endeavor after self-preservation is the essence itself of a thing (Prop. 7, pt. 3). If, therefore, any virtue could be conceived prior to this of self-preservation, the essence itself of the thing would be conceived (Def. 8, pt. 4) as prior to itself, which (as is self-evident) is absurd. No virtue, therefore, etc. — Q.E.D.

Corollary. The endeavor after self-preservation is the primary and only foundation of virtue. For prior to this principle no other can be conceived (Prop. 22, pt. 4), and without it (Prop. 21, pt. 4) no virtue can be conceived.

PROPOSITION XXIII. *A man cannot be absolutely said to act in conformity with virtue, in so far as he is determined to any action because he has inadequate ideas, but only in so far as he is determined because he understands.*

Demonstration. In so far as a man is determined to action because he has inadequate ideas (Prop. 1, pt. 3), he is passive, that is to say (Defs. 1 and 2, pt. 3), he does something which through his essence alone cannot be perceived, that is to say (Def. 8, pt. 4), which does not follow from his virtue. But in so far as he is determined to any action because he understands, he acts (Prop. 1, pt. 3), that is to say (Def. 2, pt. 3), he does something which is perceived through his essence alone, or (Def. 8, pt. 4) which adequately follows from his virtue. — Q.E.D.

PROPOSITION XXIV. *To act absolutely in conformity with virtue is ,in us, nothing but acting, living, and preserving our being (these three things have the same meaning) as reason directs, from the ground of seeking our own profit.*

Demonstration. To act absolutely in conformity with virtue is nothing (Def. 8, pt. 4) but acting according to the laws of our own proper nature. But only in so far as we understand do we act (Prop. 3, pt. 3). Therefore, to act in conformity with virtue is nothing but acting, living, and preserving our being as reason directs, and doing so (Corol. Prop. 22, pt. 4) from the ground of seeking our own profit. — Q.E.D.

PROPOSITION XXV. *No one endeavors to preserve his own being for the sake of another object.*

Demonstration. The effort by which any object strives to persevere in its own being is limited solely by the essence of the object itself (Prop. 7, pt. 3), and from this given essence alone it necessarily follows — and not from the essence of any other object — (Prop. 6, pt. 3) that each object strives to preserve its being. This proposition is also evident from Corol. Prop. 22, pt. 4. For if a man endeavored to preserve his being for the sake of any other object, this object would then become the primary foundation of virtue (as is self-evident), which (by the Corol. just quoted) is an absurdity. No one, therefore, endeavors to preserve his being, etc. — Q.E.D.

PROPOSITION XXVI. *All efforts which we make through reason are nothing but efforts to understand, and the mind, in so far as it uses reason, adjudges nothing as profitable to itself except that which conduces to understanding.*

Demonstration. The endeavour after self-preservation is nothing but the essence of the object itself (Prop. 7, pt. 3), which, in so far as it exists, is conceived to have power to persevere in existence (Prop. 6, pt. 3), and to do those things which necessarily follow from its given nature. (See the definition of desire in Note, Prop. 9, pt. 3.) But the essence of reason is nothing but our mind in so far as it clearly and distinctly understands. (See definition of clear and distinct understanding in Note 2, Prop. 40, pt. 2.) Therefore (Prop. 40, pt. 2), all efforts which we make through reason are nothing else than efforts to understand. Again, since this effort of the mind, by which the mind, in so far as it reasons, endeavors to preserve its being, is nothing but the effort to understand (by the first part of this demonstration), it follows (Corol. Prop. 22, pt. 4), that this effort to understand is the primary and sole foundation of virtue, and that (Prop. 25, pt. 4) we do not endeavor to understand things for the sake of any end, but, on the contrary, the mind, in so far as it reasons, can conceive nothing as being good for itself except that which conduces to understanding (Def. 1, pt. 4). — Q.E.D.

PROPOSITION XXVII. *We do not know that anything is certainly good or evil except that which actually conduces to understanding, or which can prevent us from understanding.*

Demonstration. The mind, in so far as it reasons, desires nothing but to understand, nor does it adjudge anything to be profitable to itself except what conduces to understanding (Prop. 26, pt. 4). But the mind (Props. 41 and 43, pt. 2, with the Note) possesses no certitude unless in so far as it possesses adequate ideas, or (which by Note, Prop. 40, pt. 2, is the same thing) in so far as it reasons. We do not know, therefore, that anything is certainly good, except that which actually conduces to understanding, and, on the other hand, we do not know that anything is evil except that which can hinder us from understanding. — Q.E.D.

PROPOSITION XXVIII. *The highest good of the mind is the knowl dge of God, and the highest virtue of the mind is to know God.*

Demonstration. The highest thing which the mind can understand is God, that is to say (Def. 6, pt. 1), Being absolutely infinite, and without whom (Prop. 15, pt. 1) nothing can be nor can be conceived, and therefore (Props. 26 and 27, pt. 4) that which is chiefly profitable to the mind, or (Def. 1, pt. 4) which is the highest good of the mind, is the knowledge of God. Again, the mind acts only in so far as it understands (Props. 1 and 3, pt. 3), and only in so far (Prop. 23, pt. 4) can it be absolutely said to act in conformity with virtue. To understand, therefore, is the absolute virtue of the mind. But the highest thing which the mind can understand is God (as we have already demonstrated), and therefore the highest virtue of the mind is to understand or know God. — Q.E.D.

PROPOSITION XXIX. *No individual object whose nature is altogether different from our own can either help or restrain our power of acting, and absolutely nothing can be to us either good or evil unless it possesses something in common with ourselves.*

Demonstration. The power of an individual object, and consequently (Corol. Prop. 10, pt. 2) that of man, by which he exists and acts, is determined only by another individual object (Prop. 28, pt. 1) whose nature (Prop. 6, pt. 2) must be understood through the same attribute as that by means of which human nature is conceived. Our power of acting, therefore, in whatever way it may be conceived, can be determined, and consequently helped or restrained, by the power of another individual object possessing something in common with us, and cannot be thus determined by the power of an object whose nature is altogether different from ours. Inasmuch, therefore, as a thing is called good or evil because it is the cause of joy or sorrow (Prop. 8, pt. 4), that is to say (Note, Prop. 11, pt. 3), because it increases or diminishes, helps or restrains, our power of action; an object whose nature is altogether different from our own cannot be either good or evil to us. — Q.E.D.

PROPOSITION XXX. *Nothing can be evil through that which it possesses in common with our nature, but in so far as a thing is evil to us is it contrary to us.*

Demonstration. We call that thing evil which is the cause of sorrow (Prop. 8, pt. 4), that is to say (by the definition of sorrow in Note, Prop. 11, pt. 3), which lessens or restrains our power of action. If, therefore, any object were evil to us through that which it possesses in common with us, it could lessen or restrain what it possesses in common with us, which (Prop. 4, pt. 3) is absurd. Nothing, therefore, through that which it possesses in common with us can be evil to us, but, on the contrary, in so far as it is evil, that is to say (as we have already shown), in so far as it can lessen or restrain our power of action (Prop. 5, pt. 3), is it contrary to us. — Q.E.D.

PROPOSITION XXXI. *In so far as an object agrees with our nature is it necessarily good.*

Demonstration. In so far as any object agrees with our nature (Prop. 30, pt. 4) it cannot be evil. It must, therefore, necessarily be either good or indifferent. If it be supposed as indifferent, that is to say, as neither good nor evil, nothing (Ax. 3, pt. 1, and Def. 1, pt. 4) will follow from its nature which conduces to the preservation of our nature, that is to say (by hypothesis), which conduces to its own preservation. But this (Prop. 6, pt. 3) is absurd, and, therefore, in so far as the object agrees with our nature, it will necessarily be good. — Q.E.D.

Corollary. Hence it follows that the more an object agrees with our own nature, the more profitable it is to us, that is to say, the better it is for us, and, conversely, the more profitable an object is to us, the more does it agree with our own nature. For in so far as it does not agree with our nature it will necessarily be either diverse from our nature or contrary to it. If diverse, it can (Prop. 29, pt. 4) be neither good nor evil, but if contrary, it will therefore be contrary also to that which agrees with our own nature, that is to say (Prop. 31, pt. 4), contrary to the good, or, in other words, it will be evil. Nothing, therefore, can be good except in so far as it agrees with our nature, and, therefore, the more an object agrees with our nature, the more profitable it will be, and *vice versa.* — Q.E.D.

PROPOSITION XXXII. *In so far as men are subject to passions, they cannot be said to agree in nature.*

Demonstration. Things which are said to agree in nature are understood to agree in power (Prop. 7, pt. 3), and not in impotence or negation, and consequently (Note, Prop. 3, pt. 3), not in passion, and therefore men, in so far as they are subject to passion, cannot be said to agree in nature. — Q.E.D.

Note. This proposition is self-evident, for he who says that black and white agree solely in the fact that neither of them is red absolutely affirms that black and white agree in nothing. So also if we say that a stone and a man agree solely in this that they are both finite or impotent or do not exist from the necessity of their nature, or are both to an indefinite extent dominated by external causes, we affirm that a stone and a man agree in nothing, for things which agree in negation only or in that which they have not, really agree in nothing.

PROPOSITION XXXIII. *Men may differ in nature from one another in so far as they are agitated by emotions which are passions, and in so far also as one and the same man is agitated by passions is he changeable and inconstant.*

Demonstration. The nature or essence of the emotions cannot be explained through our essence or nature alone (Defs. 1 and 2, pt. 3), but must be determined by the power, that is to say (Prop. 7, pt. 3), the nature of external causes compared with our own nature. Hence it follows that there are as many kinds of each emotion as there are kinds of objects by which we are affected (Prop. 56, pt. 3); that men are affected in different ways by one and the same object (Prop. 51, pt. 3), and so far differ in nature; and, finally, that one and the same man (Prop. 51, pt. 3) is affected in different ways towards the same object, and so far is changeable and inconstant. — Q.E.D.

PROPOSITION XXXIV. *In so far as men are agitated by emotions which are passions can they be contrary to one another.*

Demonstration. A man, Peter, for example, may be a cause of sorrow to Paul because he possesses something resembling that which Paul hates (Prop. 16, pt. 3), or because he alone possesses something which Paul himself also loves (Prop. 32, pt. 3, with its Note), or for other reasons (the chief of which are mentioned in Note, Prop. 55, pt. 3). Hence it will come to pass (Def. 7 of the emotions) that Paul hates Peter, and, consequently, it will easily happen (Prop. 40, pt. 3, with its Note) that Peter in turn hates Paul, and that they endeavor (Prop. 39, pt. 3) to injure one another, or, in other words (Prop. 30, pt. 4), that they are contrary to one another. But the emotion of sorrow is always a passion (Prop. 59, pt. 3), and therefore men, in so far as they are agitated by emotions which are passions, can be contrary to one another. — Q.E.D.

Note. I have said that Paul hates Peter because he imagines that Peter possesses something which he himself loves, from which at first sight it appears to follow that, because they both love the same thing and, consequently, agree in nature with one another, they are, therefore, injurious to one another; and if this be true, Props. 30 and 31, pt. 4, would be false. But if we will examine the matter impartially, we shall see that all these things are quite in accord. For Peter and Paul are not injurious to one another in so far as they agree in nature, that is to say, in so far as they both love the same object, but in so far as they differ from one another. For in so far as they both love the same object is the love of each strengthened (Prop. 31, pt. 3), that is to say (Def. 6 of the emotions), so far is the joy of both increased. It is far from true, therefore, that in so far as they love the same object and agree in nature they are injurious to one another. They are injurious to one another, on the contrary, as I have said, solely because they are supposed to differ in nature. For we suppose Peter to have an idea of a beloved object which he now possesses, and Paul, on the other hand, to have an idea of a beloved object which he has lost. The former, therefore, is affected with joy, and the latter, on the contrary, with sorrow, and so far they are contrary to one another. In this manner we can easily show that the other causes of hatred depend solely on the fact that men differ by nature and not on anything in which they agree.

PROPOSITION XXXV. *So far as men live in conformity with the guidance of reason, in so far only do they always necessarily agree in nature.*

Demonstration. In so far as men are agitated by emotions which are passions can they differ in nature (Prop. 33, pt. 4) and be contrary to one another (Prop. 34, pt. 4). But men are said to act only in so far as they live according to the guidance of reason (Prop. 3, pt. 3), and, therefore, whatever follows from human nature, in so far as it is determined by reason (Def. 2, pt. 3), must be understood through human nature alone as through its proximate cause. But because everyone, according to the laws of his own nature, desires that which he adjudges to be good, and endeavors to remove that which he adjudges to be evil (Prop. 19, pt. 4), and because that which from the dictates of reason we judge to be good or evil is necessarily good or evil (Prop. 41, pt. 2), it follows that men, only in so far as they live according to the guidance of reason, necessarily do those things which are good to human nature, and consequently to each man, that is to say (Corol. Prop. 31, pt. 4), which agree with the nature of each man, and therefore also men necessarily always agree with one another in so far as they live according to the guidance of reason. — Q.E.D.

Corollary 1. There is no single thing in Nature which is more profitable to man than a man who lives according to the guidance of reason. For that is most profitable to man which most agrees with his own nature (Corol. Prop. 31, pt. 4), that is to say, man (as is self-evident). But a man acts absolutely from the laws of his own nature when he lives according to the guidance of reason (Def. 2, pt. 3), and so far only does he always necessarily agree with the nature of another man (Prop. 35, pt. 4); therefore there is no single thing more profitable to a man than a man, etc. — Q.E.D.

Corollary 2. When each man seeks most that which is profitable to himself, then are men most profitable to one another; for the more each man seeks his own profit and endeavors to preserve himself, the more virtue does he possess (Prop. 20, pt. 4), or, in other words (Def. 8, pt. 4), the more power does he possess to act according to the laws of his own nature, that is to say (Prop. 3, pt. 3), to live according to the guidance of reason. But men most agree in nature when they live according to the guidance of reason (Prop. 35, pt. 4), therefore (by the previous Corol.) men will be most profitable to one another when each man seeks most what is profitable to himself. — Q.E.D.

Note. To what we have just demonstrated daily experience itself testifies by so many and such striking proofs that it is in almost everybody's mouth that man is a god to man. It is very seldom indeed that men live according to the guidance of reason; on the contrary, it so happens that they are generally envious and injurious to one another. But, nevertheless, they are scarcely ever able to lead a solitary life, so that to most men the definition of man that he is a social animal entirely commends itself, and indeed it is the case that far more advantages than disadvantages arise from the common society of men. Let satirists therefore scoff at human affairs as much as they please, let theologians denounce them, and let the melancholy praise as much as they can a life rude and without refinement, despising men and admiring the brutes, men will nevertheless find out that by mutual help they can much more easily procure the things they need, and that it is only by their united strength they can avoid the dangers which everywhere threaten them, to say nothing about its being far nobler and worthier of our knowledge to meditate upon the doings of men than upon those of brutes. But more of this elsewhere.

PROPOSITION XXXVI. *The highest good of those who follow after virtue is common to all, and all may equally enjoy it.*

Demonstration. To act in conformity with virtue is to act according to the guidance of reason (Prop. 24, pt. 4), and every effort which we make through reason is an effort to understand (Prop. 26, pt. 4), and therefore (Prop. 28, pt. 4) the highest good of those who follow after virtue is to know God, that is to say (Prop. 47, pt. 2, with its Note), it is a good which is common to all men, and can be equally possessed by all men in so far as they are of the same nature. — Q.E.D.

Note. If anybody asks, What if the highest good of those who follow after virtue were not common to all? — would it not thence follow (as above, see Prop. 34, pt. 4) that men who live according to the guidance of reason, that is to say (Prop. 35, pt. 4), men in so far as they agree in nature, would be contrary to one another? We reply that it arises from no accident, but from the nature itself of reason, that the highest good of man is common to all, inasmuch as it is deduced from the human essence itself, in so far as it is determined by reason, and also because man could not be nor be conceived if he had not the power of rejoicing in this highest good. For it pertains (Prop. 47, pt. 2) to the essence of the human mind to have an adequate knowledge of the eternal and infinite essence of God.

PROPOSITION XXXVII. *The good which every one who follows after virtue seeks for himself he will desire for other men; and his desire on their behalf will be greater in proportion as he has a greater knowledge of God.*

Demonstration. Men are most profitable to man in so far as they live according to the guidance of reason (Corol. 1, Prop. 35, pt. 4), and therefore (Prop. 19, pt. 4), according to the guidance of reason, we necessarily endeavor to cause men to live according to the guidance of reason. But the good which each person seeks who lives according to the dictates of reason, that is to say (Prop. 24, pt. 4), who follows after virtue, is to understand (Prop. 26, pt. 4), and therefore the good which each person seeks who follows after virtue he will also desire for other men. Again, desire, in so far as it is related to the mind, is the essence itself of the mind (Def. 1 of the emotions). But the essence of the mind consists in knowledge (Prop. 11, pt. 2), which involves the knowledge of God (Prop. 47, pt. 2), and without this knowledge the essence of the mind can neither be nor be conceived (Prop. 15, pt. 1); and therefore the greater the knowledge of God which the essence of the mind involves, the greater will be the desire with which he who follows after virtue will desire for another the good which he seeks for himself. — Q.E.D.

Another Demonstration. The good which a man seeks for himself and which he loves he will love more unchangeably if he sees that others love it (Prop. 31, pt. 3), and therefore (Corol. Prop. 31, pt. 3) he will endeavor to make others love it; and because this good (Prop. 36, pt. 4) is common to all and all can rejoice in it, he will endeavor (by the same reasoning) to cause all to rejoice in it, and (Prop. 37, pt. 3) he will do so the more, the more he rejoices in this good himself. — Q.E.D.

Note 1. He who strives from an emotion alone to make others love what he himself loves, and to make others live according to his way of thinking, acts from mere impulse, and is therefore hateful, especially to those who have other tastes, and who therefore also desire, and by the same impulse strive to make others live according to their way of thinking.

Again, since the highest good which men seek from an emotion is often such that only one person can possess it, it follows that persons who love are not consistent with themselves, and, whilst they delight to recount the praises of the beloved object, fear lest they should be believed. But he who endeavors to lead others by reason does not act from impulse, but with humaneness and kindness, and is always consistent with himself.

Everything which we desire and do, of which we are the cause in so far as we possess an idea of God, or in so far as we know God, I refer to "religion." The desire of doing well which is born in us, because we live according to the guidance of reason, I call "piety." The desire to join others in friendship to himself, with which a man living according to the guidance of reason is possessed, I call "honor." I call that thing "honorable" which men who live according to the guidance of reason praise; and that thing, on the contrary, I call "base" which sets itself against the formation of friendship. Moreover, I have also shown what are the foundations of a State.

The difference also between true virtue and impotence may, from what has already been said, be easily seen to be this — that true virtue consists in living according to the guidance of reason alone, and that impotence therefore consists in this alone that a man allows himself to be led by things which are outside himself, and by them to be determined to such actions as the common constitution of external things demands, and not to such as his own nature considered in itself alone demands. These are the things which I promised in Note, Prop. 18, pt. 4, I would demonstrate. From them we see that the law against killing animals is based upon an empty superstition and womanish tenderness rather than upon sound reason. A proper regard, indeed, to one's own profit teaches us to unite in friendship with men, and not with brutes, nor with things whose nature is different from human nature. It teaches us, too, that the same right which they have over us we have over them. Indeed, since the right of any person is limited by his virtue or power, men possess a far greater right over brutes than brutes possess over men. I by no means deny that brutes feel, but I do deny that, on this account, it is unlawful for us to consult our own profit by using them for our own pleasure and treating them as is most convenient for us, inasmuch as they do not agree in nature with us, and their feelings are different from our emotions (Note, Prop. 57, pt. 3).

It now remains that I should explain what are justice, injustice, crime, and, finally, merit. With regard to these, see the following note.

Note 2. In the Appendix to the First Part I promised I would explain what are praise and blame, merit and crime, justice and injustice. I have already shown what is the meaning of praise and blame in Note, Prop. 29, pt. 3, and this will be a fitting place for the explanation of the rest. A few words must, however, first be said about the natural and civil state of man.

It is by the highest right of Nature that each person exists, and consequently it is by the highest right of Nature that each person does those things which follow from the necessity of his nature; and therefore it is by the highest right of Nature that each person judges what is good and what is evil, consults his own advantage as he thinks best (Props. 19 and 20, pt. 4), avenges himself (Corol. 2, Prop. 40, pt. 3), and endeavors to preserve what he loves and to destroy what he hates (Prop. 28, pt. 3). If men lived according to the guidance of reason, everyone would enjoy this right without injuring any one else (Corol. 1, Prop. 35, pt. 4). But because men are subject to emotions (Corol. Prop. 4, pt. 4), which far surpass human power or virtue (Prop. 6, pt. 4), they are often drawn in different directions (Prop. 33, pt. 4), and are contrary to one another (Prop. 34, pt. 4), although they need one another's help (Note, Prop. 35, pt. 4).

In order, then, that men may be able to live in harmony and be a help to one another, it is necessary for them to cede their natural right, and beget confidence one in the other that they will do nothing by which one can injure the other. In what manner this can be done, so that men who are necessarily subject to emotions (Corol. Prop. 4, pt. 4), and are uncertain and changeable (Prop. 33, pt. 4), can beget confidence one in the other and have faith in one another, is evident from Prop. 7, pt. 4, and Prop. 39, pt. 3. It is there shown that no emotion can be restrained unless by a stronger and contrary emotion, and that every one abstains from doing an injury through fear of a greater injury. By this law, therefore, can society be strengthened, if only it claims for itself the right which every individual possesses of avenging himself and deciding what is good and what is evil, and provided, therefore, that it possess the power of prescribing a common rule of life, of promulgating laws and supporting them, not by reason, which cannot restrain the emotions (Note, Prop. 17, pt. 4), but by penalties.

This society, firmly established by law and with a power of self-preservation, is called a "State," and those who are protected by its right are called "citizens." We can now easily see that in the natural state there is nothing which by universal consent is good or evil, since everyone in a natural state consults only his own profit, deciding according to his own way of thinking what is good and what is evil with reference only to his own profit, and is not bound by any law to obey anyone but himself. Hence in a natural state sin cannot be conceived, but only in a civil state where it is decided by universal consent what is good and what is evil, and where everyone is bound to obey the State. "Sin," therefore, is nothing but disobedience, which is punished by the law of the State alone; obedience, on the other hand, being regarded as a *merit* in a citizen, because on account of it he is considered worthy to enjoy the privileges of the State. Again, in a natural state no one by common consent is the owner of anything, nor is there anything in Nature which can be said to be the rightful property of this and not of that man, but all things belong to all, so that in a natural state it is impossible to conceive a desire of rendering to each man his own or taking from another that which is his; that is to say, in a natural state there is nothing which can be called just or unjust, but only in a civil state, in which it is decided by universal consent what is one person's and what is another's. Justice and injustice, therefore, sin and merit, are external notions, and not attributes, which manifest the nature of the mind. But enough of these matters.

PROPOSITION XXXVIII. *That which so disposes the human body that it can be affected in many ways, or which renders it capable of affecting external bodies in many ways, is profitable to man, and is more profitable in proportion as by its means the body becomes better fitted to be affected in many ways and to affect other bodies; on the other hand, that thing is injurious which renders the body less fitted to affect or be affected.*

Demonstration. In proportion as the body is rendered more fitted for this is the mind rendered more capable of perception (Prop. 14, pt. 2), and, therefore, whatever disposes the body in this way and renders it fitted for this is necessarily good or profitable (Props. 26

and 27, pt. 4), and is more profitable in proportion to its power of rendering the body more fitted for this, while, on the contrary (by Prop. 14, pt. 2, conversely, and Props. 26 and 27, pt. 4), it is injurious if it renders the body less fitted for this. — Q.E.D.

PROPOSITION XXXIX. *Whatever is effective to preserve the proportion of motion and rest which the parts of the human body bear to each other is good, and, on the contrary, that is evil which causes the parts of the human body to h̴ e a different proportion of motion and rest to each other.*

Demonstration. The human body needs for its preservation very many other bodies (Post. 4, pt. 2). But what constitutes the form of the human body is this that its parts communicate their motions to one another in a certain fixed proportion (Def. preceding Lem. 4, following Prop. 13, pt. 2). Whatever, therefore, is effective to preserve the proportion of motion and rest which the parts of the human body bear to each other preserves the form of the human body, and, consequently (Posts. 3 and 6, pt. 2), is effective to enable the body to be affected in many ways, and to affect external bodies in many ways, and, therefore (Prop. 38, pt. 4), is good. Again, whatever causes the parts of the human body to get a different proportion of motion and rest (by the definition just quoted) causes the human body to assume another form, that is to say (as is self-evident, and as we observed at the end of the preface to this part), causes the human body to be destroyed, rendering it consequently incapable of being affected in many ways, and is, therefore (Prop. 38, pt. 4), bad. — Q.E.D.

Note. In what degree these things may injure or profit the mind will be explained in the Fifth Part. Here I observe merely that I understand the body to die when its parts are so disposed as to acquire a different proportion of motion and rest to each other. For I dare not deny that the human body, though the circulation of the blood and the other things by means of which it is thought to live be preserved, may, nevertheless, be changed into another nature altogether different from its own. No reason compels me to affirm that the body never dies unless it is changed into a corpse. Experience, indeed, seems to teach the contrary. It happens sometimes that a man undergoes such changes that he cannot very well be said to be the same man, as was the case with a certain Spanish poet of whom I have heard, who was seized with an illness and, although he recovered, remained, nevertheless, so oblivious of his past life that he did not believe the tales and tragedies he had composed were his own, and he might, indeed, have been taken for a grown-up child if he had also forgotten his native tongue. But if this seems incredible, what shall we say of children? The man of mature years believes the nature of children to be so different from his own that it would be impossible to persuade him he had ever been a child if he did not conjecture regarding himself from what he sees of others. But in order to avoid giving to the superstitious matter for new questions, I prefer to go no further in the discussion of these matters.

PROPOSITION XL. *Whatever conduces to the universal fellowship of men, that is to say, whatever causes men to live in harmony with one another, is profitable, and, on the contrary, whatever brings discord into the State is evil.*

Demonstration. For whatever causes men to live in harmony with one another causes them to live according to the guidance of reason (Prop. 35, pt. 4), and, therefore (Props. 26 and 27, pt. 4), is good, and (by the same reasoning) those things are evil which excite discord. — Q.E.D.

PROPOSITION XLI. *Joy is not directly evil but good; sorrow, on the other hand, is directly evil.*

Demonstration. Joy (Prop. 11, pt. 3, with its Note) is an emotion by which the body's power of action is increased or assisted. Sorrow, on the other hand, is an emotion by which the body's power of action is lessened or restrained, and, therefore (Prop. 38, pt. 4), joy is directly good. — Q.E.D.

PROPOSITION XLII. *Cheerfulness can never be excessive, but is always good; melancholy, on the contrary, is always evil.*

Demonstration. Cheerfulness (see its definition in Note, Prop. 11, pt. 3) is joy which, in so far as it is related to the body, consists in this that all the parts of the body are equally affected, that is to say (Prop. 11, pt. 3), the body's power of action is increased or assisted, so that all the parts acquire the same proportion of motion and rest to each other. Cheerfulness, therefore (Prop. 39, pt. 4), is always good and can never be excessive. But melancholy (see its definition in Note, Prop. 11, pt. 3) is sorrow, which, in so far as it is related to the body, consists in this that the body's power of action is absolutely lessened or restrained, and melancholy, therefore (Prop. 38, pt. 4), is always evil. — Q.E.D.

PROPOSITION XLIII. *Pleasurable excitement may be excessive and an evil, and pain may be good in so far as pleasurable excitement or joy is evil.*

Demonstration. Pleasurable excitement is joy which, in so far as it is related to the body, consists in this that one or some of the parts of the body are affected more than others (see Def. in Note, Prop. 11, pt. 3). The power of this emotion may, therefore, be so great as to overcome the other actions of the body (Prop. 6, pt. 4); it may cling obstinately to the body; it may impede the body in such a manner as to render it less capable of being affected in many ways, and therefore (Prop. 38, pt. 4) may be evil. Again, pain, which, on the contrary, is sorrow, considered in itself alone cannot be good (Prop. 41, pt. 4). But because its power and increase is limited by the power of an external cause compared with our own power (Prop. 5, pt. 4), we can therefore conceive infinite degrees of strength of this emotion, and infinite kinds of it (Prop. 3, pt. 4), and we can therefore conceive it to be such that it can restrain an excess of pleasurable excitement, and so far (by the first part of this proposition) preventing the body from becoming less capable. So far, therefore, will pain be good. — Q.E.D.

PROPOSITION XLIV. *Love and desire may be excessive.*

Demonstration. Love is joy (Def. 6 of the emotions) with the accompanying idea of an external cause. Pleasurable excitement, therefore

(Note, Prop. 11, pt. 3), with the accompanying idea of an external cause, is love, and therefore love (Prop. 43, pt. 4) may be excessive. Again, desire is greater as the emotion from which it springs is greater (Prop. 37, pt. 3). Inasmuch, therefore, as an emotion (Prop. 6, pt. 4) may overpower the other actions of a man, so also the desire which springs from this emotion may also overpower the other desires, and may therefore exist in the same excess which we have shown (in the preceding proposition) that pleasurable excitement possesses. — Q.E.D.

Note. Cheerfulness, which I have affirmed to be good, is more easily imagined than observed; for the emotions by which we are daily agitated are generally related to some part of the body which is affected more than the others, and therefore it is that the emotions exist for the most part in excess, and so hold the mind down to the contemplation of one object alone that it can think about nothing else; and although men are subject to a number of emotions, and therefore few are found who are always under the control of one and the same emotion, there are not wanting those to whom one and the same emotion obstinately clings. We see men sometimes so affected by one object that, although it is not present, they believe it to be before them; and if this happens to a man who is not asleep, we say that he is delirious or mad. Nor are those believed to be less mad who are inflamed by love, dreaming about nothing but a mistress or harlot day and night, for they excite our laughter. But the avaricious man who thinks of nothing else but gain or money, and the ambitious man who thinks of nothing but glory, inasmuch as they do harm and are, therefore, thought worthy of hatred, are not believed to be mad. In truth, however, avarice, ambition, lust, etc., are a kind of madness, although they are not reckoned amongst diseases.

PROPOSITION XLV. *Hatred can never be good.*

Demonstration. The man whom we hate we endeavor to destroy (Prop. 39, pt. 3), that is to say (Prop. 37, pt. 4), we endeavor to do something which is evil. Therefore hatred, etc. — Q.E.D.

Note. It is to be observed that here and in the following propositions I understand by "hatred," hatred toward men only.

Corollary 1. Envy, mockery, contempt, anger, revenge, and the other emotions which are related to hatred or arise from it are evil. This is also evident from Prop. 39, pt. 3, and Prop. 37, pt. 4.

Corollary 2. Everything which we desire because we are affected by hatred is base and unjust in the State. This is also evident from Prop. 39, pt. 3, and from the definition in Note, Prop. 37, pt. 4, of what is base and unjust.

Note. I make a great distinction between mockery (which I have said, in Corol. 1 of this Prop., is bad) and laughter; for laughter and merriment are nothing but joy, and therefore, provided they are not excessive, are in themselves good (Prop. 41, pt. 4). Nothing but a gloomy and sad superstition forbids enjoyment. For why is it more seemly to extinguish hunger and thirst than to drive away melancholy? My reasons and my conclusions are these: No God and no human being, except an envious one, is delighted by my impotence or my trouble, or esteems as any virtue in us tears, sighs, fears, and other things of this kind, which are signs of mental impotence; on the contrary, the greater the joy with which we are affected, the greater the perfection to which we pass thereby, that is to say, the more do we necessarily partake of the divine nature. To make use of things, therefore, and to delight in them as much as possible (provided we do not disgust ourselves with them, which is not delighting in them), is the part of a wise man. It is the part of a wise man, I say, to refresh and invigorate himself with moderate and pleasant eating and drinking, with sweet scents and the beauty of green plants, with ornament, with music, with sports, with the theater, and with all things of this kind which one man can enjoy without hurting another. For the human body is composed of a great number of parts of diverse nature, which constantly need new and varied nourishment in order that the whole of the body may be equally fit for everything which can follow from its nature, and consequently that the mind may be equally fit to understand many things at once. This mode of living best of all agrees both with our principles and with common practice; therefore this mode of living is the best of all, and is to be universally commended. There is no need, therefore, to enter more at length into the subject.

PROPOSITION XLVI. *He who lives according to the guidance of reason strives as much as possible to repay the hatred, anger, or contempt of others toward himself with love or generosity.*

Demonstration. All emotions of hatred are evil (Corol. 1, Prop. 45, pt. 4), and, therefore, the man who lives according to the guidance of reason will strive as much as possible to keep himself from being agitated by the emotions of hatred (Prop. 19, pt. 4), and, consequently (Prop. 37, pt. 4), will strive to keep others from being subject to the same emotions. But hatred is increased by reciprocal hatred, and, on the other hand, can be extinguished by love (Prop. 43, pt. 3), so that hatred passes into love (Prop. 44, pt. 3). Therefore he who lives according to the guidance of reason will strive to repay the hatred of another, etc., with love, that is to say, with generosity (see definition of generosity in Note, Prop. 59, pt. 3). — Q.E.D.

Note. He who wishes to avenge injuries by hating in return does indeed live miserably. But he who, on the contrary, strives to drive out hatred by love fights joyfully and confidently, with equal ease resisting one man or a number of men, and needing scarcely any assistance from fortune. Those whom he conquers yield gladly, not from defect of strength, but from an increase of it. These truths, however, all follow so plainly from the definitions alone of love and the intellect that there is no need to demonstrate them singly.

PROPOSITION XLVII. *The emotions of hope and fear cannot be good of themselves.*

Demonstration. The emotions of hope and fear cannot exist without sorrow, for fear (Def. 13 of the emotions) is sorrow, and hope (see the explanation of Defs. 12 and 13 of the emotions) cannot exist without fear. Therefore (Prop. 41, pt. 4), these emotions cannot be good of themselves, but only in so far as they are able to restrain the excesses of joy (Prop. 43, pt. 4). — Q.E.D.

Note. We may here add that these emotions indicate want of knowledge and impotence of mind, and, for the same reason, confidence, despair, gladness, and remorse are signs of weakness of mind. For although confidence and gladness are emotions of joy, they nevertheless suppose that sorrow has preceded them, namely, hope or fear. In proportion, therefore, as we endeavor to live according to the guidance of reason, shall we strive as much as possible to depend less on hope, to liberate ourselves from fear, to rule fortune, and to direct our actions by the sure counsels of reason.

PROPOSITION XLVIII. *The emotions of overestimation and contempt are always evil.*

Demonstration. These emotions (Defs. 21 and 22 of the emotions) are opposed to reason and therefore (Props. 26 and 27, pt. 4) are evil. — Q.E.D.

PROPOSITION XLIX. *Overestimation easily renders the man who is overestimated proud.*

Demonstration. If we see that a person, through love, thinks too much of us, we shall easily glorify ourselves (Note, 41, pt. 3), or, in other words, be affected with joy (Def. 30 of the emotions), and easily believe the good which we hear others affirm of us (Prop. 25, pt. 3), and, consequently, through self-love, we shall think too much of ourselves, that is to say (Def. 28 of the emotions), we shall easily grow proud. — Q.E.D.

PROPOSITION L. *Pity in a man who lives according to the guidance of reason is in itself evil and unprofitable.*

Demonstration. Pity (Def. 18, of the emotions) is sorrow, and therefore (Prop. 41, pt. 4) is in itself evil. The good, however, which issues from pity, namely, that we endeavor to free from misery the man we pity (Corol. 3, Prop. 27, pt. 3), we desire to do from the dictate of reason alone (Prop. 37, pt. 4); nor can we do anything except by the dictate of reason alone, which we are sure is good (Prop. 27, pt. 4). Pity, therefore, in a man who lives according to the guidance of reason is in itself bad and unprofitable. — Q.E.D.

Corollary. Hence it follows that a man who lives according to the dictates of reason endeavors as much as possible to prevent himself from being touched by pity.

Note. The man who has properly understood that everything follows from the necessity of the divine nature, and comes to pass according to the eternal laws and rules of Nature, will in truth discover nothing which is worthy of hatred, laughter, or contempt, nor will he pity anyone, but, so far as human virtue is able, he will endeavor to *do well,* as we say, and to *rejoice.* We must add also that a man who is easily touched by the emotion of pity, and is moved by the misery or tears of another, often does something of which he afterward repents, both because from an emotion we do nothing which we certainly know to be good and also because we are so easily deceived by false tears. But this I say expressly of the man who lives according to the guidance of reason. For he who is moved neither by reason nor pity to be of any service to others is properly called inhuman; for (Prop. 27, pt. 3) he seems to be unlike a man.

PROPOSITION LI. *Favor is not opposed to reason but agrees with it, and may arise from it.*

Demonstration. Favor is love toward him who does good to another (Def. 19 of the emotions), and therefore can be related to the mind in so far as it is said to act (Prop. 59, pt. 3), that is to say (Prop. 3, pt. 3), in so far as it understands, and therefore favor agrees with reason. — Q.E.D.

Another Demonstration. If we live according to the guidance of reason, we shall desire for others the good which we seek for ourselves (Prop. 37, pt. 4). Therefore if we see one person do good to another, our endeavor to do good is assisted, that is to say (Note, Prop. 11, pt. 3), we shall rejoice, and our joy (by hypothesis) will be accompanied with the idea of the person who does good to the other, that is to say (Def. 19 of the emotions), we shall favor him. — Q.E.D.

Note. Indignation, as it is defined by us (Def. 20 of the emotions), is necessarily evil (Prop. 45, pt. 4); but it is to be observed that when the supreme authority, constrained by the desire of preserving peace, punishes a citizen who injures another, I do not say that it is indignant with the citizen, since it is not excited by hatred to destroy him, but punishes him from motives of piety.

PROPOSITION LII. *Self-satisfaction may arise from reason, and the self-satisfaction alone which arises from reason is the highest which can exist.*

Demonstration. Self-satisfaction is the joy which arises from a man's contemplating himself and his power of action (Def. 25 of the emotions). But man's true power of action or his virtue is reason itself (Prop. 3, pt. 3), which he contemplates clearly and distinctly (Props. 40 and 43, pt. 2). Self-satisfaction therefore arises from reason. Again, man, when he contemplates himself, perceives nothing clearly and distinctly or adequately except those things which follow from his power of action (Def. 2, pt. 3), that is to say (Prop. 3, pt. 3), those things which follow from his power of understanding; and therefore from this contemplation alone the highest satisfaction which can exist arises. — Q.E.D.

Note. Self-satisfaction is indeed the highest thing for which we can hope, for (as we have shown in Prop. 25, pt. 4) no one endeavors to preserve his being for the sake of any end. Again, because this self-satisfaction is more and more nourished and strengthened by praise (Corol. Prop. 53, pt. 3), and, on the contrary (Corol. Prop. 55, pt. 3), more and more disturbed by blame, therefore we are principally led by glory, and can scarcely endure life with disgrace.

PROPOSITION LIII. *Humility is not a virtue, that is to say, it does not spring from reason.*

Demonstration. Humility is sorrow which springs from this that a man contemplates his own weakness (Def. 26 of the emotions). But in so far as a man knows himself by true reason is he supposed to understand his essence, that is to say (Prop. 7, pt. 3), his power. If, therefore, while contemplating himself, he perceives any impotence of his, this is not due to his understanding himself, but, as we have shown (Prop. 55, pt. 3), to the fact that his power of action is restrained.

But if we suppose that he forms a conception of his own impotence because he understands something to be more powerful than himself, by the knowledge of which he limits his own power of action, in this case we simply conceive that he understands himself distinctly (Prop. 26, pt. 4), and his power of action is increased. Humility or sorrow, therefore, which arises because a man contemplates his own impotence does not spring from true contemplation or reason, and is not a virtue, but a passion. — Q.E.D.

PROPOSITION LIV. *Repentance is not a virtue, that is to say, it does not spring from reason; on the contrary, the man who repents of what he has done is doubly wretched or impotent.*

Demonstration. The first part of this proposition is demonstrated in the same manner as the preceding proposition. The second part follows from the definition alone of this emotion (Def. 27 of the emotions.) For, in the first place, we allow ourselves to be overcome by a depraved desire, and, in the second place, by sorrow.

Note. Inasmuch as men seldom live as reason dictates, therefore these two emotions, humility and repentance, together with hope and fear, are productive of more profit than disadvantage, and therefore, since men must sin, it is better that they should sin in this way. For if men, impotent in mind, were all equally proud, were ashamed of nothing, and feared nothing, by what bonds could they be united or constrained? The multitude becomes a thing to be feared if it has nothing to fear. It is not to be wondered at, therefore, that the prophets, thinking rather of the good of the community than of a few, should have commended so greatly humility, repentance, and reverence. Indeed, those who are subject to these emotions can be led much more easily than others, so that, at last, they come to live according to the guidance of reason, that is to say, become free men and enjoy the life of the blessed.

PROPOSITION LV. *The greatest pride or the greatest despondency is the greatest ignorance of one's self.*

Demonstration. This is evident from Defs. 28 and 29 of the emotions.

PROPOSITION LVI. *The greatest pride or despondency indicates the greatest impotence of mind.*

Demonstration. The primary foundation of virtue is the preservation of our being (Corol. Prop. 22, pt. 4) according to the guidance of reason (Prop. 24, pt. 4). The man, therefore, who is ignorant of himself is ignorant of the foundation of all the virtues, and consequently is ignorant of all the virtues. Again, to act in conformity with virtue is nothing but acting according to the guidance of reason (Prop. 24, pt. 4), and he who acts according to the guidance of reason must necessarily know that he acts according to the guidance of reason (Prop. 43, pt. 2). He, therefore, who is ignorant of himself, and consequently (as we have just shown) altogether ignorant of all the virtues, cannot in any way act in conformity with virtue, that is to say (Def. 8, pt. 4), is altogether impotent in mind. Therefore (Prop. 55, pt. 4), the greatest pride or despondency indicates the greatest impotence of mind. — Q.E.D.

Corollary. Hence follows, with the utmost clearness, that the proud and the desponding are above all others subject to emotions.

Note. Despondency, nevertheless, can be corrected more easily than pride, since the former is an emotion of sorrow, while the latter is an emotion of joy, and is, therefore (Prop. 18, pt. 4), stronger than the former.

PROPOSITION LVII. *The proud man loves the presence of parasites or flatterers, and hates that of the noble-minded.*

Demonstration. Pride is joy arising from a man's having too high an opinion of himself (Defs. 28 and 6 of the emotions). This opinion a proud man will endeavor, as much as he can, to cherish (Note, Prop. 13, pt. 3), and, therefore, will love the presence of parasites or flatterers (the definitions of these people are omitted because they are too well known), and will shun that of the noble-minded who think of him as is right. — Q.E.D.

Note. It would take too much time to enumerate here all the evils of pride, for the proud are subject to all emotions, but to none are they less subject than to those of love and pity. It is necessary, however, to observe here that a man is also called proud if he thinks too little of other people, and so, in this sense, pride is to be defined as joy which arises from the false opinion that we are superior to other people, while despondency, the contrary to this pride, would be defined as sorrow arising from the false opinion that we are inferior to other people. This being understood, it is easy to see that the proud man is necessarily envious (Note, Prop. 55, pt. 3), and that he hates those above all others who are the most praised on account of their virtues. It follows, too, that his hatred of them is not easily overcome by love or kindness (Note, Prop. 41, pt. 3), and that he is delighted by the presence of those only who humor his weakness, and from a fool make him a madman. Although despondency is contrary to pride, the despondent man is closely akin to the proud man. For since the sorrow of the despondent man arises from his judging his own impotence by the power or virtue of others, his sorrow will be mitigated, that is to say, he will rejoice, if his imagination be occupied in contemplating the vices of others. Hence the proverb, "It is a consolation to the wretched to have had companions in their misfortunes." On the other hand, the more the despondent man believes himself to be below other people the more will he sorrow; and this is the reason why none are more prone to envy than the despondent, and why they, above all others, try to observe men's actions with a view to finding fault with them rather than correcting them, so that at last they praise nothing but despondency and glory in it; but in such a manner, however, as always to seem despondent.

These things follow from this emotion as necessarily as it follows from the nature of a triangle that its three angles are equal to two right angles. It is true, indeed, that I have said that I call these and the like emotions evil, in so far as I attend to human profit alone; but the laws of Nature have regard to the common order of Nature of which man is a part — a remark I desired to make in passing lest it should be thought that I talk about the vices and absurdities of men rather than attempt to demonstrate the nature and properties of things. As I said in the Preface to the Third Part, I consider human emotions and their properties precisely as I consider other natural objects; and, indeed, the emotions of man, if they do not show his power, show at least the power and workmanship of Nature, no less than many other things which we admire and delight to contemplate.

I proceed, however, to notice those things connected with the emotions which are productive either of profit or loss to man.

PROPOSITION LVIII. *Self-exaltation is not opposed to reason, but may spring from it.*

Demonstration. This is plain from Def. 30 of the emotions, and also from the definition of honor in Note 1, Prop. 37, pt. 4.

Note. What is called "vainglory" is self-satisfaction nourished by nothing but the good opinion of the multitude, so that, when that is withdrawn, the satisfaction, that is to say (Note, Prop. 52, pt. 4), the chief good which every one loves, ceases. For this reason those who glory in the good opinion of the multitude anxiously and with daily care strive, labor, and struggle to preserve their fame. For the multitude is changeable and fickle, so that fame, if it be not preserved, soon passes away. As everyone, moreover, is desirous to catch the praises of the people, one person will readily destroy the fame of another, and, consequently, as the object of contention is what is commonly thought to be the highest good, a great desire arises on the part of everyone to keep down his fellows by every possible means, and he who at last comes off conqueror boasts more because he has injured another person than because he has profited himself. This glory of self-satisfaction, therefore, is indeed vain, for it is really no glory. What is worthy of notice with regard to shame may easily be gathered from what has been said about compassion and repentance. I will only add that pity, like shame, although it is not a virtue, is nevertheless good in so far as it shows that a desire of living uprightly is present in the man who is possessed with shame, just as pain is called good in so far as it shows that the injured part has not yet putrefied. A man, therefore, who is ashamed of what he has done, although he is sorrowful, is nevertheless more perfect than the shameless man who has no desire of living uprightly. These are the things which I undertook to establish with regard to the emotions of joy and sorrow. With reference to the desires, these are good or evil as they spring from good or evil emotions. All of them, however, in so far as they are begotten in us of emotions wherein the mind is passive, are blind (as may easily be inferred from what has been said in Note, Prop. 44, pt. 4), nor would they be of any use if men could be easily persuaded to live according to the dictates of reason alone, as I shall show in a few words.

PROPOSITION LIX. *To all actions to which we are determined by an emotion wherein the mind is passive we may, without the emotion, be determined by reason.*

Demonstration. To act according to reason is nothing (Prop. 3, and Def. 2, pt. 3) but to do those things which follow from the necessity of our nature considered in itself alone. But sorrow is evil so far as it lessens or restrains this power of action (Prop. 41, pt. 4); therefore, we can be determined by this emotion to no action which we could not perform if we were led by reason. Again, joy is evil so far only as it hinders our fitness for action (Props. 41 and 43, pt. 4); and therefore also we can so far be determined to no action which we could not do if we were led by reason. Finally, in so far as joy is good, so far it agrees with reason (for it consists in this that a man's power of action is increased or assisted), and the mind is not passive therein unless in so far as man's power of action is not increased sufficiently for him to conceive adequately himself and his actions (Prop. 3, pt. 3, with its Note). If, therefore, a man affected with joy were led to such perfection as to conceive adequately himself and his actions, he would be fitted — better even than before — for the performance of those actions to which he is now determined by the emotions wherein the mind is passive. But all the emotions are related to joy, sorrow, or desire (see the explanation of Def. 4 of the emotions), and desire (Def. 1 of the emotions) is nothing but the endeavor itself to act; therefore to all actions to which we are determined by an emotion wherein the mind is passive we may without the emotion be determined by reason alone. — Q.E.D.

Another Demonstration. Any action is called evil in so far as it arises from our being affected with hatred or some evil emotion (Corol. 1, Prop. 45, pt. 4). But no action considered in itself alone is either good or evil (as we have already shown in the preface to this part), but one and the same action is sometimes good and sometimes evil. Therefore we may be led by reason (Prop. 19, pt. 4) to that same action which is sometimes evil or which arises from some evil emotion. — Q.E.D.

Note. This can be explained more clearly by an example. The action of striking, for instance, in so far as it is considered physically, and we attend only to the fact that a man raises his arm, closes his hand, and forcibly moves the whole arm downwards, is a virtue which is conceived from the structure of the human body. If, therefore, a man agitated by anger or hatred is led to close the fist or move the arm, this comes to pass, as we have shown in the Second Part, because one and the same action can be joined to different images of things, and therefore we may be led to one and the same action as well by the images of things which we conceive confusedly as by those which we conceive clearly and distinctly. It appears, therefore, that every desire which arises from an emotion wherein the mind is passive would be of no use if men could be led by reason. We shall now see why a desire which arises from an emotion wherein the mind is passive is called blind.

PROPOSITION LX. *The desire which arises from joy or sorrow, which is related to one or to some, but not to all, the parts of the body, has no regard to the profit of the whole man.*

Demonstration. Let it be supposed that a part of the body — A, for example — is so strengthened by the force of some external cause that it prevails over the others (Prop. 6, pt. 4). It will not endeavor, therefore, to lose its strength in order that the remaining parts of the body may perform their functions, for in that case it would have a force or power of losing its strength, which (Prop. 6, pt. 3) is absurd. It will endeavor, therefore, and consequently (Props. 7 and 12, pt. 3) the mind also will endeavor, to preserve this same state; and so the desire which arises from such an emotion of joy has no regard to the whole man. If, on the other hand, it be supposed that the part A is restrained so that the other parts prevail, it can be demonstrated in the same way that the desire which springs from sorrow has no regard to the whole man. — Q.E.D.

Note. Since, therefore, joy is most frequently related to one part of the body (Note, Prop. 44, pt. 4), we generally desire to preserve our being without reference to our health as a whole; and, moreover, the desires by which we are chiefly controlled (Corol. Prop. 9, pt. 4) have regard to the present only, and not to the future.

PROPOSITION LXI. *A desire which springs from reason can never be in excess.*

Demonstration. Desire (Def. 1 of the emotions), absolutely considered, is the very essence of man, in so far as he is conceived as determined in any way whatever to any action, and therefore the desire which springs from reason, that is to say (Prop. 3, pt. 3), which is begotten in us in so far as we act, is the very essence or nature of man in so far as it is conceived as determined to actions which are adequately conceived by the essence of man alone (Def. 2, pt. 3). If, therefore, this desire could be in excess, it would be possible for human nature, considered in itself alone, to exceed itself, or, in other words, more would be possible to it than is possible, which is a manifest contradiction, and therefore this desire can never be in excess. — Q.E.D.

PROPOSITION LXII. *In so far as the conception of an object is formed by the mind according to the dictate of reason, the mind is equally affected, whether the idea be that of something future, past, or present.*

Demonstration. Everything which the mind, under the guidance of reason, conceives, it conceives under the same form of eternity or necessity (Corol. 2, Prop. 44, pt. 2), and it is affected with the same certainty (Prop. 43, pt. 2, and its Note). Therefore, whether the idea be one of a future, past, or present object, the mind conceives the object with the same necessity, and is affected with the same certainty; and whether the idea be that of a future, past, or present object, it will nevertheless be equally true (Prop. 41, pt. 2), that is to say (Def. 4, pt. 2), it will always have the same properties of an adequate idea. Therefore, in so far as the conception of an object is formed by the mind according to the dictates of reason, the mind will be affected in the same way whether the idea be that of something future, past, or present. — Q.E.D.

Note. If it were possible for us to possess an adequate knowledge concerning the duration of things and to determine by reason the periods of their existence, we should contemplate with the same emotion objects future and present; and the good which the mind conceived to be future, it would seek just as it would seek the present good. Consequently, it would necessarily neglect the present good for the sake of a greater future good, and would, as we shall presently show, be very little disposed to seek a good which was present, but which would be a cause of any future evil. But it is not possible for us to have any other than a very inadequate knowledge of the duration of things (Prop. 31, pt. 2), and we determine (Note, Prop. 44, pt. 2) the periods of the existence of objects by the imagination alone, which is not affected by the image of a present object in the same way as it is by that of a future object. Hence it comes to pass that the true knowledge of good and evil which we possess is only abstract or universal; and the judgment we pass upon the order of things and the connection of causes, so that we may determine what is good for us in the present and what is evil, is rather imaginary than real. It is not, therefore, to be wondered at if the desire which arises from a knowledge of good and evil, in so far as this knowledge has regard to the future, is capable of being easily restrained by the desire of objects which are sweet to us at the present moment. (See Prop. 16, pt. 4.)

PROPOSITION LXIII. *He who is led by fear and does what is good in order that he may avoid what is evil is not led by reason.*

Demonstration. All the emotions which are related to the mind, in so far as it acts, that is to say (Prop. 3, pt. 3), which are related to reason, are no other than emotions of joy and desire (Prop. 59, pt. 3); and therefore (Def. 13 of the emotions), he who is led by fear and does good through fear of evil is not led by reason. — Q.E.D.

Note. The superstitious, who know better how to rail at vice than to teach virtue, and who study not to lead man by reason, but to hold him in through fear, in order that he may shun evil rather than love virtue, aim at nothing more than that others should be as miserable as themselves, and, therefore, it is not to be wondered at if they generally become annoying and hateful to men.

Corollary. By the desire which springs from reason we follow good directly and avoid evil indirectly.

Demonstration. For the desire which springs from reason cannot spring from sorrow, but only from an emotion of joy, in which the mind is not passive (Prop. 59, pt. 3), that is to say, from joy which cannot be in excess (Prop. 61, pt. 4). This desire springs, therefore (Prop. 8, pt. 4), from the knowledge of good, and not from the knowledge of evil, and therefore, according to the guidance of reason, we seek what is good directly, and so far only do we shun what is evil. — Q.E.D.

Note. This corollary is explained by the example of a sick man and a healthy man. The sick man, through fear of death, eats what he dislikes; the healthy man takes a pleasure in his food, and so enjoys life more than if he feared death and directly desired to avoid it. So also the judge who condemns a guilty man to death, not from hatred or anger, but solely from love for the public welfare, is led by reason alone.

PROPOSITION LXIV. *The knowledge of evil is inadequate knowledge.*

Demonstration. The knowledge of evil (Prop. 8, pt. 4) is sorrow itself, in so far as we are conscious of it. But sorrow is the passage to a less perfection (Def. 3 of the emotions), and it cannot, therefore, be understood through the essence itself of man (Props. 6 and 7, pt. 3). It is, therefore (Def. 2, pt. 3), a passive state which (Prop. 3, pt. 3) depends upon inadequate ideas, and consequently (Prop. 29, pt. 2) the knowledge of sorrow, that is to say, the knowledge of evil, is inadequate. — Q.E.D.

Corollary. Hence it follows that if the human mind had none but adequate ideas it would form no notion of evil.

PROPOSITION LXV. *According to the guidance of reason, of two things which are good, we shall follow the greater good, and of two evils, we shall follow the less.*

Demonstration. The good which hinders us from enjoying a greater good is really an evil, for good and evil (as we have shown in the preface to this part) are affirmed of things in so far as we compare them with one another. By the same reasoning a less evil is really a good, and therefore (Corol. Prop. 63, pt. 4), according to the guidance of reason, we shall seek or follow the greater good only and the lesser evil. — Q.E.D.

Corollary. According to the guidance of reason, we shall follow a lesser evil for the sake of a greater good, and a lesser good which is the cause of a greater evil we shall neglect. For the evil which we here call less is really a good, and the good, on the other hand, is evil; and therefore (Corol. Prop. 63, pt. 4) we shall seek the former and neglect the latter. — Q.E.D.

PROPOSITION LXVI. *According to the guidance of reason, we shall seek the greater future good before that which is less and present, and we shall seek also the less and present evil before that which is greater and future.*

Demonstration. If it were possible for the mind to have an adequate knowledge of a future object, it would be affected by the same emotion toward the future object as toward a present object (Prop. 62, pt. 4). Therefore, in so far as we attend to reason itself, as we are supposing in this proposition that we do, it is the same thing whether the greater good or evil be supposed to be future or present, and therefore (Prop. 65, pt. 4) we shall seek the greater future good before that which is less and present, etc. — Q.E.D.

Corollary. According to the guidance of reason we shall seek the lesser present evil which is the cause of the greater future good, and the lesser present good which is the cause of a greater future evil we shall neglect. This corollary is connected with the foregoing proposition in the same way as Corol. Prop. 65 is connected with Prop. 65.

Note. If what has been said here be compared with what has been demonstrated about the strength of the passions in the first eighteen Props., pt. 4. and in Note, Prop. 18, pt. 4, it will easily be seen in what consists the difference between a man who is led by emotion or opinion alone and one who is led by reason. The former, whether he wills it or not, does those things of which he is entirely ignorant, but the latter does the will of no one but himself, and does those things only which he knows are of greatest importance in life, and which he therefore desires above all things. I call the former, therefore, a slave, and the latter free.

I will add here a few words concerning the character of the free man and his manner of life.

PROPOSITION LXVII. *A free man thinks of nothing less than of death, and his wisdom is not a meditation upon death but upon life.*

Demonstration. A free man, that is to say, a man who lives according to the dictates of reason alone, is not led by the fear of death (Prop. 63, pt. 4), but directly desires the good (Corol. Prop. 63, pt. 4), that is to say (Prop. 24, pt. 4), desires to act, to live, and to preserve his being in accordance with the principle of seeking his own profit. He thinks, therefore, of nothing less than of death, and his wisdom is a meditation upon life. — Q.E.D.

PROPOSITION LXVIII. *If men were born free, they would form no conception of good and evil so long as they were free.*

Demonstration. I have said that that man is free who is led by reason alone. He, therefore, who is born free and remains free has no other than adequate ideas, and therefore has no conception of evil (Corol. Prop. 64, pt. 4), and consequently (as good and evil are correlative) no conception of good. — Q.E.D.

Note. It is clear from Prop. 4, pt. 4, that the hypothesis of this proposition is false, and cannot be conceived unless in so far as we regard human nature alone or rather God, not in so far as He is infinite, but in so far only as He is the cause of man's existence. This (together with the other things we have before demonstrated) appears to have been what was meant by Moses in that history of the first man. In that history no other power of God is conceived except that by which He created man, that is to say, the power with which He considered nothing but the advantage of man. Therefore we are told that God forbad free man to eat of the tree of knowledge of good and evil, and warned him that as soon as he ate of it he would immediately dread death rather than desire to live. Afterwards we are told that when man found a wife who agreed entirely with his nature, he saw that there could be nothing in Nature which could be more profitable to him than his wife. But when he came to believe that the brutes were like himself, he immediately began to imitate their emotions (Prop. 27, pt. 3) and to lose his liberty, which the Patriarchs afterwards recovered, being led by the spirit of Christ, that is to say, by the idea of God, which alone can make a man free, and cause him to desire for other men the good he desires for himself, as (Prop. 37, pt. 4) we have already demonstrated.

PROPOSITION LXIX. *The virtue of a free man is seen to be as great in avoiding danger as in overcoming it.*

Demonstration. An emotion cannot be restrained or removed unless a contrary and stronger emotion restrains it (Prop. 7, pt. 4); but blind audacity and fear are emotions which may be conceived as being equally great (Props. 5 and 3, pt. 4). The virtue or strength of mind, therefore (for the definition of this, see Note, Prop. 59, pt. 3), which is required to restrain audacity must be equally great with that which is required to restrain fear, that is to say (Defs. 40 and 41 of the emotions), a free man avoids danger by the same virtue of the mind as that by which he seeks to overcome it. — Q.E.D.

Corollary. Flight at the proper time, just as well as fighting, is to be reckoned, therefore, as showing strength of mind in a man who is free, that is to say, a free man chooses flight by the same strength or presence of mind as that by which he chooses battle.

Note. What strength of mind is or what I understand by it, I have explained in Note, Prop. 59, pt. 3. By danger I understand anything which may be the cause of sorrow, hatred, discord, or any other evil like them.

PROPOSITION LXX. *The free man who lives amongst those who are ignorant strives as much as possible to avoid their favors.*

Demonstration. Everyone, according to his own disposition, judges what is good (Note, Prop. 39, pt. 3). The ignorant man, therefore, who has conferred a favor on another person will value it according to his own way of thinking, and he will be sad if a less value seems to be placed upon it by the person who has received it (Prop. 42, pt. 3). But a free man strives to unite other men with himself by friendship (Prop. 37, pt. 4), and not to return to them favors which they, according to their emotions, may consider to be equal to those which they have bestowed. He desires rather to govern himself and others by the free decisions of reason, and to do those things only which he has discovered to be of the first importance. A free man, therefore, in order that he may not be hated by the ignorant, nor yet yield to their appetites, but only to reason, will endeavor as much as possible to avoid their favors. — Q.E.D.

Note. I say "as much as possible." For although men are ignorant, they are nevertheless men, who, when we are in straits, are able to afford us human assistance — the best assistance which man can receive. It is often necessary, therefore, to receive a favor from the ignorant and to thank them for it according to their taste; and besides this, care must be used, even in declining favors, not to seem either to despise the givers or through avarice to dread a return, so that we may not, while striving to escape their hatred, by that very act incur their displeasure. In avoiding favors, therefore, we must be guided by a consideration of what is profitable and honorable.

PROPOSITION LXXI. *None but those who are free are very grateful to one another.*

Demonstration. None but those who are free are very profitable to one another or are united by the closest bond of friendship (Prop. 35, pt. 4, and Corol. 1), or with an equal zeal of love strive to do good to one another (Prop. 37, pt. 4), and therefore (Def. 34 of the emotions) none but those who are free are very grateful to one another. — Q.E.D.

Note. The gratitude to one another of men who are led by blind desire is generally a matter of business or a snare rather than gratitude. Ingratitude, it is to be observed, is not an emotion. It is nevertheless base because it is generally a sign that a man is too much affected by hatred, anger, pride, or avarice. For he who through stupidity does not know how to return a gift is not ungrateful; and much less is he ungrateful who is not moved by the gifts of a harlot to serve her lust, nor by those of a thief to conceal his thefts, nor by any other gifts of

a similar kind.   On the contrary, a man shows that he possesses a
steadfast mind if he does not suffer himself to be enticed by any gifts
to his own or the common ruin.

PROPOSITION LXXII. *A free man never acts deceitfully, but always
    honorably.*

Demonstration. If a free man did anything deceitfully, in so far as
he is free, he would do it at the bidding of reason (for so far only do
we call him free); and therefore to act deceitfully would be a virtue
(Prop. 24, pt. 4), and consequently (by the same proposition) it would
be more advantageous to every one, for the preservation of his being,
to act deceitfully, that is to say (as is self-evident), it would be more
advantageous to men to agree only in words and to be opposed in
reality, which (Corol. Prop. 31, pt. 4) is absurd.   A free man, therefore,
etc. — Q.E.D.

Note. If it be asked whether, if a man by breach of faith could
escape from the danger of instant death, reason does not counsel him,
for the preservation of his being, to break faith, I reply in the same
way that if reason gives such counsel she gives it to all men, and reason
therefore generally counsels men to make no agreements for uniting
their strength and possessing laws in common except deceitfully, that
is to say, to have in reality no common laws, which is absurd.

PROPOSITION LXXIII. *A man who is guided by reason is freer in a
    State where he lives according to the common laws than he is in
    solitude, where he obeys himself alone.*

Demonstration. A man who is guided by reason is not led to obey
by fear (Prop. 63, pt. 4), but in so far as he endeavors to preserve his
being in accordance with the bidding of reason, that is to say (Note,
Prop. 66, pt. 4), in so far as he endeavors to live in freedom, does he
desire to have regard for the common life and the common profit
(Prop. 37, pt. 4); and consequently (as we have shown in Note 2,
Prop. 37, pt. 4) he desires to live according to the common laws of
the State.   A man, therefore, who is guided by reason desires, in order

that he may live more freely, to maintain the common rights of the State. — Q.E.D.

Note. These, and the like things which we have demonstrated concerning the true liberty of man, are related to fortitude, that is to say (Note, Prop. 59, pt. 3), to strength of mind and generosity. Nor do I think it worth while to demonstrate here, one by one, all the properties of fortitude, and still less to show how its possessor can hate no one, be angry with no one, can neither envy, be indignant with nor despise anybody, and can least of all be proud. For all this, together with truths of a like kind which have to do with the true life and religion, are easily deduced from Props. 37 and 46, pt. 4, which show that hatred is to be overcome by love, and that everyone who is guided by reason desires for others the good which he seeks for himself. In addition, we must remember what we have already observed in Note, Prop. 50, pt. 4, and in other places, that the brave man will consider above everything that all things follow from the necessity of the divine nature; and that, consequently, whatever he thinks injurious and evil, and, moreover, whatever seems to be impious, dreadful, unjust, or wicked, arises from this that he conceives things in a disturbed, mutilated, and confused fashion. For this reason, his chief effort is to conceive things as they are in themselves, and to remove the hindrances to true knowledge, such as hatred, anger, envy, derision, pride, and others of this kind which we have before noticed; and so he endeavors, as we have said, as much as possible to do well and rejoice. How far human virtue reaches in the attainment of these things, and what it can do, I shall show in the following part.

APPENDIX

My observations in this part concerning the true method of life have not been arranged so that they could be seen at a glance, but have been demonstrated here and there according as I could more easily deduce one from another. I have determined, therefore, here to collect them, and reduce them under principal heads.

I.

All our efforts or desires follow from the necessity of our nature in such a manner that they can be understood either through it alone as their proximate cause, or in so far as we are a part of Nature, which part cannot be adequately conceived through itself and without the other individuals.

II.

The desires which follow from our nature in such a manner that they can be understood through it alone are those which are related to the mind, in so far as it is conceived to consist of adequate ideas. The remaining desires are not related to the mind, unless in so far as it conceives things inadequately, whose power and increase cannot be determined by human power, but by the power of objects which are without us. The first kind of desires, therefore, are properly called actions, but the latter passive states, for the first always indicate our power, and the latter, on the contrary, indicate our impotence and imperfect knowledge.

III.

Our actions, that is to say, those desires which are determined by man's power or reason, are always good; the others may be good as well as evil.

IV.

It is therefore most profitable to us in life to make perfect the intellect or reason as far as possible, and in this one thing consists the highest happiness or blessedness of man; for blessedness is nothing but the peace of mind which springs from the intuitive knowledge of God, and to perfect the intellect is nothing but to understand God, together with the attributes and actions of God which flow from the necessity of His nature. The final aim, therefore, of a man who is guided by reason, that is to say, the chief desire by which he strives to govern all his other desires, is that by which he is led adequately to conceive himself and all things which can be conceived by his intelligence.

V.

There is no rational life therefore, without intelligence, and things are good only in so far as they assist man to enjoy that life of the mind which is determined by intelligence. Those things alone, on the other hand, we call evil which hinder man from perfecting his reason and enjoying a rational life.

VI.

But because all those things of which man is the efficient cause are necessarily good, it follows that no evil can happen to man except from external causes, that is to say, except in so far as he is a part of the whole of Nature, whose laws human nature is compelled to obey — compelled also to accommodate himself to this whole of Nature in almost an infinite number of ways.

VII.

It is impossible that a man should not be a part of Nature and follow her common order; but if he be placed amongst individuals who agree with his nature, his power of action will by that very fact be assisted and supported. But if, on the contrary, he be placed amongst individuals who do not in the least agree with his nature, he will scarcely be able without great change on his part to accommodate himself to them.

VIII.

Anything that exists in Nature which we judge to be evil or able to hinder us from existing and enjoying a rational life, we are allowed to remove from us in that way which seems the safest; and whatever, on the other hand, we judge to be good or to be profitable for the preservation of our being or the enjoyment of a rational life, we are permitted to take for our use and use in any way we may think proper; and absolutely, everyone is allowed by the highest right of Nature to do that which he believes contributes to his own profit.

IX.

Nothing, therefore, can agree better with the nature of any object than other individuals of the same kind, and so (see §7) there is nothing more profitable to man for the preservation of his being and the enjoyment of a rational life than a man who is guided by reason. Again, since there is no single thing we know which is more excellent than a man who is guided by reason, it follows that there is nothing by which a person can better show how much skill and talent he possesses than by so educating men that at last they will live under the direct authority of reason.

X.

In so far as men are carried away by envy or any emotion of hatred toward one another, so far are they contrary to one another, and, consequently, so much the more are they to be feared, as they have more power than other individual parts of Nature.

XI.

Minds, nevertheless, are not conquered by arms, but by love and generosity.

XII.

Above all things it is profitable to men to form communities and to unite themselves to one another by bonds which may make all of them as one man; and, absolutely, it is profitable for them to do whatever may tend to strengthen their friendships.

XIII.

But to accomplish this, skill and watchfulness are required; for men are changeable (those being very few who live according to the laws of reason), and nevertheless generally envious and more inclined to vengeance than pity. To bear with each, therefore, according to his disposition and to refrain from imitating his emotions requires a singular power of mind. But those, on the contrary, who know how to revile men, to denounce vices rather than teach virtues, and not to strengthen men's minds but to weaken them, are injurious both to themselves and others, so that many of them, through an excess of impatience and a false zeal for religion, prefer living with brutes rather than amongst men; just as boys or youths, unable to endure with equanimity the rebukes of their parents, fly to the army, choosing the discomforts of war and the rule of a tyrant rather than the comforts of home and the admonitions of a father, suffering all kinds of burdens to be imposed upon them in order that they may revenge themselves upon their parents.

XIV.

Although, therefore, men generally determine everything by their pleasure, many more advantages than disadvantages arise from their common union. It is better, therefore, to endure with equanimity the injuries inflicted by them, and to apply our minds to those things which subserve concord and the establishment of friendship.

XV.

The things which beget concord are those which are related to justice, integrity, and honor; for besides that which is unjust and injurious, men take ill also anything which is esteemed base, or that anyone should despise the received customs of the State. But in order to win love, those things are chiefly necessary which have reference to religion and piety. (See Notes 1 and 2, Prop. 37; Note, Prop. 46, and Note, Prop. 73, pt. 4.)

XVI.

Concord, moreover, is often produced by fear, but it is without good faith. It is to be observed, too, that fear arises from impotence of mind, and therefore is of no service to reason; nor is pity, although it seems to present an appearance of piety.

XVII.

Men also are conquered by liberality, especially those who have not the means wherewith to procure what is necessary for the support of life. But to assist every one who is needy far surpasses the strength or profit of a private person, for the wealth of a private person is altogether insufficient to supply such wants. Besides, the power of any one man is too limited for him to be able to unite every one with himself in friendship. The care, therefore, of the poor is incumbent on the whole of society and concerns only the general profit.

XVIII.

In the receipt of benefits and in returning thanks, care altogether different must be taken — concerning which see Note, Prop. 70, and Note, Prop. 71, pt. 4.

XIX.

The love of a harlot, that is to say, the lust of sexual intercourse, which arises from mere external form, and absolutely all love which recognizes any other cause than the freedom of the mind, easily passes into hatred unless, which is worse, it becomes a species of delirium, and thereby discord is cherished rather than concord (Corol. Prop. 31, pt. 3).

XX.

With regard to marriage, it is plain that it is in accordance with reason if the desire of connection is engendered not merely by external form, but by a love of begetting children and wisely educating them; and if, in addition, the love both of the husband and wife has for its cause not external form merely, but chiefly liberty of mind.

XXI.

Flattery, too, produces concord, but only by means of the disgraceful crime of slavery or perfidy; for there are none who are more taken by flattery than the proud, who wish to be first and are not so.

XXII.

There is a false appearance of piety and religion in dejection; and although dejection is the opposite of pride, the humble, dejected man is very near akin to the proud (Note, Prop. 57, pt. 4).

XXIII.

Shame also contributes to concord, but only with regard to those matters which cannot be concealed. Shame, too, inasmuch as it is a kind of sorrow, does not belong to the service of reason.

XXIV.

The remaining emotions of sorrow which have man for their object are directly opposed to justice, integrity, honor, piety, and religion; and although indignation may seem to present an appearance of equity, yet there is no law where it is allowed to everyone to judge the deeds of another, and to vindicate his own or another's right.

XXV.

Affability, that is to say, the desire of pleasing men, which is determined by reason, is related to piety (Note, Prop. 37, pt. 4). But if affability arise from an emotion, it is ambition or desire, by which men, generally under a false pretence of piety, excite discords and seditions. For he who desires to assist other people, either by advice or by deed, in order that they may together enjoy the highest good, will strive, above all things, to win their love, and not to draw them into admiration, so that a doctrine may be named after him, nor absolutely to give any occasion for envy. In common conversation, too, he will avoid referring to the vices of men, and will take care only sparingly to speak of human impotence, while he will talk largely of human virtue or power, and of the way by which it may be made perfect, so that men, being moved not by fear or aversion but solely by the emotion of joy, may endeavor as much as they can to live under the rule of reason.

XXVI.

Except man, we know no individual thing in Nature in whose mind we can take pleasure, nor anything which we can unite with ourselves by friendship or any kind of intercourse, and therefore regard to our own profit does not demand that we should preserve anything which exists in Nature except men, but teaches us to preserve it or destroy it in accordance with its varied uses, or to adapt it to our own service in any way whatever.

XXVII.

The profit which we derive from objects without us, over and above the experience and knowledge which we obtain because we observe them and change them from their existing forms into others, is chiefly the preservation of the body, and for this reason those objects are the most profitable to us which can feed and nourish the body, so that all its parts are able properly to perform their functions. For the more capable the body is of being affected in many ways, and affecting external bodies in many ways, the more capable of thinking is the mind (Props. 38 and 39, pt. 4). But there seem to be very few things in Nature of this kind, and it is consequently necessary for the requisite nourishment of the body to use many different kinds of food, for the human body is composed of a great number of parts of different nature, which need constant and varied food in order that the whole of the body may be equally adapted for all those things which can follow from its nature, and consequently that the mind also may be equally adapted to conceive many things.

XXVIII.

The strength of one man would scarcely suffice to obtain these things if men did not mutually assist one another. As money has presented us with an abstract of everything, it has come to pass that its image above every other usually occupies the mind of the multitude because they can imagine hardly any kind of joy without the accompanying idea of money as its cause.

XXIX.

This, however, is a vice only in those who seek money not from poverty or necessity, but because they have learned the arts of gain by which they keep up a grand appearance. As for the body itself, they feed it in accordance with custom, but sparingly because they believe that they lose so much of their goods as they spend upon the preservation of their body. Those, however, who know the true use of money, and regulate the measure of wealth according to their needs, live contented with few things.

XXX.

Since, therefore, those things are good which help the parts of the body to perform their functions, and since joy consists in this that

the power of man, in so far as he is made up of mind and body, is
helped or increased, it follows that all those things which bring joy
are good. But inasmuch as things do not work to this end — that
they may affect us with joy — nor is their power of action guided in
accordance with our profit, and finally, since joy is generally related
chiefly to some one part of the body, it follows that generally the
emotions of joy (unless reason and watchfulness be present), and
consequently the desires which are begotten from them, are excessive.
It is to be added that an emotion causes us to put that thing first
which is sweet to us in the present, and that we are not able to judge
the future with an equal emotion (Note, Prop. 44, and Note, Prop.
60, pt. 4).

XXXI.

Superstition, on the contrary, seems to affirm that what brings
sorrow is good, and, on the contrary, that what brings joy is evil.
But, as we have already said (Note, Prop. 45, pt. 4), no one except
an envious man is delighted at my impotence or disadvantage, for
the greater the joy with which we are affected, the greater the perfection to which we pass, and consequently the more do we participate
in the divine nature; nor can joy ever be evil which is controlled by
a true consideration for our own profit. On the other hand, the man
who is led by fear and does what is good that he may avoid what is
evil, is not guided by reason.

XXXII.

But human power is very limited and is infinitely surpassed by the
power of external causes, so that we do not possess an absolute power
to adapt to our service the things which are without us. Nevertheless
we shall bear with equanimity those things which happen to us contrary to what a consideration of our own profit demands if we are
conscious that we have performed our duty, that the power we have
could not reach so far as to enable us to avoid those things, and that
we are a part of the whole of Nature, whose order we follow. If we
clearly and distinctly understand this, the part of us which is deter-

mined by intelligence, that is to say, the better part of us, will be entirely satisfied therewith, and in that satisfaction will endeavor to persevere; for, in so far as we understand, we cannot desire anything except what is necessary, nor, absolutely, can we be satisfied with anything but the truth. Therefore, in so far as we understand these things properly, will the efforts of the better part of us agree with the order of the whole of Nature.

PART FIVE

Of the Power of the Intellect;
or of Human Freedom

PREFACE

I PASS at length to the other part of Ethics which concerns the method or way which leads to freedom. In this part, therefore, I shall treat of the power of reason, showing how much reason itself can control the emotions, and then what is freedom of mind or blessedness. Thence we shall see how much stronger the wise man is than the ignorant. In what manner and in what way the intellect should be rendered perfect, and with what art the body is to be cared for in order that it may properly perform its functions, I have nothing to do with here; for the former belongs to logic, the latter to medicine. I shall occupy myself here, as I have said, solely with the power of the mind or of reason, first of all showing the extent and nature of the authority which it has over the emotions in restraining them and governing them; for that we have not absolute authority over them we have already demonstrated. The Stoics indeed thought that the emotions depend absolutely on our will, and that we are absolutely masters over them; but they were driven, by the contradiction of experience, though not by their own principles, to confess that not a little practice and study are required in order to restrain and govern the emotions. This one of them attempted to illustrate, if I remember rightly, by the example of two dogs, one of a domestic and the other of a hunting breed; for he was able by habit to make the house-dog hunt, and the hunting dog, on the contrary, to desist from running after hares. To the Stoical opinion Descartes much inclines. He affirms that the soul or mind is united specially to a certain part of the brain called the pineal gland, which the mind by the mere exercise of the will is able to move in different ways, and by whose help the mind perceives all the movements which are excited in the body and external objects. This gland he affirms is suspended in the middle of the brain in such a manner that it can be moved by the least motion of the animal spirits. Again, he affirms that any variation in the manner in which the animal spirits impinge upon this gland is followed by a variation in the manner in which it is suspended in the middle of the brain, and moreover that the number of different impressions on the gland is the same as that of the different external objects which propel the animal spirits towards it. Hence it comes to pass that if the gland, by the will of the soul moving it in different directions, be afterwards suspended in this or that way in which it had once been suspended by the spirits agitated in this or that way, then the gland itself will propel and determine the animal spirits themselves in the same way as that in which they had before been repelled by a similar suspension of the gland. Moreover, he affirmed that each volition of the mind is united in nature to a certain motion of the gland. For example, if a person wishes to behold a remote object, this volition will cause the pupil of the eye to dilate, but if he thinks merely of the dilation of the pupil, to have that volition will profit him nothing because Nature has not connected a motion of the gland which serves to impel the animal spirits toward the optic nerve in a way suitable for dilation or contraction of the pupil with the volition of dilation or contraction, but only with the volition of beholding objects afar off or close at hand. Finally, he maintained that, although each motion of this gland appears to be connected by Nature from the commencement of our life with an individual thought, these motions can nevertheless be connected by habit with other thoughts — a proposition which he attempts to demonstrate in his "Passions of the Soul," art. 50, pt. 1.

From this he concludes that there is no mind so feeble that it cannot, when properly directed, acquire absolute power over its passions; for passions, as defined by him, are "perceptions or sensations, or emotions of the soul which are related to it specially, and which (N.B.) are produced, preserved, and strengthened by some motion of the spirits." (See the "Passions of the Soul," art. 27, pt. 1.) But since it is possible to join to a certain volition any motion of the gland and, consequently, of the spirits, and since the determination of the will depends solely on our power, we shall be able to acquire absolute mastery over our passions provided only we determine our will by fixed and firm decisions by which we desire to direct our actions and bind with these decisions the movements of the passions we wish to have. So far as I can gather from his own words, this is the opinion of that distinguished man, and I could scarcely have believed it possible for one so great to have put it forward if it had been less subtle. I can hardly wonder enough that a philosopher who firmly resolved to make no deduction except from self-evident principles, and to affirm nothing but what he clearly and distinctly perceived, and who blamed all the schoolmen because they desired to explain obscure matters by occult qualities, should accept a hypothesis more occult than any occult quality. What does he understand, I ask, by the union of the mind and body? What clear and distinct conception has he of thought intimately connected with a certain small portion of matter? I wish that he had explained this union by its proximate cause. But he conceived the mind to be so distinct from the body that he was able to assign no single cause of this union, nor of the mind itself, but was obliged to have recourse to the cause of the whole universe, that is to say, to God. Again, I should like to know how many degrees of motion the mind can give to that pineal gland, and with how great a power the mind can hold it suspended. For I do not understand whether this gland is acted on by the mind more slowly or more quickly than by the animal spirits, and whether the movements of the passions, which we have so closely bound with firm decisions, might not be separated from them again by bodily causes, from which it would follow that although the mind had firmly determined to meet danger, and had joined to this decision the motion of boldness, the sight of the danger might cause the gland to be suspended in such a manner that the mind could think of nothing but flight. Indeed, since there is no relation between the will and motion, so there is no comparison between the power or strength of the body and that of the mind, and consequently the strength of the body can never be determined by the strength of the mind. It is to be remembered also that this gland is not found to be so situated in the middle of the brain that it can be driven about so easily and in so many ways, and that all the nerves are not extended to the cavities of the brain. Lastly, I omit all that Descartes asserts concerning the will and the freedom of the will, since I have shown over and over again that it is false. Therefore, inasmuch as the power of the mind, as I have shown above, is determined by intelligence alone, we shall determine by the knowledge of the mind alone the remedies against the emotions — remedies which every one, I believe, has experienced, although there may not have been any accurate observation or distinct perception of them, and from this knowledge of the mind alone shall we deduce everything which relates to its blessedness.

AXIOMS

1. If two contrary actions be excited in the same subject, a change must necessarily take place in both, or in one alone, until they cease to be contrary.

2. The power of an emotion is limited by the power of its cause, in so far as the essence of the emotion is manifested or limited by the essence of the cause itself.

This axiom is evident from Prop. 7, pt. 3.

PROPOSITIONS

PROPOSITION I. *As thoughts and the ideas of things are arranged and connected in the mind, exactly so are the modifications of the body or the images of things arranged and connected in the body.*

Demonstration. The order and connection of ideas is the same (Prop. 7, pt. 2) as the order and connection of things, and, *vice versa,* the order and connection of things is the same (Corol. Props. 6 and 7, pt. 2) as the order and connection of ideas. Therefore, as the order and connection of ideas in the mind is according to the order and connection of the modifications of the body (Prop. 18, pt. 2), it follows, *vice versa* (Prop. 2, pt. 3), that the order and connection of the modifications of the body is according to the order and connection in the mind of the thoughts and ideas of things. — Q.E.D.

PROPOSITION II. *If we detach a perturbation of the mind or an emotion from the thought of an external cause and connect it with other thoughts, then the love or hatred toward the external cause and the fluctuations of the mind which arise from these emotions will be destroyed.*

Demonstration. That which constitutes the form of love or hatred is joy or sorrow, accompanied with the idea of an external cause (Defs. 6 and 7 of the emotions). If this idea therefore be taken away, the form of love or hatred is also removed, and therefore these emotions and any others which arise from them are destroyed. — Q.E.D.

PROPOSITION III. *An emotion which is a passion ceases to be a passion as soon as we form a clear and distinct idea of it.*

Demonstration. An emotion which is a passion is a confused idea (by the general definition of the emotions). If, therefore, we form a clear and distinct idea of this emotion, the idea will not be distinguished — except by reason — from this emotion, in so far as the emotion is related to the mind alone (Prop. 21, pt. 2, with its Note), and therefore (Prop. 3, pt. 3) the emotion will cease to be a passion. — Q.E.D.

Corollary. In proportion, then, as we know an emotion better is it more within our control, and the less does the mind suffer from it.

PROPOSITION IV. *There is no modification of the body of which we cannot form some clear and distinct conception.*

Demonstration. Those things which are common to all cannot be otherwise than adequately conceived (Prop. 38, pt. 2), and therefore (Prop. 12, and Lem. 2, following Note, Prop. 13, pt. 2) there is no modification of the body of which we cannot form some clear and distinct conception. — Q.E.D.

Corollary. Hence it follows that there is no emotion of which we cannot form some clear and distinct conception. For an emotion is an idea of a modification of the body (by the general definition of the emotions), and this idea therefore (Prop. 4, pt. 5) must involve some clear and distinct conception.

Note. Since nothing exists from which some effect does not follow (Prop. 36, pt. 1), and since we understand clearly and distinctly everything which follows from an idea which is adequate in us (Prop. 40, pt. 2), it is a necessary consequence that everyone has the power, partly at least, if not absolutely, of understanding clearly and distinctly himself and his emotions, and consequently of bringing it to pass that he suffers less from them. We have therefore mainly to strive to acquire a clear and distinct knowledge as far as possible of each emotion, so that the mind may be led to pass from the emotion to think those things which it perceives clearly and distinctly, and with which it is entirely satisfied, and to strive also that the emotion may be separated from the thought of an external cause and connected with true thoughts. Thus not only love, hatred, etc. will be destroyed (Prop. 2, pt. 5), but also the appetites or desires to which the emotion gives rise cannot be excessive (Prop. 61, pt. 4). For it is above everything to be observed that the appetite by which a man is said to act is one and the same appetite as that by which he is said to suffer. For example, we have shown that human nature is so constituted that every one desires that other people should live according to his way of thinking (Note, Prop. 31, pt. 3), a desire which in a man who is not guided by reason is a passion which is called ambition, and is not very different from pride; while, on the other hand, in a man who lives according to the dictates of reason it is an action or virtue which is called piety (Note, 1 Prop. 37, pt. 4, and Demonst. 2 of the same Prop.). In the same manner, all the appetites or desires are passions only in so far as they arise from inadequate ideas, and are classed among the virtues whenever they are excited or begotten by adequate ideas; for all the desires by which we are determined to any action may arise either from adequate or inadequate ideas (Prop. 59, pt. 4). To return, therefore, to the point from which we set out: there is no remedy within our power which can be conceived more excellent for the emotions than that which consists in a true knowledge of them, since the mind possesses no other power than that of thinking and forming adequate ideas, as we have shown above (Prop. 3, pt. 3).

PROPOSITION V. *An emotion toward an object which we do not imagine as necessary, possible, or contingent, but which we simply imagine, is, other things being equal, the greatest of all.*

Demonstration. The emotion toward an object which we imagine to be free is greater than toward one which is necessary (Prop. 49, pt. 3), and consequently still greater than toward one which we imagine as possible or contingent (Prop. 11, pt. 4). But to imagine an object as free can be nothing else than to imagine it simply, while we know not the causes by which it was determined to action. (See Note, Prop. 35, pt. 2.) An emotion, therefore, toward an object which we simply imagine is, other things being equal, greater than toward one which we imagine as necessary, possible, or contingent, and consequently greatest of all. — Q.E.D.

PROPOSITION VI. *In so far as the mind understands all things as necessary, so far has it greater power over the emotions, or suffers less from them.*

Demonstration. The mind understands all things to be necessary (Prop. 29, pt. 1), and determined by an infinite chain of causes to existence and action (Prop. 28, pt. 1), and, therefore (Prop. 5, pt. 5), so far enables itself to suffer less from the emotions which arise from these things, and (Prop. 48, pt. 3) to feel less emotion toward them. — Q.E.D.

Note. The more this knowledge that things are necessary is applied to individual things which we imagine more distinctly and more vividly, the greater is this power of the mind over the emotions — a fact to which experience also testifies. For we see that sorrow for the loss of anything good is diminished if the person who has lost it considers that it could not by any possibility have been preserved. So also we see that nobody pities an infant because it does not know how to speak, walk, or reason, and lives so many years not conscious, as it were, of itself; but if a number of human beings were born adult, and only a few here and there were born infants, everyone would pity the infants because we should then consider infancy not as a thing natural and necessary, but as a defect or fault of Nature. Many other facts of a similar kind we might observe.

PROPOSITION VII. *The emotions which spring from reason or which are excited by it are, if time be taken into account, more powerful than those which are related to individual objects which we contemplate as absent.*

Demonstration. We do not contemplate an object as absent by reason of the emotion by which we imagine it, but by reason of the fact that the body is affected with another emotion which excludes the existence of that object (Prop. 17, pt. 2). The emotion, therefore, which is related to an object which we contemplate as absent is not of such a nature as to overcome the other actions and power of man (concerning these things see Prop. 6, pt. 4), but, on the contrary, is of such a nature that it can in some way be restrained by those emotions which exclude the existence of its external cause (Prop. 9, pt. 4). But the emotion which arises from reason is necessarily related to the common properties of things (see definition of reason in Note 2, Prop. 40, pt. 2) which we always contemplate as present (for nothing can exist which excludes their present existence), and which we always imagine in the same way (Prop. 38, pt. 2). This emotion, therefore, always remains the same, and consequently (Ax. 1, pt. 5) the emotions which are contrary to it, and which are not maintained by their external cause, must more and more accommodate themselves to it until they are no longer contrary to it. So far, therefore, the emotion which springs from reason is the stronger. — Q.E.D.

PROPOSITION VIII. *The greater the number of the causes which simultaneously concur to excite any emotion, the greater it will be.*

Demonstration. A number of simultaneous causes can do more than if they were fewer (Prop. 7, pt. 3), and therefore (Prop. 5, pt. 4) the greater the number of the simultaneous causes by which an emotion is excited, the greater it is. — Q.E.D.

Note. This proposition is also evident from Ax. 2, pt. 5.

PROPOSITION IX. *If we are affected by an emotion which is related to many and different causes which the mind contemplates at the same time with the emotion itself, we are less injured, suffer less from it,*

and are less affected therefore toward each cause than if we were
affected by another emotion equally great which is related to one
cause only or to fewer causes.

Demonstration. An emotion is bad or injurious only in so far as it hinders the mind from thinking (Props. 26 and 27, pt. 4), and therefore that emotion by which the mind is determined to the contemplation of a number of objects at the same time is less injurious than another emotion equally great which holds the mind in the contemplation of one object alone or of a few objects, so that it cannot think of others. This is the first thing we had to prove. Again, since the essence of the mind, that is to say (Prop. 7, pt. 3), its power, consists in thought alone (Prop. 11, pt. 2), the mind suffers less through an emotion by which it is determined to the contemplation of a number of objects at the same time than through an emotion equally great which holds it occupied in the contemplation of one object alone or of a few objects. This is the second thing we had to prove. Finally, this emotion (Prop. 48, pt. 3), in so far as it is related to a number of external causes, is therefore less toward each. — Q.E.D.

PROPOSITION X. *So long as we are not agitated by emotions which are contrary to our nature do we possess the power of arranging and connecting the modifications of the body according to the order of the intellect.*

Demonstration. The emotions which are contrary to our nature, that is to say (Prop. 30, pt. 4), which are evil, are evil so far as they hinder the mind from understanding (Prop. 27, pt. 4). So long, therefore, as we are not agitated by emotions which are contrary to our nature, so long the power of the mind by which it endeavors to understand things (Prop. 26, pt. 4) is not hindered, and therefore so long does it possess the power of forming clear and distinct ideas and of deducing them the one from the other (see Note 2, Prop. 40, and Note, Prop. 47, pt. 2). So long, consequently (Prop. 1, pt. 5), do we possess the power of arranging and connecting the modifications of the body according to the order of the intellect. — Q.E.D.

Note. Through this power of properly arranging and connecting the modifications of the body we can prevent ourselves from being easily affected by evil emotions. For (Prop. 7, pt. 5) a greater power is required to restrain emotions which are arranged and connected according to the order of the intellect than is required to restrain those which are uncertain and unsettled. The best thing, therefore, we can do, so long as we lack a perfect knowledge of our emotions, is to conceive a right rule of life or sure maxims (*dogmata*) of life — to commit these latter to memory, and constantly to apply them to the particular cases which frequently meet us in life, so that our imagination may be widely affected by them, and they may always be ready to hand. For example, amongst the maxims of life we have placed this (see Prop. 46, pt. 4, with its Note) — that hatred is to be conquered by love or generosity, and is not to be met with hatred in return. But in order that we may always have this prescript of reason in readiness whenever it will be of service, we must think over and often meditate upon the common injuries inflicted by men, and consider how and in what way they may best be repelled by generosity; for thus we shall connect the image of injury with the imagination of this maxim, and (Prop. 18, pt. 2) it will be at hand whenever an injury is offered to us. If we also continually have regard to our own true profit and the good which follows from mutual friendship and common fellowship, and remember that the highest peace of mind arises from a right rule of life (Prop. 52, pt. 4), and also that man, like other things, acts according to the necessity of nature, then the injury or the hatred which usually arises from that necessity will occupy but the least part of the imagination, and will be easily overcome; or supposing that the anger which generally arises from the greatest injuries is not so easily overcome, it will nevertheless be overcome, although not without fluctuation of mind, in a far shorter space of time than would have been necessary if we had not possessed those maxims on which we had thus meditated beforehand. This is evident from Props. 6, 7, and 8, pt. 5.

Concerning strength of mind, we must reflect in the same way for the purpose of getting rid of fear, that is to say, we must often enumerate and imagine the common dangers of life, and think upon the manner in which they can best be avoided and overcome by presence of mind and courage. It is to be observed, however, that in the ordering of our thoughts and images we must always look (Corol. Prop.

63, pt. 4, and Prop. 59, pt. 3) to those qualities which in each thing are good, so that we may be determined to action always by an emotion of joy.

For example, if a man sees that he pursues glory too eagerly, let him think on its proper use, for what end it is to be followed, and by what means it can be obtained; but let him not think upon its abuse and vanity, and on the inconstancy of men and things of this sort, about which no one thinks unless through disease of mind; for with such thoughts do those who are ambitious greatly torment themselves when they despair of obtaining the honors for which they are striving, and, while they vomit forth rage, wish to be thought wise. Indeed, it is certain that those covet glory the most who are loudest in declaiming against its abuse and the vanity of the world. Nor is this a peculiarity of the ambitious, but is common to all to whom fortune is adverse and who are impotent in mind; for we see that a poor and avaricious man is never weary of speaking about the abuse of money and the vices of the rich, thereby achieving nothing save to torment himself and show to others that he is unable to bear with equanimity not only his own poverty but also the wealth of others. So also a man who has not been well received by his mistress thinks of nothing but the fickleness of women, their faithlessness, and their other oft-proclaimed failings — all of which he forgets as soon as he is taken into favor by his mistress again. He, therefore, who desires to govern his emotions and appetites from a love of freedom alone will strive as much as he can to know virtues and their causes, and to fill his mind with that joy which springs from a true knowledge of them. Least of all will he desire to contemplate the vices of men and disparage men, or to delight in a false show of freedom. He who will diligently observe these things (and they are not difficult) and will continue to practise them will assuredly in a short space of time be able for the most part to direct his actions in accordance with the command of reason.

PROPOSITION XI. *The greater the number of objects to which an image is related, the more constant is it, or the more frequently does it present itself, and the more does it occupy the mind.*

Demonstration. The greater the number of objects to which an image or emotion is related, the greater is the number of causes by which it can be excited and cherished. All these causes the mind contemplates simultaneously by means of the emotion (by hypothesis), and therefore the more constant is the emotion or the more frequently does it present itself, and the more does it occupy the mind (Prop. 8, pt. 5). — Q.E.D.

PROPOSITION XII. *The images of things are more easily connected with those images which are related to things which we clearly and distinctly understand than with any others.*

Demonstration. Things which we clearly and distinctly understand are either the common properties of things or what are deduced from them (see the definition of reason in Note 2, Prop. 40, pt. 2), and consequently (Prop. 11, pt. 5) are more frequently excited in us; and therefore it is easier for us to contemplate other things together with these which we clearly and distinctly understand than with any others, and consequently (Prop. 18, pt. 2) it is easier to connect things with these which we clearly and distinctly understand than with any others. — Q.E.D.

PROPOSITION XIII. *The greater the number of other things with which any image is connected, the more frequently does it present itself.*

Demonstration. For the greater the number of other things with which an image is connected, the greater is the number of causes (Prop. 18, pt. 2) by which it may be excited. — Q.E.D.

PROPOSITION XIV. *The mind can cause all the modification of the body or the images of things to be related to the idea of God (ideam Dei).*[1]

Demonstration. There is no modification of the body of which the mind cannot form some clear and distinct conception (Prop. 4, pt. 5),

[1] See note, p. 60. — TR.

and therefore (Prop. 15, pt. 1) it can cause all the modifications of the
body to be related to the idea of God. — Q.E.D.

PROPOSITION XV. *He who clearly and distinctly understands himself
and his emotions loves God, and loves Him better the better he understands himself and his emotions.*

Demonstration. He who clearly and distinctly understands himself
and his emotions rejoices (Prop. 53, pt. 3), and his joy is attended
with the idea of God (Prop. 14, pt. 5), therefore (Def. 6 of the emotions)
he loves God, and (by the same reasoning) loves Him better the better
he understands himself and his emotions. — Q.E.D.

PROPOSITION XVI. *This love of God above everything else ought to occupy
the mind.*

Demonstration. For this love is connected with all the modifications
of the body (Prop. 14, pt. 5), by all of which it is cherished (Prop. 15,
pt. 5), and therefore (Prop. 11, pt. 5) above everything else ought to
occupy the mind. — Q.E.D.

PROPOSITION XVII. *God is free from passions, nor is He affected with
any emotion of joy or sorrow.*

Demonstration. All ideas, in so far as they are related to God, are
true (Prop. 32, pt. 2), that is to say (Def. 4, pt. 2), are adequate, and
therefore (by the general definition of the emotions) God is free from
passions. Again, God can neither pass to a greater nor to a less perfection (Corol. 2, Prop. 20, pt. 1), and therefore (Defs. 2 and 3 of the
emotions) He cannot be affected with any emotion of joy or sorrow.
— Q.E.D.

Corollary. Properly speaking, God loves no one and hates no one;
for God (Prop. 17, pt. 5) is not affected with any emotion of joy or
sorrow, and consequently (Defs. 6 and 7 of the emotions) He neither
loves nor hates anyone.

PROPOSITION XVIII. *No one can hate God.*

Demonstration. The idea of God which is in us is adequate and perfect (Props. 46 and 47, pt. 2), and, therefore, in so far as we contemplate God do we act (Prop. 3, pt. 3), and consequently (Prop. 59, pt. 3) no sorrow can exist with the accompanying idea of God, that is to say (Def. 7 of the emotions), no one can hate God. — Q.E.D.

Corollary. Love of God cannot be turned into hatred.

Note. But some may object that, if we understand God to be the cause of all things, we do for that very reason consider Him to be the cause of sorrow. But I reply that in so far as we understand the causes of sorrow it ceases to be a passion (Prop. 3, pt. 5), that is to say (Prop. 59, pt. 3), it ceases to be sorrow; and, therefore, in so far as we understand God to be the cause of sorrow do we rejoice.

PROPOSITION XIX. *He who loves God cannot strive that God should love him in return.*

Demonstration. If a man were to strive after this, he would desire (Corol. Prop. 17, pt. 5) that God, whom he loves, should not be God, and consequently (Prop. 19, pt. 3) he would desire to be sad, which (Prop. 28, pt. 3) is absurd. Therefore he who loves God, etc. — Q.E.D.

PROPOSITION XX. *This love of God cannot be defiled either by the emotion of envy or jealousy, but is the more strengthened, the more people we imagine to be connected with God by the same bond of love.*

Demonstration. This love of God is the highest good which we can seek according to the dictate of reason (Prop. 28, pt. 4), is common to all men (Prop. 36, pt. 4), and we desire that all may enjoy it (Prop. 37, pt. 4). It cannot, therefore (Def. 23 of the emotions), be sullied by the emotion of envy, nor (Prop. 18, pt. 5, and Def. of Jealousy in Note, Prop. 35, pt. 3) by that of jealousy, but, on the contrary (Prop. 31, pt. 3), it must be the more strengthened, the more people we imagine to rejoice in it. — Q.E.D.

Note. It is possible to show in the same manner that there is no emotion directly contrary to this love and able to destroy it, and so we may conclude that this love of God is the most constant of all the emotions, and that, in so far as it is related to the body, it cannot be destroyed unless with the body itself. What its nature is, in so far as it is related to the mind alone, we shall see hereafter.

I have, in what has preceded, included all the remedies for the emotions, that is to say, everything which the mind, considered in itself alone, can do against them. It appears therefrom that the power of the mind over the emotions consists —

1. In the knowledge itself of the emotions. (See Note, Prop. 4, pt. 5.)

2. In the separation by the mind of the emotions from the thought of an external cause, which we imagine confusedly. (See Prop. 2, pt. 5, and Note, Prop. 4, pt. 5.)

3. In duration, in which the modifications[2] which are related to objects we understand surpass those related to objects conceived in a mutilated or confused manner (Prop. 7, pt. 5.).

4. In the multitude of causes by which the modifications[2] which are related to the common properties of things or to God are nourished (Props. 9 and 11, pt. 5.).

5. In the order in which the mind can arrange its emotions and connect them one with the other. (Note, Prop. 10, pt. 5, and see also Props. 12, 13, and 14, pt. 5.)

But that this power of the mind over the emotions may be better understood, it is to be carefully observed that we call the emotions great when we compare the emotion of one man with that of another, and see that one man is agitated more than another by the same emotion, or when we compare the emotions of one and the same man with one another, and discover that he is affected or moved by one emotion more than by another.

For (Prop. 5, pt. 4) the power of any emotion is limited by the power of the external cause as compared with our own power. But the power of the mind is limited solely by knowledge, whilst impotence or passion is estimated solely by privation of knowledge or, in other words, by that through which ideas are called inadequate; and it therefore follows that that mind suffers the most whose largest part consists of inadequate ideas, so that it is distinguished by what it suffers rather than by what it does, while, on the contrary, that mind

---

[2] *Affectiones.* Probably a misprint, however, for *Affectus.* — TR.

acts the most whose largest part consists of adequate ideas, so that, although it may possess as many inadequate ideas as the first, it is nevertheless distinguished by those which belong to human virtue rather than by those which are a sign of human impotence. Again, it is to be observed that our sorrows and misfortunes mainly proceed from too much love toward an object which is subject to many changes, and which we can never possess. For no one is troubled or anxious about any object he does not love, neither do wrongs, suspicions, hatreds, etc., arise except from love toward objects of which no one can be truly the possessor.

From all this we easily conceive what is the power which clear and distinct knowledge, and especially that third kind of knowledge (see Note, Prop. 47, pt. 2) whose foundation is the knowledge itself of God possesses over the emotions — the power, namely, by which it is able, in so far as they are passions, if not actually to destroy them (see Prop. 3, pt. 5, with the Note to Prop. 4, pt. 5), at least to make them constitute the smallest part of the mind (see Prop. 14, pt. 5). Moreover, it begets a love toward an immutable and eternal object (see Prop. 15, pt. 5) of which we are really partakers (see Prop. 45, pt. 2) — a love which therefore cannot be vitiated by the defects which are in common love, but which can always become greater and greater (Prop. 15, pt. 5), occupy the largest part of the mind (Prop. 16, pt. 5) and thoroughly affect it.

I have now concluded all that I had to say relating to this present life. For any one who will attend to what has been urged in this Note, and to the definition of the mind and its emotions, and to Props. 1 and 3, pt. 3, will easily be able to see the truth of what I said in the beginning of the Note — that in these few words all the remedies for the emotions are comprehended. It is time, therefore, that I should now pass to the consideration of those matters which appertain to the duration of the mind without relation to the body.

PROPOSITION XXI. *The mind can imagine nothing, nor can it recollect anything that is past, except while the body exists.*

Demonstration. The mind does not express the actual existence of its body, nor does it conceive as actual the modifications of the body, except while the body exists (Corol. Prop. 8, pt. 2), and consequently (Prop. 26, pt. 2) it conceives no body as actually existing except while its own body exists. It can therefore imagine nothing (see the definition of "imagination" in Note, Prop. 17, pt. 2), nor can it recollect anything that is past, except while the body exists (see the definition of "memory" in Note, Prop. 18, pt. 2). — Q.E.D.

PROPOSITION XXII. *In God, nevertheless, there necessarily exists an idea which expresses the essence of this or that human body under the form of eternity.*

Demonstration. God is not only the cause of the existence of this or that human body, but also of its essence (Prop. 25, pt. 1), which therefore must necessarily be conceived through the essence of God itself (Ax. 4, pt. 1) and by a certain eternal necessity (Prop. 16, pt. 1). This conception, moreover, must necessarily exist in God (Prop. 3, pt. 2). — Q.E.D.

PROPOSITION XXIII. *The human mind cannot be absolutely destroyed with the body, but something of it remains which is eternal.*

Demonstration. In God there necessarily exists a conception or idea which expresses the essence of the human body (Prop. 22, pt. 5). This conception or idea is therefore necessarily something which pertains to the essence of the human mind (Prop. 13, pt. 2). But we ascribe to the human mind no duration which can be limited by time unless in so far as it expresses the actual existence of the body, which is manifested through duration and which can be limited by time, that is to say (Corol. Prop. 8, pt. 2), we cannot ascribe duration to the mind except while the body exists.

But nevertheless, since this something is that which is conceived by a certain eternal necessity through the essence itself of God (Prop. 22, pt. 5), this something which pertains to the essence of the mind will necessarily be eternal. — Q.E.D.

Note. This idea which expresses the essence of the body under the form of eternity is, as we have said, a certain mode of thought which pertains to the essence of the mind, and is necessarily eternal. It is impossible, nevertheless, that we should recollect that we existed before the body because there are no traces of any such existence in the body, and also because eternity cannot be defined by time or have any relationship to it. Nevertheless, we feel and know by experience that we are eternal. For the mind is no less sensible of those things which it conceives through intelligence than of those which it remembers, for demonstrations are the eyes of the mind by which it sees and observes things.

Although, therefore, we do not recollect that we existed before the body, we feel that our mind, in so far as it involves the essence of the body under the form of eternity, is eternal, and that this existence of the mind cannot be limited by time nor manifested through duration. Only in so far, therefore, as it involves the actual existence of the body can the mind be said to possess duration, and its existence be limited by a fixed time, and so far only has it the power of determining the existence of things in time, and of conceiving them under the form of duration.

PROPOSITION XXIV. *The more we understand individual objects, the more we understand God.*

Demonstration. This is evident from Corol. Prop. 25, pt. 1.

PROPOSITION XXV. *The highest effort of the mind and its highest virtue is to understand things by the third kind of knowledge.*

Demonstration. The third kind of knowledge proceeds from an adequate idea of certain attributes of God to an adequate knowledge of the essence of things (see its definition in Note, 2, Prop. 40, pt. 2); and the more we understand things in this manner (Prop. 24, pt. 5), the more we understand God; and therefore (Prop. 28, pt. 4), the highest virtue of the mind, that is to say (Def. 8, pt. 4), the power or nature of the mind, or (Prop. 7, pt. 3) its highest effort, is to understand things by the third kind of knowledge. — Q.E.D.

PROPOSITION XXVI. *The better the mind is adapted to understand things by the third kind of knowledge, the more it desires to understand them by this kind of knowledge.*

Demonstration. This is evident; for in so far as we conceive the mind to be adapted to understand things by this kind of knowledge do we conceive it to be determined to understand things by this kind of knowledge, and consequently (Def. 1 of the emotions) the better the mind is adapted to this way of understanding things, the more it desires it. — Q.E.D.

PROPOSITION XXVII. *From this third kind of knowledge arises the highest possible peace of mind.*

Demonstration. The highest virtue of the mind is to know God (Prop. 28, pt. 4) or to understand things by the third kind of knowledge (Prop. 25, pt. 5). This virtue is greater the more the mind knows things by this kind of knowledge (Prop. 24, pt. 5), and therefore he who knows things by this kind of knowledge passes to the highest human perfection, and consequently (Def. 2 of the emotions) is affected with the highest joy which is accompanied with the idea of himself and his own virtue (Prop. 43, pt. 2); and therefore (Def. 25 of the emotions), from this kind of knowledge arises the highest possible peace of mind. — Q.E.D.

PROPOSITION XXVIII. *The effort or the desire to know things by the third kind of knowledge cannot arise from the first kind, but may arise from the second kind of knowledge.*

Demonstration. This proposition is self-evident; for everything that we clearly and distinctly understand we understand either through itself or through something which is conceived through itself; or, in other words, ideas which are clear and distinct in us or which are related to the third kind of knowledge (Note 2, Prop. 40, pt. 2) cannot follow from mutilated and confused ideas, which (by the same Note) are related to the first kind of knowledge, but from adequate ideas, that is to say (by the same Note), from the second and third kinds of knowledge. Therefore (Def. 1 of the emotions), the desire of knowing things by the third kind of knowledge cannot arise from the first kind, but may arise from the second. — Q.E.D.

PROPOSITION XXIX. *Everything which the mind understands under the form of eternity, it understands not because it conceives the present actual existence of the body, but because it conceives the essence of the body under the form of eternity.*

Demonstration. In so far as the mind conceives the present existence of its body does it conceive duration which can be determined in time, and so far only has it the power of conceiving things in relation to time (Prop. 21, pt. 5, and Prop. 26, pt. 2). But eternity cannot be manifested through duration (Def. 8, pt. 1, and its explanation), therefore the mind so far has not the power of conceiving things under the form of eternity; but because it is the nature of reason to conceive things under the form of eternity (Corol. 2, Prop. 44, pt. 2), and because it also pertains to the nature of the mind to conceive the essence of the body under the form of eternity (Prop. 23, pt. 5), and except these two things nothing else pertains to the nature of the mind (Prop. 13, pt. 2), therefore this power of conceiving things under the form of eternity does not pertain to the mind except in so far as it conceives the essence of the body under the form of eternity. — Q.E.D.

Note. Things are conceived by us as actual in two ways — either in so far as we conceive them to exist with relation to a fixed time and place or in so far as we conceive them to be contained in God and to follow from the necessity of the divine nature. But those thing which are conceived in this second way as true or real we conceive under the form of eternity, and their ideas involve the eternal and infinite essence of God, as we have shown in Prop. 45, pt. 2, to the Note of which proposition the reader is also referred.

PROPOSITION XXX. *Our mind, in so far as it knows itself and the body under the form of eternity, necessarily has a knowledge of God, and knows that it is in God and is conceived through Him.*

Demonstration. Eternity is the very essence of God, in so far as that essence involves necessary existence (Def. 8, pt. 1). To conceive things therefore under the form of eternity is to conceive them in so far as they are conceived through the essence of God as actually existing things, or in so far as through the essence of God they involve existence. Therefore our mind, in so far as it conceives itself and its body under the form of eternity, necessarily has a knowledge of God, and knows etc. — Q.E.D.

PROPOSITION XXXI. *The third kind of knowledge depends upon the mind as its formal cause, in so far as the mind itself is eternal.*

Demonstration. The mind conceives nothing under the form of eternity unless in so far as it conceives the essence of its body under the form of eternity (Prop. 29, pt. 5), that is to say (Props. 21 and 23, pt. 5), unless in so far as it is eternal. Therefore (Prop. 30, pt. 5), in so far as the mind is eternal it has a knowledge of God, which is necessarily adequate (Prop. 46, pt. 2), and therefore, in so far as it is eternal it is fitted to know all those things which can follow from this knowledge of God (Prop. 40, pt. 2), that is to say, it is fitted to know things by the third kind of knowledge (see the definition of this kind of knowledge in Note 2, Prop. 40, pt. 2), of which (Def. 1, pt. 3), in so far as the mind is eternal, it is the adequate or formal cause. — Q.E.D.

Note. As each person therefore becomes stronger in this kind of knowledge, the more is he conscious of himself and of God, that is to say, the more perfect and the happier he is — a truth which will still more clearly appear from what follows. Here, however, it is to be observed that although we are now certain that the mind is eternal in so far as it conceives things under the form of eternity, yet, in order that what we wish to prove may be more easily explained and better understood, we shall consider the mind, as we have hitherto done, as if it had just begun to be, and had just begun to understand things under the form of eternity. This we can do without any risk of error, provided only we are careful to conclude nothing except from clear premises.

PROPOSITION XXXII. *We delight in whatever we understand by the third kind of knowledge, and our delight is accompanied with the idea of God as its cause.*

Demonstration. From this kind of knowledge arises the highest possible peace of mind, that is to say (Def. 25 of the emotions), the highest joy, attended, moreover, with the idea of one's self (Prop. 27, pt. 5), and consequently (Prop. 30, pt. 5) attended with the idea of God as its cause. — Q.E.D.

Corollary. From the third kind of knowledge necessarily springs the intellectual love of God. For from this kind of knowledge arises (Prop. 32, pt. 5) joy attended with the idea of God as its cause, that is to say (Def. 6 of the emotions), the love of God, not in so far as we imagine Him as present (Prop. 29, pt. 5), but in so far as we understand that He is eternal; and that is what I call the intellectual love of God.

PROPOSITION XXXIII. *The intellectual love of God which arises from the third kind of knowledge is eternal.*

Demonstration. The third kind of knowledge (Prop. 31, pt. 5, and Ax. 3, pt. 1) is eternal, and therefore (by the same axiom) the love which springs from it is necessarily eternal. — Q.E.D.

Note. Although this love of God has no beginning (Prop. 33, pt. 5), it nevertheless has all the perfections of love, just as if it had originated — as we supposed in the corollary of Prop. 32, pt. 5. Nor is there here any difference except that the mind has eternally possessed these same perfections which we imagined as now accruing to it, and has possessed them with the accompanying idea of God as the eternal cause. And if joy consist in the passage to a greater perfection, blessedness must indeed consist in this that the mind is endowed with perfection itself.

PROPOSITION XXXIV. *The mind is subject to emotions which are related to passions only so long as the body exists.*

Demonstration. An imagination is an idea by which the mind contemplates any object as present (see its definition in Note, Prop. 17, pt. 2). This idea nevertheless indicates the present constitution of the human body rather than the nature of the external object (Corol. 2, Prop. 16, pt. 2). An emotion, therefore (by the general definition of the emotions), is an imagination in so far as it indicates the present constitution of the body, and therefore (Prop. 21, pt. 5) the mind only so long as the body exists is subject to emotions which are related to passions. — Q.E.D.

Corollary. Hence it follows that no love except intellectual love is eternal.

Note. If we look at the common opinion of men we shall see that they are indeed conscious of the eternity of their minds, but they confound it with duration and attribute it to imagination or memory, which they believe remain after death.

PROPOSITION XXXV. *God loves Himself with an infinite intellectual love.*

Demonstration. God is absolutely infinite (Def. 6, pt. 1), that is to say (Def. 6, pt. 2), the nature of God delights in infinite perfection accompanied (Prop. 3, pt. 2) with the idea of Himself, that is to say (Prop. 11, and Def. 1, pt. 1), with the idea of Himself as cause, and this is what, in Corol. Prop. 32, pt. 5, we have called intellectual love.

PROPOSITION XXXVI. *The intellectual love of the mind toward God is the very love with which He loves Himself, not in so far as He is infinite, but in so far as He can be manifested through the essence of the human mind, considered under the form of eternity; that is to say, the intellectual love of the mind toward God is part of the infinite love with which God loves Himself.*

Demonstration. This love of the mind must be related to the actions of the mind (Corol. Prop. 32, pt. 5, and Prop. 3, pt. 3), and it is therefore an action by which the mind contemplates itself; and which is accompanied with the idea of God as cause (Prop. 32, pt. 5, with the Corol.), that is to say (Corol. Prop. 25, pt. 1, and Corol. Prop. 11, pt. 2), it is an action by which God, in so far as He can be manifested through the human mind, contemplates Himself, the action being accompanied with the idea of Himself; and therefore (Prop. 35, pt. 5), this love of the mind is part of the infinite love with which God loves Himself. — Q.E.D.

Corollary. Hence it follows that God, in so far as He loves Himself, loves men, and consequently that the love of God toward men and the intellectual love of the mind toward God are one and the same thing.

Note. Hence we clearly understand that our salvation, or blessedness, or freedom consists in a constant and eternal love toward God, or in the love of God toward men. This love or blessedness is called "glory" in the sacred writings, and not without reason. For whether it be related to God or to the mind, it may properly be called repose of mind, which (Defs. 25 and 30 of the emotions) is, in truth, not distinguished from glory. For in so far as it is related to God it is (Prop. 35, pt. 5) joy (granting that it is allowable to use this word) accompanied with the idea of Himself, and it is the same thing when it is related to the mind (Prop. 27, pt. 5). Again, since the essence of our mind consists in knowledge alone, whose beginning and foundation is God (Prop. 15, pt. 1, and Note, Prop. 47, pt. 2), it is clear to us in what manner and by what method our mind, with regard both to essence and existence, follows from the divine nature and continually depends upon God. I thought it worth while for me to notice this here in order that I might show, by this example, what that knowledge of individual objects which I have called intuitive or of the third kind (Note 2, Prop. 40, pt. 2) is able to do, and how much more potent it is than the universal knowledge which I have called knowledge of the second kind. For although I have shown generally in the First Part that all things, and consequently also the human mind, depend upon God both with regard to existence and essence, yet that demonstration, although legitimate and placed beyond the possibility of a doubt, does not, nevertheless, so affect our mind as a proof from the essence itself of any individual object which we say depends upon God.

PROPOSITION XXXVII. *There is nothing in Nature which is contrary to this intellectual love, or which can negate it.*

Demonstration. This intellectual love necessarily follows from the nature of the mind in so far as it is considered, through the nature of God, as an eternal truth (Props. 33 and 29, pt. 5). If there were anything, therefore, contrary to this love, it would be contrary to the truth, and consequently whatever might be able to negate this love would be able to make the true false, which (as is self-evident) is absurd. There exists, therefore, nothing in Nature, etc. — Q.E.D.

Note. The axiom of the Fourth Part refers only to individual objects, in so far as they are considered in relation to a fixed time and place. This, I believe, no one can doubt.

PROPOSITION XXXVIII. *The more objects the mind understands by the second and third kinds of knowledge, the less it suffers from those emotions which are evil, and the less it fears death.*

Demonstration. The essence of the mind consists in knowledge (Prop. 11, pt. 2). The more things, therefore, the mind knows by the second and third kinds of knowledge, the greater is that part which abides (Props. 29 and 23, pt. 5), and consequently (Prop. 37, pt. 5) the greater is that part which is not touched by emotions which are contrary to our nature, that is to say (Prop. 30, pt. 4), which are evil. The more things, therefore, the mind understands by the second and third kinds of knowledge, the greater is that part which remains unharmed, and the less consequently does it suffer from the emotions. — Q.E.D.

Note. We are thus enabled to understand that which I touched upon in Note, Prop. 39, pt. 4, and which I promised to explain in this part, namely, that death is by so much the less injurious to us as the clear and distinct knowledge of the mind is greater, and consequently as the mind loves God more. Again, since (Prop. 27, pt. 5) from the third kind of knowledge there arises the highest possible peace, it follows that it is possible for the human mind to be of such a nature that that part of it which we have shown perishes with its body (Prop. 21, pt. 5), in comparison with the part of it which remains, is of no consequence. But more fully upon this subject presently.

PROPOSITION XXXIX. *He who possesses a body fit for many things possesses a mind of which the greater part is eternal.*

Demonstration. He who possesses a body fitted for doing many things is least of all agitated by those emotions which are evil (Prop. 38, pt. 4), that is to say (Prop. 30, pt. 4), by emotions which are contrary to our nature, and therefore (Prop. 10, pt. 5) he possesses the power of arranging and connecting the modifications of the body according to the order of the intellect, and consequently (Prop. 14, pt. 5) of causing all the modifications of the body to be related to the idea of God (Prop. 15, pt. 5); in consequence of which he is affected with a love to God, which (Prop. 16, pt. 5) must occupy or form the greatest part of his mind, and therefore (Prop. 33, pt. 5) he possesses a mind of which the greatest part is eternal. — Q.E.D.

Note. Inasmuch as human bodies are fit for many things, we cannot doubt the possibility of their possessing such a nature that they may be related to minds which have a large knowledge of themselves and of God, and whose greatest or principal part is eternal, so that they scarcely fear death. To understand this more clearly it is to be here considered that we live in constant change, and that according as we change for the better or the worse we are called happy or unhappy. For he who passes from infancy or childhood to death is called unhappy, and, on the other hand, we consider ourselves happy if we can pass through the whole period of life with a sound mind in a sound body. Moreover, he who, like an infant or child, possesses a body fit for very few things, and almost altogether dependent on external causes, has a mind which, considered in itself alone, is almost entirely unconscious of itself, of God, and of objects. On the other hand, he who possesses a body fit for many things possesses a mind which, considered in itself alone, is largely conscious of itself, of God, and of objects. In this life, therefore, it is our chief endeavor to change the body of infancy, so far as its nature permits and is conducive thereto, into another body which is fitted for many things, and which is related to a mind conscious as much as possible of itself, of God, and of objects, so that everything which is related to its memory or imagination, in comparison with the intellect, is scarcely of any moment, as I have already said in the Note of the preceding proposition.

PROPOSITION XL. *The more perfection a thing possesses, the more it acts and the less it suffers; and conversely the more it acts, the more perfect it is.*

Demonstration. The more perfect a thing is, the more reality it possesses (Def. 6, pt. 2), and consequently (Prop. 3, pt. 3, with the Note), the more it acts and the less it suffers. Inversely also it may be demonstrated in the same way that the more a thing acts, the more perfect it is. — Q.E.D.

Corollary. Hence it follows that that part of the mind which abides, whether great or small, is more perfect than the other part. For the part of the mind which is eternal (Props. 23 and 29, pt. 5) is the intellect, through which alone we are said to act (Prop. 3, pt. 3), but that part which, as we have shown, perishes is the imagination itself (Prop. 21, pt. 5), through which alone we are said to suffer (Prop. 3, pt. 3, and the general definition of the emotions). Therefore (Prop. 40, pt. 5), that part which abides, whether great or small, is more perfect than the latter. — Q.E.D.

Note. These are the things I proposed to prove concerning the mind, in so far as it is considered without relation to the existence of the body, and from these, taken together with Prop. 21, pt. 1, and other propositions, it is evident that our mind, in so far as it understands, is an eternal mode of thought which is determined by another eternal mode of thought, and this again by another, and so on *ad infinitum*, so that all taken together form the eternal and infinite intellect of God.

PROPOSITION XLI. *Even if we did not know that our mind is eternal, we should still consider as of primary importance piety and religion, and absolutely everything which in the Fourth Part we have shown to be related to strength of mind and generosity.*

Demonstration. The primary and sole foundation of virtue or of the proper conduct of life (by Corol. Prop. 22, and Prop. 24, pt. 4) is to seek our own profit. But in order to determine what reason prescribes as profitable, we had no regard to the eternity of the mind, which we did not recognize till we came to the Fifth Part. Therefore, although we were at that time ignorant that the mind is eternal, we considered as of primary importance those things which we have shown are related to strength of mind and generosity; and therefore, even if we were now ignorant of the eternity of the mind, we should consider those commands of reason as of primary importance. — Q.E.D.

Note. The creed of the multitude seems to be different from this, for most persons seem to believe that they are free in so far as it is allowed them to obey their lusts, and that they give up a portion of their rights, in so far as they are bound to live according to the commands of divine law. Piety, therefore, and religion, and absolutely all those things that are related to greatness of soul, they believe to be burdens which they hope to be able to lay aside after death, hoping also to receive some reward for their bondage, that is to say, for their piety and religion. It is not merely this hope, however, but also and chiefly fear of dreadful punishments after death by which they are induced to live according to the commands of divine law, that is to say, as far as their feebleness and impotent mind will permit; and if this hope and fear were not present to them, but if they, on the contrary, believed that minds perish with the body, and that there is no prolongation of life for miserable creatures exhausted with the burden of their piety, they would return to ways of their own liking — they would prefer to let everything be controlled by their own passions and to obey fortune rather than themselves.

This seems to me as absurd as if a man, because he does not believe that he will be able to feed his body with good food to all eternity, should desire to satiate himself with poisonous and deadly drugs, or as if, because he sees that the mind is not eternal or immortal, he should therefore prefer to be mad and to live without reason — absurdities so great that they scarcely deserve to be repeated.

PROPOSITION XLII. *Blessedness is not the reward of virtue but is virtue itself; nor do we delight in blessedness because we restrain our lusts, but, on the contrary, because we delight in it, therefore are we able to restrain them.*

Demonstration. Blessedness consists in love toward God (Prop. 36, pt. 5, and its Note) which arises from the third kind of knowledge

(Corol. Prop. 32, pt. 5), and this love, therefore (Props. 59 and 3, pt. 3), must be related to the mind in so far as it acts. Blessedness, therefore (Def. 8, pt. 4), is virtue itself, which was the first thing to be proved. Again, the more the mind delights in this divine love or blessedness, the more it understands (Prop. 32, pt. 5), that is to say (Corol. Prop. 3, pt. 5), the greater is the power it has over its emotions, and (Prop. 38, pt. 5) the less it suffers from emotions which are evil. Therefore, it is because the mind delights in this divine love or blessedness that it possesses the power of restraining the lusts; and because the power of man to restrain the emotions is in the intellect alone, no one, therefore, delights in blessedness because he has restrained his emotions, but, on the contrary, the power of restraining his lusts springs from blessedness itself. — Q.E.D.

Note. I have finished everything I wished to explain concerning the power of the mind over the emotions and concerning its freedom. From what has been said we see what is the strength of the wise man, and how much he surpasses the ignorant who is driven forward by lust alone. For the ignorant man is not only agitated by external causes in many ways, and never enjoys true peace of soul, but lives also ignorant, as it were, both of God and of things, and as soon as he ceases to suffer ceases also to be. On the other hand, the wise man, in so far as he is considered as such, is scarcely ever moved in his mind, but, being conscious by a certain eternal necessity of himself, of God, and of things, never ceases to be, and always enjoys true peace of soul. If the way which, as I have shown, leads hither seem very difficult, it can nevertheless be found. It must indeed be difficult since it is so seldom discovered, for if salvation lay ready to hand and could be discovered without great labor, how could it be possible that it should be neglected almost by everybody? But all noble things are as difficult as they are rare.

INDEX